THE LANDLORD'S GAME

Strategies, Stories, and Tips for the Novice Real Estate Investor

W.R. Cheltenham

Banana-Lake Publishing

Copyright © 2022 Banana-Lake Publishing

All rights reserved

No part of this book may be reproduced, or stored in a retrieval system, or transmitted in any form or by any means, electronic, mechanical, photocopying, recording, or otherwise, without express written permission of the publisher.

To Sarge Turner...

...may he rest in peace

"Some books should be tasted, some devoured, but only a few should be chewed and digested thoroughly."

SIR FRANCIS BACON

CONTENTS

Title Page
Copyright
Dedication
Epigraph
PRELUDE ... 1
Note From the Author ... 4
PART 1: PREPARATION & EDUCATION ... 6
CHAPTER ONE - Planting A Seed ... 7
CHAPTER TWO - Why Real Estate? ... 11
CHAPTER THREE - Preparation and Personal Finances ... 28
CHAPTER FOUR – Market Research ... 47
CHAPTER FIVE - Building a Team ... 54
PART 2: THE PURSUIT ... 60
CHAPTER SIX – Pre-Approval and Criteria ... 61
CHAPTER SEVEN - Sources for Funding a Deal ... 69
CHAPTER EIGHT - Sources for Finding a Deal ... 74
CHAPTER NINE - Viewing Properties and Learning What to Look For ... 80
CHAPTER TEN - Structuring Offers ... 89
CHAPTER ELEVEN - Acceptance of Offer ... 105
CHAPTER TWELVE - Closing ... 125

PART THREE: LANDLORDING	130
CHAPTER THIRTEEN – Early Days	131
CHAPTER FOURTEEN - Marketing an Apartment	140
CHAPTER FIFTEEN - Leasing a Unit	170
CHAPTER SIXTEEN – Expenses of Real Estate Ownership	190
CHAPTER SEVENTEEN – Growth: The Next Steps in Building an Empire	211
CHAPTER EIGHTEEN – Landlording Through a Pandemic	232
CHAPTER NINETEEN - What's Next?	243
APPENDIX	258
About the Author	272

PRELUDE

One of the most enduring board games of the past century, one that has transcended decade-by-decade cultural changes, is the game of Monopoly. Bringing families together and tearing them apart since the early 1900's, Monopoly is a staple of the American family home. The history behind the game is slightly more cynical than what most know, and somewhat more shrouded in question that most have been taught.

Contrary to popular belief, the concept of the game Monopoly was not invented by Charles Darrow in the 1930's, but rather decades earlier by a little know mover-and-shaker named Elizabeth Magie. At the time of its creation America was experiencing the huge economic boom known as the Second Industrial Revolution. Names like Rockefeller, Carnegie, Ford and others dominated the front pages. Elizabeth Magie, a far cry from the tycoons previously mentioned, was determined to do her part to help the common citizen counter what she saw as the overbearing control of the industrialists and elites of the day.

Magie lived on the East Coast where in cities like New York, perhaps more apparent than anywhere else in the world at that time, living conditions were an atrocity.

Millions of low wage workers, immigrants and their families lived in tenement housing and the city was bursting at the seams. Families would pack into apartments that commonly did not have toilets or running water. Having a window was considered a luxury and coal-burning stoves caked

the walls & ceilings with soot. It wasn't until 1901 that the New York State Tenement House Act required fire escapes in apartment buildings.

Disease was rampant and death was a common occurrence. Seeing these atrocities and wanting to bring some sense of happiness to the harsh realty these tenants faced, while simultaneously helping them learn about managing money, Magie decided to create a board game. In a satirical jab to her current day and age, it was called "The Landlord's Game".

The game was originally intended to show that rents "enriched the property owners and impoverished the tenants" by having properties along the game path that players could purchase" and charge rent to their opponents. The Landlord's Game was one of the first board games created with a continuous path, meaning there was no defined end point and players traveled around the board in a loop. Magie was quoted as saying "It might well have been called the 'Game of Life', as it contains all the elements of success and failure in the real world…"

The first patent for the game was filed by Magie in 1903, but it was not an immediate success. The board and pieces were created by hand, and often times passed around from family to family. Multiple iterations of the game were created with rules that were slightly tweaked throughout the years. The game could be played as one of two versions: Monopolist and Anti-Monopolist. Oddly enough it was the former of the two, which sought to show the ruthlessness of the robber barons of the age, which caught on most. It wasn't until the 1930's that a down and out man named Charles Darrow was said to have "invented" the game which most closely resembles the version we know today and sold it to Parker Brothers for millions. Magie would go to her grave receiving a mere $500 for her patent rights and without proper recognition for nearly 75 years.

Real estate investing seems at odds with the very core of the message that Magie was trying to spread. Yet when done with an ethical intent, real estate investing can, and indeed should, be pursued to enrich the lives of not only the property owners, as Magie described, but of the tenants as well. A life in real estate investing can accomplish both and will provide you with a roadmap similar to the "continuous path" of the board game that can create wealth that lasts for generations.

NOTE FROM THE AUTHOR

It should be known that there are a few overriding facts about myself and this book that the reader must consider. First and foremost, I am neither an attorney nor an accountant. The content within this book is a compilation of research, as well as opinion at times. With that in mind, realize that I am not providing legal advice or accounting advice, and as such urge you to discuss all topics as they relate to your personal situation with your attorney and/or certified professional accountant.

Secondly, it will become apparent that I have a significant bias towards real estate in the Chicago market. This is not because I think the Chicago market is somehow better than other markets in the country, but simply because it is where I live and where I do my investing. This book is not specific to Chicago in terms of the overall goals and benefits of real estate investing. Rather, the information and lessons provided within can be applied to any market across the country. The numbers may be different, but the principles are the same. Apply them to your own local market and find out the specifics that may be unique there.

Lastly, recognize the fact that at the time of writing this book, I am what most would consider a novice real estate investor. I own three properties consisting of 13 apartments, so my portfolio is a far cry from most who have written books on the subject. This book in particular is intended to help the reader learn from my experiences and mistakes, as well as gain insight into the research I have compiled to further the knowledge base of other aspiring real estate investors. This book is not intended for the seasoned veteran. I have attempted to provide information highlighting both sides of an argument when providing any opinion. This book is far from all-encompassing and certainly has portions that could be debated as to what the best method is. Take this information, analyze it, and go on to read more about real estate investing so you can become well rounded and determine what works best for you.

PART 1: PREPARATION & EDUCATION

CHAPTER ONE - PLANTING A SEED

The idea of real estate investing was sown in my mind long before I knew where I would end up with it, in fact, long before I even knew I wanted to pursue it. The notion of investing in real estate was a seed planted in my head when I was only about 14 years old. My dad had casually mentioned to me "I could see you owning an apartment building like these one day" while driving past the classic, brick "3-flat" apartments that Chicago is inundated with. Intrigued, I asked, "what do you mean?" At one time his dream was to own and manage apartment buildings, creating a real estate portfolio to one day retire on.

My dad owned a small heating and air conditioning company and in the early 90's one of his clients at the time happened to be the owner of a small apartment complex. He would do regular service calls at the buildings and came to know the owner on a personal level. Through this relationship he was able to find out that the owner eventually had had enough and was wanting out. It was his perfect opportunity to get into real estate.

While running the HVAC company, my dad was doing what he could to help my mom raise 5 young boys. My mom, who to this day I will never understand how she did it short of being a saint, looked after us boys during the days and then often went to work as a caterer at nights and on weekends. Even at an early age I realized the toll this took on her, but it was a sacrifice she was willing to make for the family. As I came to find out later, my mom and dad had further conversations about the apartment building and eventually decided that the headaches of owning rental properties would not be best for the family, and the opportunity was turned down.

Fast forward about ten years and I find myself with my dad, driving past those brick apartment buildings listening to him explain how I could one day own apartment buildings to create a real estate portfolio to retire on. I realize now that if he wasn't going to be able to pursue real estate investing himself, he thought perhaps one of his sons might be interested in it the same way he is. It was probably through osmosis that I came to be interested in real estate. I listened intently to his explanation, thought it was a cool idea for a fleeting moment, and quickly moved on to other thoughts. However, this one conversation, as brief as it was and as long ago as it may have been, was the seed that was planted in my head which over time would wait for the right moment to sprout. Little did I know that that seed would sprout on the other side of the world.

A few years later I was at college earning a degree in construction management. While I was at school two of my brothers had taken a year off to go to New Zealand to play rugby (they both claim they were fired from their respective jobs, coincidentally on the same day, but there's some doubt surrounding that narrative). To understand us you must know that we are somewhat of a rugby family. Four of the five of us boys played rugby at some point in time. I had played from high school, through college, and continued on playing for a men's club after graduating. However, still being at college at the time, I didn't have the opportunity to go with them to New Zealand, and subsequently found myself in the working world a few years later wanting a similar experience.

By 2012 I had graduated and was working for a large general contractor in Chicago. I was doing the daily grind of a W2 job (as I still do now) thinking there must be more to life than doing this every day until I'm 65. And so, within the span of about a month and a half, I quit my job, packed my bags and found myself standing in the arrivals terminal of the Sydney International Airport in Australia, not knowing a single person on the entire continent.

Much like my brothers, I was in Australia to play rugby, but also to enjoy life as young man in a place where the people sound different, and the cars drive on the other side of the road. I've done a good deal of traveling while playing rugby, and this latest adventure had taken me about as far as I could geographically go. I had connected with a team in Sydney who was nice enough to accommodate me with a room in one of their rugby houses and take me on as a player. My first month in the country was spent looking for a job in construction. My thought was if I could stay in the same industry I had worked in at home, I could come back without having missed a beat. My job had become finding a job. Every day I flooded online job postings with my resume and even went as far as walking on to construction sites to hand my resume to project managers. Often times they were impressed with my experience. The problem was that my visa only allowed me to work for 6 months before requiring me to change jobs, done so to protect Australian citizens also seeking work. No one was willing to hire me for a skilled job only to have me leave in 6 months.

Throughout all this searching I also had a lot of time on my hands. This "sabbatical", as I liked to call it, was turning out to be a great decision. I was glad I didn't find work! Someone who had lived in the rugby house before me had left behind the autobiography of Arnold Schwarzenegger- *Total Recall*. The book was dauntingly thick,

but I had nothing but time on the beach and an endless supply of sun lotion, so I jumped right into it. To my surprise, I learned that at the age of 27 Arnold had owned apartment buildings. To be honest, I was surprised. How was it that someone new to the country who at the time spoke broken English and spent his days

> Stop reading this book. Put it down, open an online savings account, and deposit $1.00. As Arnold said in *Predator*, "DO IT NOW!"

pumping iron, could own and manage apartment buildings? I was captivated.

To his credit Arnold Schwarzenegger is an intelligent man, but I must say I did not expect real estate investing at such a young age to be part of his story. In my mind I thought "if he can do it, I can surely do it". I began thinking again about that conversation my dad and I had so many years ago. I cruised through the rest of Arnold's book and immediately headed to the library. I had real estate on my mind. I began checking out real estate investing books to learn more. Even though some of the Australian terminology may have been different (although at the time I wouldn't have known) it was the basic concepts that mattered. I also decided to start saving away some money for a future down payment, albeit in very small amounts. I reduced my student loan payments to the minimum required and started saving tens of dollars! But it didn't matter how much money was being set aside; it was the practice of saving that had the real value at that point in time. T. Harv Ecker states it perfectly in his book *Secrets of the Millionaire Mind* – "You must acquire the habits and skills of managing a small amount of money before you can have a large amount...the habit of managing your money is more important than the amount."

By the end of my year-long sabbatical in Australia I had a couple hundred more dollars stowed away and completed a handful of books to start my education. More importantly though was I now had a burning desire to learn more.

CHAPTER TWO - WHY REAL ESTATE?

There are various options when thinking about how to secure the financial stability of your future. There are also varying opinions on which is the most effective method. I call these various methods the "Whats". Before determining which "What" is right for you, you have to determine your "Why". You can research all the "Whats" in the world and come to a consensus of which "What" works best for you, but only you can determine your "Why" and why a certain "What" is the best method to achieve your "Why".

Got all that? Me neither. In this section I'll briefly discuss some of the popular "Whys" that drive many people in their pursuit of financial stability. Then I'll go into further detail on the "Whats" and why Real Estate should be considered as your method to achieve your "Why". Let's get started.

The "Whys"

Each person will have a different "Why" that drives him or her. For some people it's financial freedom. This is my personal "Why". I'd like to have the ability to not work if I so chose to. For others, they may truly love their career and want to continue working but have a sound investment portfolio for life after work. Others still may be driven by their family; to provide college education for their children, to lessen the burden of old age, and so on. As mentioned before, only you can determine the

"Why" that will keep you bound and determined to succeed with whatever "What" you chose.

My goal is not to help determine your "Why". If you haven't determined this yet, then I suggest you do so before going on. One of the best books I've read that helped me in this area is "The One Thing" by Gary Keller and Jay Papasan. In their book, Keller and Papasan discuss not only the big "Why" that drives you through life, but also the little "Whys" that lead you across the daily stepping stones to keep you focused in the short term. Think about what is important to you. Find a reason for getting up each day and pushing on through the ups and downs. Determine your "Why".

The "Whats"

Once you've determined your "Why" you need to choose a path to get you there. These are what I call the "Whats". By reading this book you already know which "What" I am going to suggest, so for the purpose of this section I will simply list some of the common options that people use as a *long-term* path to achieve their "Why", as well as some of the drawbacks to each. I emphasize long term because some of these methods can be helpful for short periods in the early stages to build up funds. I do suggest you still research all of these methods and determine which works best for you and your appetite for risk in the long term. This list is not exhaustive, simply some of the common options available. You're likely already familiar with all of these methods, so this just serves as a quick reminder.

Company 401k – Today most salaried positions at companies offer 401k retirement plans. Some of the great benefits of these plans are that they are pre-tax dollars, and many companies offer a matching program. Some people chose to hire professional managers to determine their investments, which can be expensive, and others manage themselves, which requires an acute understanding of the market and economic influences around the world. A war in the Middle East or a trade embargo in China can affect your future at home in the States. 401k's also tend to be limited to only a handful of investment funds which can box you in.

Individual Retirement Account – Abbreviated as an IRA, this option allows people who don't have a company plan to invest for retirement. There are Traditional and Roth IRA's, which are pre-tax and post-tax contributions, respectively. Unlike a 401k, an IRA allows you to invest in stocks and bonds. Stocks are highly liquid assets and can be bought and sold with ease. Again, without professional management or knowledge this can become expensive with trade commissions. Stocks can also be highly volatile and heavily influenced by consumer confidence. I will never forget during the mortgage crisis of 2008 when I contributed to the nationwide evaporation of wealth. As I watched the markets go into a freefall, I was gripped with fear and with the click of a button sold my position in stocks and in doing so allowed the value of my portfolio to decrease by more than 50%. Contrasting with the liquidity and volatility of stocks is the slow and steadiness (or boringness) of bonds. Bonds are government-backed investments that are considered guaranteed returns based on the good word of the US Government. Bonds have minimum maturity lengths and pay very low interest rates.

Pension Plans – Pension plans, though becoming increasingly rare, were once the standard for retirement. Now utilized mostly by government bodies and unions, pensions are board-managed retirement pools funded by member dues. Members have little, if any, influence on the investment selections of the board. Unfunded pension liabilities, commonly associated with my home city of Chicago, are ballooning into catastrophes ready to pop. Take the Chicago Teacher's Union, for example, which has been dipped into by local governments for years as a piggybank for various reasons and has a taken on a liability into the hundreds of millions of dollars. As a result, taxes are raised as a method to fund these liabilities. There is a very real possibility that these pensions will not exist by the time many members reach retirement age.

Social Security – The Social Security Administration was created in 1935 in response to the Great Depression and the need for a safety net to combat unemployment, poverty, disability and old age. The largest component of Social Security is retirement benefits through old age. Similar to pension plans, Social Security has been the piggybank for the federal government and according to Social Security's Board of Trustees 2018 annual report, the fund will become insolvent by 2034. Unfortunately for the time being, we are all contributing to Social Security as one of the "Whats" whether we like it or not, and with the knowledge that we may never see a penny of it in the future.

> Australia has a compulsory retirement safety net (like Social Security) called a Superannuation Fund. Federal law dictates the percentage of income the employee must contribute from their paycheck. Employers are also required to contribute on behalf of their employees. What really intrigues me about the program is that each individual is able to see exactly how much is in their account and can further contribute over and above the federal minimum, with added tax benefits. Rather than being managed by the government, these funds are most commonly managed by private financial institutions and therefor are not subject to being exploited by the government.
>
> After having left Australia I actually received a check in the mail for the amount my employer and I had contributed. Imagine trying to do that with Social Security!

Cash Savings – For those people who lack the ability or willingness to invest in the stock market, or simply have a fear of potential losses, there is always the "cash-under-the-bed" method of a savings account. Held by banks and paid miniscule interest rates, savings accounts are nearly as ineffective as hiding money under your bed, as the interest rates paid are less than that of the rate of inflation, meaning your money is growing slower than the rate at which money decreases in purchasing power. While this may seem to contradict what I suggested earlier by opening a savings account, it is best used in the short term or for building a habit. In the long term, cash savings are a counterproductive method.

Real Estate Investing – Best for last (as I see it at least) is real estate investing. Real estate investing, like all of the other "Whats", has its risks and downsides, however I believe these are far outweighed by the benefits. Let's dive in deeper to explore the seven most beneficial reasons why I think real estate investing is the most effective "What" to help achieve your "Why".

1. **Control** – Real estate is a physical, tangible asset. It's bricks & mortar (or studs & siding) and whenever desired you can inspect the condition of the asset. Unique to real estate and to real estate alone is also the ability to *influence the value*. The spending habits of the population as a whole will influence the stock market, but you as an individual, try as you might, cannot spend enough money to have even the smallest effect on the stocks you may own. The value of real estate, on the other hand, can be directly and immediately influenced by the owner by forced appreciation. Some of the ways this can be done are renovating a kitchen, bathroom, building out storage space in a basement, adding laundry machines or anything that can immediately drive-up rent or decrease operating expenses.

   With real estate you have the ability to immediately increase your realized gains through the increase of cash flow, while simultaneously increasing the long-term unrealized gains of appreciation, which we'll get to next. The physical nature of real estate allows you to inspect, maintain and care for your investment to ensure its profitability. This control, which is non-existent in stock market trading and other forms of investments, is very real and tangible in real estate investing.

2. **Appreciation / Historical Performance** – Whereas higher rents produce an immediate, realized monetary return on real estate via cashflow, appreciation is the behind-the-scenes, unrealized benefit of owning real estate. Generally speaking, appreciation is something in which the benefits are reaped after a relatively long period of time. Like other investments, real estate is subject to drastic swings in value, up or down, depending on market conditions. That being said, changes in real estate values are typically a slower, less volatile fluctuations that lag behind changes seen in the stock market, for example. Let's consider the two ways a property can appreciate.

   i. **Macro Level** – When we look at the housing market as a whole, we are looking at real estate on the macro level. The economy, government monetary policy and consumer confidence are all factors influencing the value of real estate. And that value, in very broad strokes, has been shown to increase over time. This is what we would consider "unforced" appreciation; increase in value from market conditions and inflation over time. Now to say that the value of real estate generally increases over time is all well and good, however that can be said of most anything that retains some sort of value as it follows the upward trend of inflation. So, in what way is the macro level appreciation of real estate better than other investable assets? An interesting and incredibly comprehensive study was performed titled "The Rate of Return of Everything, 1870-2015" by individuals from leading universities, the federal reserve bank of San Francisco and Deutsche Bundesbank, the central bank of Germany. The study attempts to show which assets "have the highest long-run returns", among other outcomes. The authors employ data from 16 nations with advanced economies, covering the span of nearly 150 years. What the data shows is perplexing, by their own admission. "In terms of total returns, residential real estate and equities have shown very similar and high real total gains, on average about 7% per year... The observation that housing returns are similar to equity returns, yet considerably less volatile, is puzzling..."

Whereas other studies of housing markets, such as the Case-Schiller index, look only at the price level of existing *single-family* homes, the Rate of Return of Everything study relies on what they call the "rent-price approach", which more accurately considers the yields from rents. This is important, particularly for the reader of this book, as we are considering real estate as an investment strategy and not just the purchase of a primary residence.

The authors go on to explain that although equities have years of rapid increase in value, they also have years of rapid decrease, and as a result returns average out very close to that of what can be achieved by real estate. And so, we see that as a long-term play, real estate can be just as effective as equities investing yet considerably more stable.

 ii. **Micro Level** – Changes in the economy and the resulting appreciation in value are the results of what is known as "the Invisible Hand". However, there is another way for real estate to appreciate, and can be done so by very visible hands; your own. When looking at appreciation on an individual property, we are looking at appreciation on the micro level. The ability to immediately influence the value of a property through renovations is what we call "forced" appreciation. Similar to the increase in rents described in the Control portion of this section, forced appreciation is done through physical improvements to a property. Somewhat obviously, renovating a kitchen might not only increase your rents, but might also immediately increase the value of a property, furthering your equity position in it. This is then compounded by the effects of the macro level appreciation described earlier.

Vital to the understanding of appreciation is the acknowledgement that the increase in value is *unrealized*, or "on paper", and therefore not utilized unless you're selling the property at that time or taking cash out through a line of credit or cash-out refinance. Most investors consider appreciation as a bonus, or the icing on the cake to the other benefits of real estate investing.

Both macro level and micro level appreciation

further the argument for real estate investing as, in my opinion, the best option for long-term wealth creation. You can liken it to a trip across the ocean. A sleek yacht (stock trading) might be the flashier and segmentally faster way to travel but is slowed by serious storms and at times is bailing water. Whereas a freight liner (real estate investing) is slow and steady and weathers the storms with relative ease. The data shows that both investment vehicles reach the shore at the same time (same average return over time). When you reach retirement age which high return asset would you rather be invested in, the volatility of stocks, or the steadiness of real estate? The steady sailing of real estate investing appreciation is a better approach.

3. **Depreciation** – It would seem that if appreciation is a beneficial to real estate investing then conversely depreciation would be detrimental. However, the opposite is true. In no other investment class can you reap the rewards of appreciating value while simultaneously taking advantage of that same asset "depreciating" in value, yet that is the curious case with real estate. It seems at odds with itself.

Given that real estate is a physical, tangible asset, the IRS has determined that a residential property has a useful life span of 27.5 years, and that in theory, during that time, the structure is decreasing in value due to wear and tear. As a result, the IRS allows the owner to deduct $1/27.5^{th}$ of the value of the structure (not including the value of the land) against his or her annual taxable income. That's huge!

Let's say you purchase a property for $400,000 and your county tax assessor values the land at a conservative 20%, or $80,000. The value of the structure then is $320,000 of which you can deduct $1/27.5^{th}$ every year, or nearly $12,000. That amount is used as a deduction against the income produced by your rentals. Often times the depreciation deduction is more than the total net operating income produced, allowing you to avoid taxes on that income entirely. Not only are you able to depreciate the value of the structure, but also capital improvements such as new kitchen cabinets or an HVAC system. These items also have a useful life span and can be deducted with similar effects. This depreciation deduction is *only available to investment properties*, not on primary residences. If you live in a property in which you are also renting (a duplex, for example) out the deduction can be captured on the percentage of the property which you are renting out.

The IRS will eventually recoup these depreciation write-offs through "depreciation recapture" upon the sale of the property. In short, the sum of deductions taken over the life of owning the property is taxed at your ordinary income tax rate, while the balance of the gain is taxed at the capital gains tax rate. This should not deter the aspiring investor though, as money saved now is money that is available now for further investing. (Pro tip: if you pass along your real estate investment to an heir after you die, the depreciation recapture is nullified.)

Depreciation could be lumped in with the other tax benefits we're about to dive into, however it's significant enough that it deserves its own category. Let's look at some of the other beneficial tax strategies that come with owning real estate.

4. **Tax Benefits** – Owning real estate again proves to have a preponderance of advantages that cannot be replicated by other investing strategies, these in the form of tax benefits. Each of these are unique to real estate. Let's have a look.

    i. **Deductions** –Deductions, deductions,

deductions. Simply put, owning real estate allows you to decrease your tax basis through deductions, meaning the amount of income that is taxed at your ordinary income tax rate is lower. This is one of my favorite benefits of owning real estate. How is this done, you ask? There are a handful of ways, some more significant than others.

- **Mortgage Interest** – The IRS allows property owners to deduct the cost of mortgage interest on the first $750,000 of a loan. The Tax Cuts and Jobs Act of 2017 reduced this down from $1,000,000, but for most of the United States, with exception of high-cost areas like San Francisco and New York, this change will do nothing to the ability to deduct 100% of mortgage interest. So, what exactly is a mortgage interest deduction? It's just one way the government incentivizes home ownership. Let's look at an example:

Let's say you purchase a property for $500,000, obtaining a loan for $450,000. In this example, the loan is a 30-year, fixed rate at 4.0%. This equates to $17,856 annually in mortgage interest (the cost of borrowing money). Since the loan amount is less than the $750,000 IRS limit, you're able to deduct 100% of that $17,856 from your taxable income.

The renter who makes $75,000 per year W2 income pays an ordinary income tax rate of 22% on that $75,000. The homeowner who earns $75,000 per year W2 income pays an ordinary income tax, also at 22%, but on $57,144 ($75,000 - $17,856), a tax savings of nearly $4,000. In certain circumstances this deduction could actually drop you into a lower tax bracket. This deduction is only available on your primary residence, not properties in which you don't live in.

		Renter	Owner	
	Taxable Income Over $41,776 but Not Over $89,075 – 22% Tax Bracket (As of 2022)			
A	Income	$75,000	$75,000	
B	Mortgage Interest Deduction	$0	$17,856	
C	Adjusted Gross Income	$75,000	$57,144	A - B
D	Baseline Tax Owed	$4,808	$4,808	Amount set by IRS
E	Balance IRS Taxable Income	$33,224	$15,368	C - $41,776
F	22% of Balance Taxable Income	$7,309	$3,381	E x 22%
G	Tax Owed Before Other Deductions	$12,117	$8,189	D + F

- **Property Taxes** - Similar to mortgage interest, the State and Local property taxes paid on your primary residence can also be deducted up to an amount of $10,000, further reducing your tax basis. Additionally, taxes owed at the closing on the sale or purchase of a property can also be deducted.
- **Miscellaneous** – There are a handful of other items that contribute to the real estate investor's ability to lessen his or her tax burden. The cost of repairs to a property, which are not improving the value of that property, are deductible. Also deductible are the costs for a home office, such as computer equipment or internet service. Utility costs such as gas and electric service are also deductible. Knowing that our strategy is to live in one of these investment properties, let's say you occupy one of the four units in a building, or 25%. In each of these items described, you're able to deduct

the cost of the first 75% of each, that which is attributable to the investment portion of your home (3 of the 4 units).

ii. **1031 Exchange** – The next tax benefit of real estate we'll discuss is a portion of the IRS Tax Code known as Section 1031 – Like-Kind Exchanges, or the 1031 Exchange for short. I'll save you the burden of digging through pages of tax code and simplify it here; in short, the 1031 Exchange allows the owner of real estate to sell a property tax free, if the proceeds of that sale are used to then purchase another property within 180 days, thus deferring capital gains and depreciation recapture. The code essentially allows an investor to swap one property for another more expensive property, and transfer 100% of the equity gained from the initial property into the next without the stifling effects of taxation. The 1031 exchange can allow for rapid portfolio growth and significantly increase the return on the initial investment. There is also no limit to how many times a 1031 Exchange can be performed.

iii. **Refinancing Tax Free** – Finally, the last tax benefit of owning real estate we'll discuss (though there are more) is the ability to refinance and pull cash out of a property, tax free. If you have enough equity built up in a property it can, at times, make sense to refinance that property and pull the equity out in the form of cash. The cash can then be used as a down payment on another property, to do improvements on the existing property, or whatever you choose. The benefit here is

that this is performed without being taxed on the cash pulled out. It's actually incredible when you think about it; anytime you receive a chunk of cash, Uncle Sam wants his cut:
- Salary – ordinary income tax
- Bonus – supplemental tax
- Commissions – flat tax
- Inheritance – estate / inheritance tax
- Cash Out Refinance – nothing!

That's right, in this case our dear old uncle looks the other way. Well, sort of. The IRS does not consider the property owner to be "making money" when pulling cash out of an asset. Rather, it is just a *repositioning* of money, and overall net worth remains unchanged. Therefore, the entire amount pulled out is available for use, tax free.

After all that talk about tax benefits it easy to forget that we're discussing *all* of the benefits of owning real estate. The tax benefits alone could be enough to fill an entire book, and indeed have. The previously discussed are just some of the major tax benefits. They only scratch the surface. We'll leave the rest to the tax experts and continue our focus on the rest of the benefits of owning real estate.

5. **Amortization / Loan Paydown** – When taking on a mortgage to purchase a property, whether that be a home for the average American family with 2.5 kids and a dog, or a rental investment property as we are seeking to do, there are four components of the mortgage payment: principal, interest, taxes and insurance, otherwise known as PITI. The portion of the payment that is decreasing the balance remaining on the loan is the "principal" portion. With each payment, the loan balance decreases by that amount

which is applied to the principal. Early on, the interest on the loan far exceeds the amount that is allocated to the principal, and on a typical 30-year loan, it will usually take as long as 12-15 years before the principal catches up and eventually surpasses the interest amount. It is this principal portion we are going to highlight, though. With each month that passes, and each portion of your payment that is applied toward the principal, your equity in that property increases, and therefore your net worth. And while that amount is small in the early years, the important part is that it your <u>tenants</u>, not you personally, that are contributing to the increase in your net worth. With each passing month you are becoming wealthier, and as time goes on this accelerates at a much more rapid pace.

6. **Leverage** – The Greek mathematician Archimedes is quoted as having said "Give me a lever long enough… and I shall move the world". I will modify that quote to make it more applicable to our discussion: Give me a willing lender, and I shall purchase large sums of real estate. We are talking here, of course, about leverage. Leverage is another of those benefits of real estate that is unique to real estate alone. So, what is leverage as it relates to real estate? In the simplest of terms, leverage is utilizing other people's money to make a purchase that you would otherwise not be able to afford solely from your own resources. Leveraging a property increases your potential return, but it does also increase the risk. Let's take a look at some examples:

Let's assume an investor has $100,000 in cash available to invest. This investor has decided on real estate as the vehicle and has a couple options for utilizing that cash.

Option 1 – purchase a property outright for cash. The investor identifies a property and pays $100,000 including all fees and closing costs. After one year that property has appreciated 5% to $105,000. On the initial investment of $100k, that is a 5% return. Not bad.

Option 2 – finance a purchase using leverage. The investor identifies a property for $500,000 and makes a 20% down payment of $100,000 including all fees and closing costs. The remaining 80% is financed by a lender. After one year that property has also appreciated 5% to $525,000. On the initial investment of $100k, that is a 25% return! Much better. And with a lower down payment, this return becomes explosive. On 5% down, the return is 100%.

Of course, with higher reward comes higher risk. That same investment might decrease in value too, thus compounding your loss. However, as we know our strategy is a long-term hold, and as we observed in Section B, this potential risk is mitigated with the safeguards of appreciation over time. Leverage is one of the most powerful tools you can use to rapidly increase your real estate portfolio and grow your net worth.

7. **Cash Flow** - The primary goal of a buy and hold property is a positive cash flow, which occurs when the total of your rental income exceeds that of your mortgage payment, taxes, insurance, utilities, reserves, maintenance and other expenses. This is the "money in your pocket" every month, otherwise known as Net Operating Income. It's the money that can be saved towards additional acquisitions, or simply spent if you felt so inclined to. In time, you may have enough properties and enough positive cash

flow that you can actually live off those profits and no longer need a W2 income. Positive cash flow is not always possible in high cost areas, but purchased correctly a property can cover all of these expenses and leave you something left at the end of the month.

After all of this, the choice should now be clear: real estate is the most versatile investment vehicle to build wealth. It's like a seven-lane highway on the way to financial success; real estate can be controlled, appreciates over time, benefits from depreciation, is tax friendly, takes advantage of amortization, can be leveraged and can produce real income. Even if only a few of these benefits can be captured, real estate is still miles ahead of the other "Whats". You've determined your "Why". You now have your "What". Let's continue this journey and cruise on along our real estate highway.

CHAPTER THREE - PREPARATION AND PERSONAL FINANCES

After a year in Australia, I found myself back home in Chicago working again for the same general contractor. The end of my Australian sabbatical and subsequent resumption of my career saw the ramping up of my savings agenda. An annual salary went a long way in helping me to grow those funds. One of the first things I did was to create a monthly budget based on my income and all projected expenses. This included rent & utilities, groceries, gym membership, cell phone bill, etc.

There are a few different schools of thought when it comes to saving money. One that you may have heard of before is the "Pay Yourself First" method. The idea is that the first money to come out of your paycheck is that which is set aside for saving/investing. The remainder is then used for paying bills, discretionary spending, etc. However, a typical argument against that method is "if I don't pay my loan or credit card, I'll get foreclosed/repossessed/etc.". And it's a fair point. You can't just choose to "pay yourself" and not to pay the bills. Often time people then revert to paying the mortgage and credit cards first and then anything left over might be put towards savings. I prefer to follow a method described in Thomas J. Stanley's book, *The Millionaire Next Door.* Stanley describes what he calls creating "an artificial economic environment of scarcity".

Let's look at an example. There are a few expenses that are absolute essentials- housing and food being at the top of the list, but let's also assume you have car payments to make as well. In a typical scenario someone might have expenses for their mortgage/rent, their weekly grocery needs, and their monthly car payment. They then go on to spend money on restaurants, entertainment, and various other non-essential expenses. At the end of the month if they're lucky to have money left over it's put into some kind of savings account.

Using the artificial scarcity method, the principle is the same, but the order is rearranged slightly. You still have to first pay for the essential items, such as housing, food and for this example a car. However, the next expenditure is a portion of your income dedicated towards savings. Shoot for a minimum of 15% of your gross take-home pay. The money left over after setting aside 15% towards saving is then used on discretionary spending. It forces you to make a decision on whether or not you should buy a new pair of sunglasses, rather than whether or not you should save additional money towards your goal. In Stanley's book his study revealed that the artificial scarcity method was used by millionaires who did *not* create budgets for themselves. However, I disagree with this thought. The fact of the matter is that in order to accomplish this method you *must* budget, even if only in an abbreviated sense, to ensure you have allocated enough money to pay for your essentials. The bottom third of the equation, the non-essentials, is what does not need to be budgeted, and therefor if the money is not there for a non-essential item, it simply doesn't get spent. Hence the "scarcity". It's a method that requires discipline and honesty with yourself when it comes to deciding what is truly necessary and what is not.

> A fantastic book on the principles of personal financial management is *The Richest Man in Babylon* by George S. Clason. The book is written as a series of parables, each focusing on different aspects of financial management and personal wealth. The principles can be applied to anything in life, not just real estate investing. In my opinion, the book should be a staple in every high school curriculum. It's an old but a goodie, and very much still applies today.

Often times coming up with the large amount of capital for a down payment proves to be one of the biggest hurdles for new investors. There are plenty of strategies for "no money down" but it is my firm belief that one must have some skin in the game to go after something this significant. It makes you work that much harder towards the success of your operation. The decisions you make when you have some of your own money on the line will vary drastically from when you have nothing to lose.

Strategies to Supplement Your Savings
Coming up with the cash to make a down payment on a multi-family property is perhaps one of slowest steps towards ultimately making that first purchase. Short of winning the lottery I found that it takes good old-fashioned hard work and a lot of patience. Traditionally a down payment on a property is 20%. In many primary markets that could mean you're trying to save over $100,000. But there are steps you can take to make this a quicker process. Some can increase the cash coming in, others can decrease the amount of cash needed going out. Perhaps you can find a way to do both

Strategy 1: Second Job - No one wants to have to consider this as an option. But you must ask yourself how serious you are (or perhaps how impatient you are) that you want to come up with more cash towards a down payment. Increasing your income is done with good offense; being on the front foot and going out to earn more. This doesn't mean taking the graveyard shift at the local factory, but maybe working in the stocking department of a grocery store on the weekends could do it. Maybe it means you work some overtime if your job pays for it. How about driving for a ride-share company? I personally did side work for an app that provides on-demand moving service for people who just need one or two things moved. I would pick up the odd job after work or on the weekends. It wasn't a lot of money, but it definitely helped. The point here is that you aren't bound by your normal weekly paycheck.

That being said, I will also play devil's advocate here and mention that you should really think about the time-value of money. If you're making a few hundred dollars extra per week, but are miserable doing it and have no down time to yourself, is it really worth it? Only you can answer that question. This is just one option. Empires are built one penny at a time.

Strategy 2: Frugal Living - If making more money is considered good offense, then living frugally would be the 1985 Chicago Bears defense. Decreasing the amount of money coming out of your pocket on a monthly basis can be the easiest option of all. According to the US Bureau of Labor Statistics, housing is the largest expense for consumers, ranging between 30-35% of total annual expenditures, when looked at as an average across the whole of the population. Transportation is next in rank, and hovers right around 16% of annual expenditures. When looking to decrease the amount of money going out, these are the two categories you should focus on most. Other categories, such as food, entertainment, apparel, etc. make up too small a percentage to make a significant impact on your annual spending habits to bother cutting back.

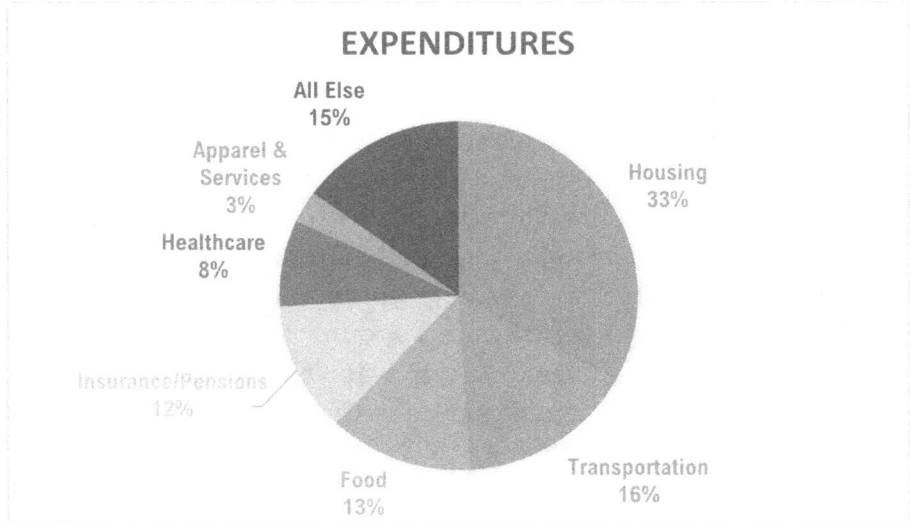

The young, future real estate investor reading this book will recognize that there are multiple ways to decrease spending in both housing and/or transportation in order to have the greatest impact on spending habits.

1. **Housing** – When I was renting, I lived in the hottest neighborhood in the city for a time. It was the epicenter of everything going on, and it was a lot of fun. But even with two roommates, rent was expensive. I later moved to one of the neighborhoods further outside of the downtown area and lived with 4 of my rugby teammates. Rent was next to nothing, not only because there were more of us paying, but also because of the geographic area. The area was still completely accessible to all the fun the city had to offer, but it was now just a short taxi or subway ride away.

   Finding ways to decrease your housing spending is the single greatest effort you can make to improve your defense. If you're able to cut your rent in half (as I was able to do in the above example) you will have about a 15% decrease in your overall spending habits.

Compare that to cutting your entertainment spending in half (at about 5% total of expenditures) and you have a 2.5% decrease in overall spending. Not only is it not as effective, but you're also impacting things you enjoy doing. There's no reason you should force yourself into cutting back on entertainment.

Options for decreasing housing expenses include moving into a less expensive area, getting roommates (sometimes known as parents), or if you already own, renting out a room to a friend to help with the mortgage payment.

2. **Transportation** – Transportation is the next largest expenditure, and unless you are working from home every day, most of that expenditure is a result of traveling to and from work. According to a study done by the US Department of Transportation, on average the American driver will spend "just under an hour driving every day... Compare that to .96 hours per day average reported in in the 2009 National Household Travel Survey, and 1.1 hours per day reported in the American Time Use Survey." If we dive further still into statistics, the average distance commuted is approximately 32 miles, round trip, according to a 2017 poll conducted by ABC News. If we apply the current federal mileage rate of 53.5 cents per mile, 5 days a week, 50 weeks per year, that equates to just over $4,000 per year in operating costs alone. Add to that the cost of fuel, your actual time spent driving and what that's worth, and the much more difficult to calculate stress of driving.

That length of time driving can be decreased by using the methods described in the Housing portion of "good defense" and moving closer to where you work, but let's say you're stuck where you are and can't move.

What can you do? Here are a few options, each getting progressively better in terms of saving money:

- Get a more fuel efficient (used) car. Is there any reason to be driving a full-size SUV or performance car if it's just to go to and from work?
- Take a bus or train to work. Now not only are you potentially eliminating a car payment, but you're also saving on operating costs, fuel and time spent sitting in traffic. Instead of paying attention to the road, you can read a book or really focus on a podcast.
- Better still, ride your bike to work. Investing in a good bike can pay for itself in a matter of months when considering the money saved in commuting costs. Not only that, but the less intentional health benefits are just a bonus. With the exception of bad weather days, you could potentially ride your bike to work every day and save a huge amount of money.

We can again reference *The Millionaire Next Door;* "Being frugal is the cornerstone of wealth-building." Between either housing or transportation, you should be able to find at least one way to decrease your expenses.

Strategy 3: Tap into other resources - This is an option that not all people may have. It is also stressed that this is used as a resource only if the circumstances are just right.

- **IRA**: If you have a traditional or Roth IRA, those funds can be used for the purchase of a property. There are a handful of sequential requirements, but meet them all and you could be looking at an additional source of funding.

- Buyers who want to tap into their IRA for the purchase of a property must be a first-time buyer. Someone who has not owned a principal residence in the prior two years also qualifies under the first-time buyer requirement. Additionally, spouses can qualify individually to draw from more than one account.
- The IRA must have been funded for at least five years before withdrawing any funds. That being said, with a Roth IRA (after tax) contributions can be withdrawn at any time, penalty free.
- The limit to withdrawing funds is $10,000. Again, the Roth IRA is slightly different here. You could potentially withdraw $10,000 in earnings *plus* whatever your contributions are.
- Once withdrawn you have 120 days to use those funds or face a penalty. I know from personal experience. More on that later.
- If you do not meet both the first-time home buyer requirement and the age of account requirement, you will be taxed at ordinary income rates (contributions and earnings on traditional IRA, earnings only for Roth IRA) as well as a 10% penalty. Careful consideration is needed before withdrawing money in this circumstance.

- **401k**: If your company offers a 401k, you can use this as an additional source of funding. Most 401k's allow the contributor to take loans out on their account. Typically, you can take a loan amount up to 50% of the value of your account. Take note that a lender recognizes that this is just another loan and takes that into account when prequalifying you, potentially effecting your interest rate.

- **Gift from family member**: Another way to supplement your down payment is a gift from a family member or person you are engaged to. If you plan on putting down 20% or more, the entire amount can be gifted (an extremely generous family member). But if you're planning on making a down payment of less than 20% then only a portion of that down payment may come in the form of a gift. Along the way proper documentation is a must. A letter must be written stating who the money is coming from, the amount, that a property purchase is the intended purpose, and most importantly that there is no expectation that it shall be repaid. That last part is key because if repayment were necessary then, similar to the 401k, the lender would simply see this as another loan therefor affecting your ability to make your mortgage payments.

Building Credit

Saving a substantial amount of money for a down payment is only one piece of a complex puzzle. Another piece that goes hand in hand is building your credit. A good credit score is vital to being approved for a loan. Getting a head start on this will pay dividends when you start actively searching for a property.

One of the best ways to build your credit is by actually using a credit card and using it often. However, the key to this is to pay it off right away. You essentially use your credit card as a glorified debit card. As soon as a purchase is made with the credit card you pay off the balance immediately, or at most within the current billing cycle. Doing this creates a track record of on time payments. Following this technique, I would never pay interest, and in fact I was getting "free" money from the credit card companies with cash back rewards programs.

A few words of caution, however, when using credit cards. An old rule of thumb is to keep your credit utilization ratio below 30%. Simply put, if your credit limit is $10,000 don't carry a balance of more than $3,000. This is easily accomplished if you are paying the balance right away. You also don't want to go opening multiple credit cards just for the sake of opening them. Not only can you get stuck paying annual fees, but an inactive credit card could actually negatively affect your credit rating. An unused card can potentially lead to the account being closed by the credit card company, which would result in a decreased average credit history and overall credit limit.

Your credit score is determined by three major credit reporting bureaus: Transunion, Equifax and Experian. You are permitted one free check of your credit score per year from each of the three bureaus without any effect on your score. The trick here is the timing. If you time it right, you can effectively get three checks per year by rotating through each bureau every four months. Another great option is using a website like Credit Karma.

These three bureaus look at six factors when determining your credit score, and each factor has a slightly different significance on your overall score, some having a higher impact than others. Each bureau scores a little bit differently but you will at least be able to see where you stand amongst their national averages as well as check for any fraudulent credit inquiries.

Credit Factors
1. **Age of Credit (moderate impact)** - The longer a credit card account is open the more favorable it is towards your credit rating. This is why you should be careful not to frequently open new credit card accounts. More "young" accounts will decrease the average age of your credit. In fact, to help this it is sometimes recommended that you never close a credit card, even if it means only using it once or twice a year to keep it active.

2. **Number of Hard Inquiries (low impact)** - Hard inquires occur when you apply for credit, such as opening a new credit card or applying for a home or car loan. Checking your credit score more than the "once per year" permitted is also recorded as a hard inquiry. Hard inquiries stay on your report for up to 2 years before being dropped from the equation. You can also appeal a hard inquiry to have it removed from your history if you believe it is illegitimate. "Soft" inquiries, such as a landlord checking credit history, do not have an effect on your credit score.

3. **Payment History (high impact)** - It goes without saying that making on-time payments is favorable and late payments are unfavorable. Given its high impact on overall credit score you should make every effort possible to make on-time payments.

4. **Credit Card Use (high impact)** – This circles back to what we discussed earlier about keeping credit card utilization below 30%, and the lower the better. Credit card use as a credit score factor is based on the percentage of use across *all* credit cards, not each one individually. So, for example you may have three credit cards with a total of $30,000 in available credit. Card A might be using 50% of its $5,000 limit, Card B using 50% of its $10,000 limit, and Card C using 10% of its $15,000 limit. In total, the $9,000 of credit being utilized is 30% of the total available credit, even though two of the cards are well above that percentage. From time to time it might make sense to have a discussion with your bank to increase your total available credit, therefor increasing the denominator by which this percentage is equated from. Just be aware that this will also come up as a hard inquiry.

5. **Derogatory Marks (high impact)** – Events such as

bankruptcies, tax liens and collections are considered derogatory marks and have a high impact on your credit score, and rightfully so. When a lender is considering loaning you money, they want to know if in the past you did not pay back a loan as agreed. A derogatory mark has a long-lasting impact on your credit and can stay on the report for as long as 7 – 10 years.

6. **Total Accounts (low impact)** – The total number of accounts includes not only those accounts which are still active and open, but those which have been closed or paid off as well. A variety of accounts (not necessarily how many), and your ability to utilize each responsibly, is beneficial to your credit score.

All the while, amongst working and saving money, I was continuing my education as an aspiring real estate investor. A friend of mine from college had been interested in doing stock market day-trading and on weekends he began going to the library for seclusion to study and create his trading strategy. I started joining him and we each studied our craft, going for hours on end without saying a word to each other, both totally focused on each unique task at hand. It was a great way to get away from any kind of distraction and in a way we both kept each other accountable for going each weekend.

Being at a library you would think I would be checking out their books for use. I never checked out a single book. Actually, I didn't even have a library card. Instead, I wanted to create my own library of real estate investing books. When I was finished with one, I would immediately move on to the next. One of my all-time favorites is *The ABCs of Real Estate Investing* by Ken McElroy. There's hordes of real estate and business books out there. Some good, some not so much. But even when I came across a book that I felt wasn't all that great I would always make a point of finishing it. If I only got just one good lesson or idea from the book, then it was worth it.

Taking on a new endeavor starts with a decision. From that decision, the self-discipline required to follow through on that decision takes dedication, which is a term that should not be used lightly. Whether it be real estate or learning a new language, it must become more than just a hobby or passing interest. It must become an obsession, a passion. It's imperative to set aside a dedicated block of time to work on this passion. That might be 30 minutes at the start of each day, or a few hours at the library each weekend. But it should be somewhere you can concentrate without distraction or interruption.

> Create your own real estate library. Whether you envision owning one property or one hundred, it is important to know where you're headed and how you plan to get there. As we discussed at the start of the book, real estate can be a means to a variety of ends. It's important, too, to understand that once you've purchased your first (or hundredth) property, it doesn't mean you stop leaning. I encourage the reader to continue his or her education by reading a variety of books, not only on real estate investing but on business and personal development as well. I have mentioned a handful of books throughout and have captured those and others in a recommended reading list in the Appendix.

Another book that I added to my library was Napoleon Hill's *A Year of Growing Rich*. And although it isn't necessarily a real estate book, it did provide a lot of good content. In particular, from his chapter on confidence, Mr. Hill goes on to say "Success doesn't crown the person who sells himself short through lack of self-confidence. It does favor the person who knows what he wants, is determined to get it and refuses to accept the word *impossible*."

Real Estate Investing Strategies

As I continued to read more about real estate investing, I began to figure out a plan for going forward. I started to learn

more about the various strategies and consider which might work best for me. There's a variety of real estate investing strategies out there, some of the most common being:
- Flipping
- Buy and hold
- Wholesaling
- Note investing

Within each of those categories there can be multiple subcategories. The challenge then is figuring out what makes the most sense for you and which path you'd like to start out with. Let's take a look at each in attempt to get a better understanding.

Flipping – This is the real estate strategy most widely recognized by the general population, and unfortunately this is due to the rise of the flipping "reality" shows. I hesitate to call it reality because so much of what happens on those shows is scripted and dramatized to provide good TV. The premise of flipping, in its simplest form, is to buy an undervalued and distressed property, renovate it, and then sell it for a profit. All of this is done in a relatively quick timeframe, usually a matter months.

Flipping requires a few things, one of the most important being guts. You have to be comfortable taking on a renovation that more likely than not will reveal unexpected problems, delays and unforeseen costs. It also requires a dedicated involvement on the part of the investor. You don't necessarily need to do the work yourself, or even know that much about the renovation process (that's what contractors are for), but you do need to be constantly involved to make decisions, manage the subcontractors, and get it all done in a timeframe that allows you to make a profit. The longer the project goes on, the more holding costs you incur, i.e. loan interest, taxes, utilities, insurance, etc.

Flipping also requires an acute knowledge of home values, market conditions and the quality of housing stock in a particular area. For instance, the ideal flip might be to buy a rundown property in an area surrounded by relatively high value homes, renovating it to that same standard, and selling it for a high margin. Conversely, if you attempted a flip in an economically depressed neighborhood, renovated it to include high end finishes and then tried to sell it, you would likely have a very hard time finding a buyer and could be looking at a dud. That may seem obvious, but it's a fine line between renovating and over-renovating. The sweet spot is getting a property to a condition where it meets the same standard or slightly better than the surrounding properties, but not vastly outpaces them. When done right flipping can be a very lucrative strategy.

Buy and Hold – If flipping is the hare in the real estate race, then buy-and-hold is the tortoise. Simply put, buy and hold real estate investing involves purchasing a property, possibly improving it if needed and the financials support it, and then retaining that property for an extended period of time, potentially never selling it and passing it down to subsequent generations. The Chicago business entrepreneur Marshall Field is quoted as having said "Buying real estate is not only the best way, the quickest way, the safest way, but the only way to become wealthy." I agree with him on every point except for the "quickest" part. Buy and hold investing is the long game- the slow, unsexy, and consistent method to accumulate great sums of wealth through real estate. In contrast to flipping, which offers a relatively quick lump sum profit from the sale of an improved property, buy and hold investing offers multiple benefits over the long run of holding the property, most of them listed in the "What" portion earlier. Deciding on buy and hold is deciding on a commitment to the long term.

Wholesaling – Another way to achieve a quick profit with relatively little involvement is done through wholesaling. Wholesaling is a method in which an investor finds a desirable property at an attractive price, gets it under contract, and then

works to achieve either two of three outcomes:
1. The contract is assigned to another buyer and the buyer pays the wholesaler an assignment fee. (Good)
2. The wholesaler completes the real estate transaction and then immediately (as in, minutes later) sells the property to a predetermined buyer for a slightly higher price. (Good)
3. The wholesaler is unable to find a buyer, or a buyer backs out and the wholesaler either loses their earnest money or is stuck with the property. (Not so good)

Wholesaling can be a lucrative option, but you need to have a network of reliable, potential buyers to really make it work.

Note Investing – "There's only three things that for sure... Taxes, death and trouble..."

Marvin Gaye was spot on in his song "Trouble Man" back in 1972. Taxes have been in place in some form or fashion since as early as the ancient Persian empires more than 8,000 years ago, according to a paper titled "A Brief History of Property Tax" by Richard Henry Carlson. And while you may be more familiar with the quote made famous by Benjamin Franklin stating "...nothing can be said to be certain, except death and taxes", the lyrics of Marvin Gaye take it one step further in that they mention one other certainty: *trouble*. Property taxes are a guaranteed part of owning real estate, yet not all people are able to keep up with paying them. Therein lies the *trouble*, and in comes the note investor. Note investing involves going to a county courthouse to purchase a "note" on a property that has become delinquent on property taxes. Counties offer the sale of this note as a way to raise revenue and eliminate the liability of collecting from the property owner. The note investor then becomes responsible for paying the property taxes on the property. Seems like a bad deal for the investor, however as holder of the note, the investor is able to collect interest from the property owner on the taxes owed over a specified length of time. If the property owner does not pay the investor, the property can be foreclosed on by the investor, in which case they essentially purchased the property for the cost of the note. Keep in mind, though, that properties in desirable neighborhoods are most often the ones that *are* paying their property taxes, meaning the note you hold could be for a property that you likely wouldn't want to buy otherwise.

Carefully reviewing and considering the options listed above, I decided the slow and steady game of cash flow & appreciation from buy and hold investing was best suited to my skills, risk tolerance and ability to manage while working a full-time job. Certainly, the other options can be lucrative, and much quicker at that, however given my career and personal commitments I decided a more passive strategy was the best fit. Research each and decide which strategy can work best for you (but also understand the intent of this book is a buy and hold strategy).

Creating A Business Plan

Once I had decided on a strategy in a broader sense, I needed to then create a plan of action going forward. What I decided to do was create a real estate investing business plan.

The plan was simple and brief, but I wanted to put my thoughts onto paper and begin taking steps to achieve it. My plan consisted of three things:

1. Mission Statement - This is your reason for doing what you are doing, your "Why" from earlier on. I described (to myself) what it was I was wanting to achieve. Mine was financial independence before the age of 40.

2. Goals - Set specific, attainable, yet challenging, goals. Setting a deadline is key to holding yourself accountable to achieving those goals in a timely manner. Your goals could be to save a certain amount of money, to buy your first property, or even just to read 5 real estate investing books. Keep track of them and put them in a place you will see them every day, so

they are ingrained into your head. There are few things I love more than checking a box on my list of goals.

3. Strategy - Here you describe the "What" you have chosen and describe how you plan to utilize it to achieve your goals. Lay it out here to give yourself a roadmap.

As you get further into the process you can continually go back to your business plan to see if you're doing what you set out to do. Naturally, plans may change over time. I enable the revisions feature on my Word document to show what the plan was originally and how it had changed over time. Creating a real estate business plan will set a solid foundation for your future endeavors.

> One simple thing you should be doing, not just in your pursuit of real estate but with life in general, is goal setting. Each year I take time to sit down to review my past year's goals, see what I accomplished or failed to accomplish, and set goals for the following year. I break it up into three categories: Financial, Career, and Personal goals. They might be things like save $25,000 for a down payment, get a promotion at work, or run a marathon. You should also be setting short-term goals to help you achieve the long-term goals. Those could be as often as daily. Keep your goals somewhere they'll be a constant visual reminder and be sure to check them off once completed.

❖ ❖ ❖

The Landlord Manifesto

We've come to the point in this book where we can ask the question, "what is the game plan?" We've looked at the various benefits of owning real estate investing, as well as the means & methods within the category of real estate as an investment strategy. At this point we can now layout the game plan for going forward. This is what is working for me and has worked very well for others too. By no means is this the only way to have success in real estate, but it is a proven model for success. Here's my *Landlord Manifesto*, in black and white:

1. Dedicate yourself to learning everything you can about purchasing and managing real estate.

2. Employ various methods of offense and defense to save a relatively substantial amount of money for a down payment.

3. Finance the purchase of a 3–4-unit multifamily property with an owner-occupied interest rate and at a low percentage down payment. The property is bought right so that rents cover expenses or come close to doing so. The purchase is intended to be a long-term hold.

4. Reside in the property as a live-in landlord gaining the "on the job" training of managing tenants and maintaining a building.

5. Accelerate your savings agenda with your ability to "live for free". This money is set aside for your next building purchase.

6. Wash, rinse, repeat.

This is our structure for success. As we get further along in the book, we'll dissect this plan a bit more to provide further detail, but this is the overarching theme and should be etched into your memory. Every step along the way needs to be for the advancement of this plan. Let's get after it.

CHAPTER FOUR – MARKET RESEARCH

Some days at the library I would read, but others I would study the local real estate market and browse listings. This helped to get a feel for pricing, housing stock, which neighborhoods I thought I could afford to buy in, and so on. I created a database of properties listed for sale and would try to gather information about the rents. There are a couple ways to get rental income data, and a reason why it's even useful.

1. I started off by emailing the listing agent or brokerage and asked for the rent roll. Often times this wasn't very successful. You'd be surprised to find out how many listing agents don't even know the rents of a particular property they're commissioned to sell. However sometimes it would work out and they'd send over the current or past year rent.
2. When the first option didn't pan out, I would investigate the rents in the area immediately surrounding the property. Websites like Craigslist, Zillow Rentals, Rentometer etc. would provide information that was close enough to what I was looking for, as long as I was sure to make like-comparisons (number of bedrooms and bathrooms).

My reason for doing this was to start analyzing the value of each specific property based on the income generated through rents. This is done through a variety of methods, and each method provides a slightly different way to analyze a property. Since I wasn't making offers quite yet, I didn't have an offer price to base it on, so I would just use the list price as a starting point. At this stage in your education of the market you'll likely be doing the same. Let's take a look at each method and what to be looking for.

Analysis Methods

>**Gross Rent Multiplier** - The Gross Rent Multiplier, or GRM, is an indication of the performance of a property as the rents relate to the market value of that property. The GRM is determined by taking the market value and dividing it by the gross annual rents, before all expenses. The resulting number is an indication of how the property performs <u>compared to other properties in the area</u>. The number itself means nothing on its own, unless you know the GRM range in your area. Let's look at a couple examples to see how it works.
>
>>Property A: 4 units
>>List Price: $600,000
>>Rent Roll: $1,200/unit x 4 units = $4,800/month x 12 months = $57,600/year
>>Local Area GRM: 9.98
>>Actual Value: $57,600 x 9.98 = $574,848
>
>>Property B: 4 units
>>List Price: $450,000
>>Area rents: $1,000/unit x 4 units = $4,000/month x 12 months = $48,000/year
>>Local Area GRM: 9.98
>>Actual Value: $48,000 x 9.98 = $479,040
>
>In these two examples, Property B would seem to indicate a better deal based on the gross rent multiplier alone. Even though Property B is achieving less gross annual rent, we can see that the actual value based on a GRM of 9.98 is higher than

what the list price is, indicating a portion of equity that can be captured on the purchase.

The GRM will vary by geographic region, current state of the market and property type. I suggest reaching out to multiple real estate agents in your area who specialize in multi-family properties to get a feel for your local GRM. Any motivated agent will not hesitate to send you information on a handful of recent sales along with the rents at the time of the sale, especially if it means potentially earning you as a client. Each agent will provide different recent sales, which in turn will equate to slightly different GRMs, but you'll get a solid range. The more of these recent sales you can get, the better. Obtaining this information from agents is critical to establishing an accurate GRM. If you bypass this step and just use *list* prices to back into a GRM you'll end up with a number that will be substantially higher, and in turn equate higher-than-actual property values.

You can also see how obtaining the actual rent roll for a property is much more precise than using a "best guess" based on other rents in the area. As a side note, if you do get a rent roll from an agent when analyzing a current listing, be sure to use the actual rental rates, not projected/stabilized. You must use the real numbers otherwise you are again inflating the value.

Cap Rate – Short for Capitalization Rate, the "cap" rate is an analysis of a property's income after all expenses are considered. A key component of this analysis is that it assumes the property is bought for cash, and that there is no financed debt, i.e. a mortgage. This is not to say that running this equation is only applicable if you purchase a property for all cash. Rather, it is a way to analyze the asset itself and eliminate the variables introduced via mortgage interest rates, terms, payment amounts, etc. Similar to the GRM, this is a method of comparison; either property vs. property, or even further as property vs. other asset classes, such as bonds.

The cap rate is determined by taking the net operating income and dividing it by the purchase price of the property. But before we can determine the cap rate, we must first determine the net operating income, or NOI. The NOI is your gross annual rent minus all expenses such as:

- Taxes
- Insurance
- Vacancy (yes, this is an expense and should absolutely be forecasted)
- Utilities
- Maintenance & repairs
- Capital expenditures

Each of these expenses introduces some sort of variable into the equation that makes it more difficult to determine the NOI. Insurance varies from property to property, and the maintenance, repairs & capital expenditures can vary wildly. So how do we get around not knowing the exact value for each of these expenses, but still get an accurate NOI in an efficient manner? We use something called the 50% Rule.

The 50% Rule states that, generally speaking, your expenses will equal roughly 50% of your gross rent, *not including the mortgage payment*. That 50% value is based on the following *approximate* figures:

- Taxes: 10% (use actual figures when available)
- Insurance: 10%
- Vacancy: 10%
- Utilities (if any): 5%
- Repairs & Maintenance: 10%
- Capital Expenses: 5%

This is only a rule of thumb, but it will get you close. So, if we use the same values from Example Property A from above, we get the following:

4 units x $1,200/month x 12 months = $57,600/year x 50%

= $28,800 Net Operating Income

With that information we are now able to determine the cap rate.

$28,800 NOI ÷ $600,000 purchase price x 100 = 4.80% Cap Rate

This percentage is the return on this particular asset at this particular point in time. Year to year the percentage will fluctuate depending on the expenses. A lower number indicates a lower return, and typically less risk. Accordingly, a higher number indicates a higher return and typically more risk. The important thing to remember is that the cap rate is a comparison tool, and you need to determine what an acceptable rate of return for yourself is. Comparing the subject property cap rate against not only other properties, but also the yield on other investments such as bank CD's and government bonds will help make a clearer picture. Furthermore, current local cap rates are publicly available via reports produced by large real estate investing firms like CBRE and Cushman & Wakefield, so you will have more data to compare your example property against.

Once you've specified an acceptable rate of return, and working in reverse, you can determine what price you are able to offer on a property. So, for example, if you decided that a 5% return is what you were seeking for this type of property in this area, $28,800 NOI ÷ .05 = $560,000 offer price (or lower, with the expectation of negotiating). Cap rates can be a useful tool for comparing properties, however more often than not they are used for larger, commercial apartment buildings of 5 units or more.

Try calculating the cap rate for Example Property B (based on list price) and see which provides a better return.

Price Per Unit – The final method is perhaps the most simplistic, and therefor least able to provide an accurate analysis of property value. It is, however, still a worthwhile exercise to gain an understanding for averages in your area. This method is the Price Per Unit analysis, or PPU. As the name implies, the PPU is simply the cost of the property divided by the number of units. If we take one last look at our example properties, this metric looks like the following:

Property A: $600,000 list price ÷ 4 units = $150,000 per unit

Property B: $450,000 list price ÷ 4 units = $112,500 per unit

You can see how this value can vary substantially for two seemingly similar properties. This metric assumes you have a reasonable sense for the condition of the units and the rent they achieve. In the scenario above, it would behoove you to ask why there is such a disparity. Does one property have much nicer finishes that the other? Is one property in a questionable area?

The best use of the PPU is to very quickly identify a property that has such an unusually high or low resultant figure that it immediately tells you to move on or investigate more in depth. Calculating a PPU on active listings, although not as accurate as recent sales, will allow you to do this.

The purpose of all of this was to help myself get more comfortable with running the numbers and gaining an understanding for what they meant. It helped define the range I could expect to see in the particular neighborhoods I was researching.

I could ask of each property "are the rents too low? Is the asking price too high? Is this property a red-hot deal?". Getting comfortable with these equations and knowing what numbers can be expected in your area will pay dividends further along in the buying process. The

> Get to know your market. Browse the local listings and run the numbers.

one thing each of these analyses have in common is that they are all based on *list price*. It has been said that a property (or anything for that matter) is only worth what someone is willing to pay for it. The listings you are viewing could be drastically overpriced or underpriced. You need to recognize that the metrics you have established for your area are for comparison purpose only, and that once a property is identified, further research is required to determine if the deal holds water. When it comes time to begin your search in earnest, these metrics will allow you to filter through a large quantity of listings and help you determine if a property is worth investigating further, and to eliminate those that are not. There are other methods that will be discussed later on that dive much deeper into the numbers. They are more useful for when you've determined your price range, loan product, etc. So, for now get comfortable with the GRM, Cap Rate and PPU in your market.

CHAPTER FIVE - BUILDING A TEAM

The continuance of my education in real estate included furthering my ability to talk the talk. I would tell people that I was studying real estate investing any chance I could get, even though I knew a purchase was still a long way off. I did this for a couple reasons. First being self-esteem. I wanted to make sure that if I went around telling people that I was going to buy a multi-unit building, that I would actually follow through with it. It gave me that extra little motivation to prove to people that I could do what I said I would do. The other reason was networking. Inevitably, when you tell someone about something you're interested in, whether that's real estate investing or figure skating, more often than not that person will either a.) listen politely, b.) lose interest quickly and steer the conversation elsewhere, or c.) tell you about someone else they know who is interested in the same thing. Scenario c is the perfect opportunity to get a name and contact info to reach out to. This is exactly what I started doing. I began setting up phone calls and meetings with anyone who was willing to give me a bit of their time.

It started off with another friend from college who had been investing in real estate with his dad since he was in high school. We met up for lunch and I picked his brain on how he got into real estate, what his strategy was and how he got to where he was at. I tried to make it less about myself and more of an interview about him, because I was genuinely interested in how he did it. Not only did the meeting fill me with great ideas, but it also provided me with a recommendation for a mortgage broker whom I would eventually use to finance the purchase of my first property.

The next conversation I had was with another landlord, one whom I didn't know or had never even met. One day a coworker of mine wanted to show me the new apartment he had just moved in to. As we were scrolling through the pictures of his new place, I noticed how simple the website was, almost as if it was made a few years after the internet was first invented. After reading the "about us" section I realized it was just some guy who owned about 20 buildings and rented them out. I had to find out how he did it. I sent a brief email telling him who I was and what it was that I wanted to do, and to my surprise he actually responded. We set up a time to talk. Once again, I made it all about him. Before the call I drafted a list of questions to ask:

What was your very first property?
How did you finance it?
Were you working a full-time job at the time?
What were some of the issues you ran in to?
What would you have done differently?

The list went on. Notice the questions weren't "How can I do this" or "Tell me how to do that". The questions were about him, and I could take his answers and learn from them. I truly believe that when you show an interest in what someone else does, they are more than happy to tell you about themself and their story. In fact, I have found that they will go out of their way to help someone who shares the same passion as they do. Perhaps he saw a younger version of himself in me.

A 20-minute call did more than just help me learn a few of the ins and outs; it was a relationship builder, and later down the road he would end up recommending the
real estate attorney I would use during my first purchase and still use to this day. These conversations were helping build my

> Reach out to other real estate investors and professionals. Make it a goal to have at least one of these conversations per month.

team a full year before I would even begin going to property showings. The more people I talked to, the more comfortable I began to feel discussing the technical terms and language of real estate.

Another conversation I had was over coffee with yet another Chicago real estate investor. I was researching methods for minimizing my down payment when I happen to come across his real estate investing blog. Once again, I casually sent out an introductory email not expecting to get a response and lo and behold, he agreed to meet up. I was on a roll! We met and discussed the properties he owned, some of the difficulties he's faced and more. I must not have looked far enough into his blog because to my surprise he was also a licensed real estate investor, and a young one at that. He would go on to be my buyer's agent in my first purchase. With each conversation I had I was gaining more confidence and seemed to be adding key members to my team along the way.

Some of the key members of your eventual team will include the following:
- Real estate agent
- Lender
- Real estate attorney
- Insurance agent
- Home inspector
- Handyman or contractor(s)

I went on to have conversations with more investors, mortgage brokers, landlords, realtors and others. Networking is key to growing your contact list, and a huge

> Start assembling a list of names for key roles on your team. Think of it as tryouts; not everyone will make your team, but you want a good pool of people to choose from.

help in getting introductions is by telling anyone and everyone what it is you do or plan to do. Referrals are perhaps the best source for building your team. You can rely on other people's experiences with professionals to find the best of the best.

Without a doubt, the two most important members of your team will be you real estate agent and lender. I spoke with them on a daily basis once I started actively shopping. You'll want to be sure you find two professionals who will be with you every step of the way and have your best interest at hand. There's a few characteristics about each you'll want to seek out when determining ultimately who to work with.

Real estate agent
- When selecting your real estate agent, it is absolutely imperative that you find one who specializes in real estate *investing*. Whether that be multi-family buildings, like in my case, or single-family homes, an agent who focuses on investment properties will provide infinitely more knowledge than your everyday agent who is just trying to sell your neighbor's home. This is more apparent when dealing with multi-family buildings, but even on single family homes, an experienced agent who regularly deals with investment properties will be privy to rental rates, improvements that will have the highest return, and other nuisances like utility metering or code violation.
- Though not a necessity, I strongly recommend finding a real estate agent who themselves owns investment properties. Their experience owning and managing properties will prove to be invaluable when in the process of shopping. They'll be able to spot problem areas that they've had issues with in the past that you might not notice. They will also be connected to a network of contractors that you know you can trust to do good work, otherwise they wouldn't refer them.

Lender
- Similar to shopping for a car you'll want to shop around

when you are looking for a mortgage lender to work with. When speaking with various lenders you will go through a process called pre-qualification. During pre-qualification you will discuss your financial situation with the lender, including income, assets, and other loans. You'll also describe the type of property you hope to purchase so they can factor in rental income. Pre-qualification typically does not include providing documents to the lender, and never includes making a hard inquiry on your credit report. A pre-qualification will provide you an estimate of what you may be able to afford, but it's not final. Shopping around for a lender will give you a better idea of who may be able to provide you to best buying power.

- Although you may be tempted to work with the lender who provides the highest pre-qualification estimate, you'll want to consider which of those lenders has the best "horsepower" so to speak. I had a few lender referrals, all of which were very capable of helping me achieve my goal. In discussing with them I would very frankly tell each lender that I was shopping around and ask them "Why should I work with you? What do you provide that gives you the upper hand over your competition?". The answer that won me over was the horsepower. I ended up working with a large, nationally recognized lender. In asking those questions I was assured of their ability to close, and to close fast; a factor desired by sellers. I was told with confidence that when the seller and their agent saw the name of the mortgage firm on my offer letter, they would know there was no chance of the deal falling through because of poor lending practices. Additionally, though I didn't know it at the time, this firm had 4 people working on my account. They were able to provide information and documentation almost instantly- a necessity when buying in a hot market. Although there may be benefits to working with a smaller lender, such as a local bank, it is my opinion that *when starting out* you should strongly consider a lender who has the horsepower to help get the deal done.

PART 2: THE PURSUIT

After nearly a year and a half of saving, studying, speaking with other investors, and absorbing everything I could about real estate, I was finally ready to jump into the market and begin actively pursuing a purchase. There's a fine line between adequately preparing yourself and perpetually preparing yourself, never getting to a point where you are ready to pull the trigger. This is what some would call "analysis paralysis". You'll never know everything you need to know, and you'll never feel 100% comfortable when dealing with something of this magnitude. Over time, however, you will learn more and you will continue to feel more comfortable to the point where most steps in the process will become second nature. Until you get there though you must at some point decide to take a leap of faith, trust your abilities and network of professionals you have surrounded yourself with, and make a move to buy your first investment property. Once you do, you'll never look back.

CHAPTER SIX – PRE-APPROVAL AND CRITERIA

At this point you have now selected your lender as well as your investment-savvy real estate agent. The next step is narrowing in on the price range of what you can afford, or in other words, the amount of risk the lender is willing to take in loaning you money. Earlier we discussed the process of pre-qualification in helping determine both the lender you would work with and a rough estimate for what you could afford. Now that you've selected your lender, you'll take it one step further with a process call pre-approval.

Pre-approval is a more precise method of determining your loan limits. It is also a conditional commitment from the lender for a loan up to a certain value. During the process you'll provide bank and credit card statements, a list of assets, and all other current loans you have. The lender will also pull your credit report, which will trigger a hard inquiry. There are multiple factors that are taken into account when determining your loan limits. Let's take a look at each and what they mean.

Credit Factors
1. **Credit Score** – As mentioned, your lender will pull your credit report which triggers a hard inquiry. Typically, the report is good for 120 days after the date of it being pulled, so you want to make sure you are relatively close to making offers. Once your lender pulls you

credit score, they are also obligated to provide this information to you.
2. **Income** – The amount of income you are grossing each month is, rather obviously, a major factor in determining "how much house" you can buy. A CEO with a six-figure salary is going to have much higher purchasing power than the recent graduate making an entry level salary. Your lender will not only verify employment but will also confirm you've been steadily employed for 2 years prior.

Interestingly, since I had only been employed for about a year and half since returning from Australia, I thought I was going to have to wait another 6 months to continue this process. Talk about a let-down! After a brief discussion with my lender, we were able to get around this. I provided a "letter of explanation" describing why my income was significantly lower in the 6 months preceding my current employment. The 2-year employment verification is more a rule of thumb than it is an outright requirement.

When analyzing your income, the lender may not consider bonuses or anticipated raises into their equation. So, if you know you receive an annual raise around the end of each year, it may be wise to time this so your new salary is taken into account.
3. **Debt-to-income Ratio** – A high powered salary means nothing if the borrower has other debt up to his eyeballs. The mortgage underwriter will look at all other loan obligations and compare this against your income to determine your debt-to-income ratio. A ratio of 43% or less is desirable. And it goes without saying that lower is better. A mortgage can still be obtained if your ratio is higher than 43%, but certain requirements must be met by the lender, and the loan is then no longer considered a "Qualified Mortgage", which is beyond the scope of this book.

> In the days leading up to the closing on my first property, I paid off a student loan via an auto-pay bank draft. When the underwriter was going through final approval of my mortgage, the absence of that one student load actually *negatively* affected my credit worthiness, causing me to pay a slightly higher interest rate. Learn from my misfortune and ensure you don't pay off and good debts immediately prior to closing.

Ironically, there are good debts to have that actually improve your loan worthiness. Something like a student loan, which typically has a low interest rate, or a history of on time payments with other loans, benefits the borrower in showing their ability to pay back a loan. Conversely, high balance revolving loans like credit cards negatively impact the borrower.

4. **Assets** – Another factor in your loan worthiness equation will be the sum of all assets you hold. These include cash savings other than what will be used for the down payment, 401k or IRA retirement funds, other property or businesses you may own, and more. The purpose of looking into these assets is for the lender to determine what, if any, assets can be pursued in the event of a loan default. These help to serve as an insurance policy for the lender. Having a greater overall value of assets assures a higher likelihood of loan approval.

All of this information will allow your lender to then provide you with a maximum loan amount, the upper limit of your price range. As mentioned before, this amount is a conditional commitment, not a guarantee. Certain criteria must still be met once a property is identified for purchase. And just because the lender has approved you up to a certain value, it does not necessarily mean you should strive to spend that much once you've identified a potential property. A lot of analysis must still be done to see if the property can sustain a certain price point, which we will get into further on. When you do get to the point of making an offer on a property you will be able to attach your lender's pre-approval letter to it, which is further assurance to the seller of your ability to close. It could give you the upper hand against other potential buyers who make an offer without the commitment of a lender behind it.

With the upper limit of your price range determined, you then should also set a lower limit of your price range. I say *should* because you could potentially set the low end at $0, but in doing so you will end up filtering through a lot of undesirable properties. The low end of your price range is very much determined by your local market. I know that in the areas of Chicago where I invest, I can't find a decent triplex for less than $500,000. Again, another key word here is "decent". Certainly, I could find a triplex for less than $500,000 but it would be in such bad shape that I wouldn't even want to bother with it, or it would be in an area that I'm not comfortable owning in. Both the condition of the building and the area it's in will be two of the criteria we discuss in the next part, and they tie directly into helping determine the low end of your price range.

Determining Criteria

The criteria you outline are going to be the parameters of your search that define exactly what it is you're looking for. Think of it as a 1-2 sentence "wanted" ad in a newspaper or on Craigslist. It's a brief, well defined description of your ideal property. There's a handful of big criteria that I suggest you use, but you could make it as specific as the color of the building if you really wanted to, though doing so would limit the results you come across.

Area – The most obvious criteria to start your list is the area in which you'd like to purchase. I have no experience in remote investing and will make the assumption that as a reader of this book you will be looking to purchase fairly close to home. So, in determining your area you first need to decide if it makes more sense to invest in the nearest major metropolitan area, or in the surrounding suburbs. For me, living and working in the city, it made the most sense to also invest in a property within the city limits. From there you can further narrow it down.

The city of Chicago has 77 uniquely defined neighborhoods that make up the city as a whole. And like any large city, some of those are good areas and some of them are not so good. The condition of any particular area can be described as Class A, B, C or D, with A being the most desirable and D being the least. These designations, of course, are subjective labels and you won't find an official designation for an area. However, with a minimal amount of research you should be able to quickly eliminate the areas where you wouldn't feel safe walking alone at night, or even during the day in some cases.

> **Generic Area Classification Descriptions**
>
> **Class A** – High-end, luxury apartments with various amenities in the most desirable areas. Least amount of inherent risk.
>
> **Class B** – Middle ground rentals with standard condo quality finishes, typically priced towards working professionals.
>
> **Class C** – Blue-collar communities with low-quality to basic level finishes, affordably to moderately priced. May be on the fringe of less desirable areas, or on the fringe of more desirable areas.
>
> **Class D** – Disinvested communities typically in high-crime areas. Most inherent risk.

Many of the best areas can also be immediately removed from your search simply by the fact that the median price range will be well above what you have been prequalified for. While you may see a lot of very desirable properties in these areas, don't even waste your time as you know you won't be able to afford them anyways. You can start honing in on an area and setting boundaries with streets on all four sides. Perhaps it's not your favorite part of the city, or exactly your first choice of where you'd like to live, but oftentimes that's the reality of shopping for real estate.

Something else that should also be taken into consideration when determining the area is the stability and trends for that area. Is it a solid, blue-collar population with a dependable pool of renters? Does it have explosive growth with new construction? Is the population migrating to other neighboring areas as local schools have been closing down? Be careful not to convince yourself of the prospect of *future growth* in a currently depressed area. That would be considered speculating, akin to gambling, and should be done only with careful research and plenty of data to support your beliefs. Instead, I recommend you stick with those mature parts of the city that are not necessarily outpacing other areas in growth but are also not declining in local population. Stay away too from the trendiest areas, as these will prove to be the most competitive and overpriced.

Size –In terms of size I'm talking about number of units, not the actual square footage of a property. Economies of scale will generally mean the more units, the better. One building with three units and one roof is generally easier to maintain than three buildings with one unit each and three roofs. Remember the vacancy rate we discussed before when determining your cash flow? Economies of scale will help in this area too. A four unit building with one vacancy (25% vacancy factor) has a much smaller effect on your cash flow than a single-family residence that sits vacant for the same period of time (100% vacancy factor).

With that being said, it's unlikely that'll you'll be purchasing a large apartment complex as your first property. Additionally, the loan type you will be pursuing will be a residential loan. Residential loans allow the purchase of buildings with 1 to 4 units. Anything 5 units or more is considered commercial and will require a commercial loan with a minimum 20% down payment, so more isn't always possible. Therefore, you should strive to get the most bang for your buck and search for buildings with 4 units. The price difference from a 2 unit to a 4 unit is typically not that much where it will throw a 4 unit building out of your price range. Plus, the management increase from 2 units to 4 units is minimal. I personally set my criteria for 3- and 4-unit buildings to ensure I wouldn't miss out on a good deal.

Something that may be considered along with the size of the building is the construction type. Construction type is the physical nature of the building. This could be masonry construction, fame construction, with or without a basement, flat roof or pitched roof, and so on. There are practical reasons for determining the construction type as a criterion, such as maintenance requirements and durability, as well as emotional reasons. I tend to focus on brick buildings as they have a much longer life span, but I also fall victim to the emotional reason of "I just like them more than a frame construction building". Real estate can be a very emotional purchase, and I love the architectural aspects of an old brick building. But I am also careful not to ignore a good deal when it presents itself, regardless of the construction type.

Condition – When considering the condition of a building, there are multiple factors to look at. The age of a building plays a key role. You may choose to only look for buildings that were built after the year 2000, for instance. In Chicago, where a majority of the housing stock is close to 100 years old, I don't have that luxury. Further still is the amount of rehab work you may or may not want to take on. This depends heavily on your level of comfort, availability of time and appetite for risk:

1. **Turnkey** – a "turnkey" property is one that requires no work once purchased. It is move-in ready, so to speak. This can be a great option if you don't want to deal with the hassles of improving a property or don't have the time to do it. Keep in mind though that you will be paying a premium for a turnkey property and the return will not be as high.

2. **Minor Improvements** – The word 'minor' is subjective, but typically a building in this condition is livable as-is, yet has room for improvement. These improvements could be cosmetic, such as a fresh coat of paint, or something more involved such as a new bathroom. In my first property I installed new air conditioning systems in each apartment where there had been none

before, and in doing so was able to increase rents. Or you could also potentially buy a property in this condition and do nothing at all.

3. **Major Rehab** – A rehab project is one that requires time, involvement and a certain ability to stomach the uncertainties of renovating. In saying that it also has the highest upside as usually these buildings can be bought at a relatively low price with the opportunity to drastically increase the return with higher rents, as well as provide a significant increase in value and equity.

Determining your criteria will set a guideline for yourself and for your realtor. You should strictly adhere to the criteria you set so that you don't get sidetracked during the search. It's easy to fall victim to bending the parameters of your criteria, especially if you've been searching in vain for an extended period of time. You've set your criteria for specific reasons, and it's important that you stick to them.

CHAPTER SEVEN - SOURCES FOR FUNDING A DEAL

Since the start of this journey, you've been slowly building up your cash savings set aside for the down payment. At this point you have determined your price range and the criteria for your ideal property. Now you need to figure out how you will fund the balance this purchase. While paying all-cash is certainly an option, it's not always the best option if you want to take advantage of leverage, as discussed before (nor is it typically realistic). Remember our Landlord Manifesto; we are seeking to use a low down payment method of financing the purchase of a property. Let's look at the some of the low down payment financing options you'll be able to consider and discuss with your lender, as well as other less conventional options.

FHA Loan: A Federal Housing Administration loan is oftentimes very attractive for the first-time homebuyer, though it is not a requirement that you be buying your first home. One of the reasons it is so attractive is that the down payment can be as little as 3.5%. It also has less restrictive requirements on credit scores. You may be inclined to write off any other options and immediately jump for an FHA loan, but consider a few things first.

> 1. An FHA buyer must reside in the property. Not a problem if you're wanting to live-and-flip or be a resident landlord. Understand that occupancy must

take place within 60 days of closing.
2. In the eyes of the lender, the lower down payment means higher risk. Enter Private Mortgage Insurance, or PMI. PMI is a monthly insurance that gets included in your escrow, on top of your regular property insurance, to protect the lender from the risk of the homeowner defaulting. This can add a couple hundred dollars to your mortgage payment every month. Depending on how your loan is structured you could be stuck paying PMI for the life of the loan.
3. Often times a seller will have a negative reception to an offer that is financed by an FHA loan, which could be more aptly named "red tape loan". For a sale to go through with an FHA loan a lot of criteria at that property must first be met. A major part of it is the health and safety inspection as a key component to the appraisal. The sale of a property could be delayed from something as seemingly insignificant as peeling paint or a missing handrail. In other scenarios these things can simply be worked out with closing credits. But for an FHA loan to go through they are required to be corrected beforehand. For a seller who doesn't have the time or motivation, your offer could be overlooked for a lower, conventional or all-cash offer.

While FHA loans offer the buyer a lower barrier of entry, they can also possibly make it more difficult to close on a property. Don't let this all scare you; they can still be a very good option.

There is also a subcategory within FHA called section 203k, which is a purchase + rehab loan. This loan product allows you to finance the purchase of a property as well as the costs of rehabbing it. There are a lot of requirements that must be met in order to obtain a 203k loan, the details of which we won't go into here, but this is another option if you're looking to purchase a property that needs work.

VA Loan: The Department of Veterans Affairs provides another avenue of financing, specifically for veterans, active military personnel and their families. Similar to an FHA loan, a VA loan is government program provided through private lenders, but unlike an FHA loan, a VA loan is partially guaranteed by the US government. The benefits of a VA loan are many:
1. Amazingly, VA loans can be secured with no money down. I expressed earlier my feelings on not having skin in the game, but this can be a viable option for military members.
2. Being partially guaranteed by the government negates the requirement for private mortgage insurance.
3. Similarly, credit rating requirements are lower because some of the reduced risk to the lender, making it easier to qualify for the loan.

Conventional 5% Down: This is perhaps one of the most straightforward options but is also more difficult to obtain. It requires a little bit more capital than previous options, but certainly not as much as the traditional 20% conventional mortgage. The lending requirements tend to be the strictest for this type of loan because of the fact that it is conventional, but the down payment is so low (more risk to the lender). Achieve the following and you could be in good shape to secure a loan:
1. The borrower must provide a 2-year employment history showing stable employment. Bouncing around to different jobs does not look good in the eyes of a lender.
2. Credit score minimums are higher. You'll want to have a score of at least 640 to be confident in getting

approved. This can be higher or lower depending on lender, but it is a good target. Remember, this is the bare minimum. A higher score increases your ability to satisfy the lender.
3. The lender will want to verify that you have cash reserves, separate from whatever you will be using for the down payment. This also increases the amount of capital required.

You will, of course, have private mortgage insurance tacked on to your monthly payment, however that can be removed once your equity in the property reaches 20%, or sometimes sooner, depending on the lender. Additionally, the interest rate tends to be bit higher with this loan type.

Other Options: Sometimes you must get creative to make a deal happen. Depending on the circumstances you might not be able to get financing, or you might be able to figure out a way to do it cheaper by not financing through a bank. Here are a couple other options that are outside of the typical financing box:
1. **Partner with someone** - Finding an investing partner can be a good option if you lack the ability to obtain a loan on your own or want the guidance of another investor. This is where networking is hugely beneficial. The more people you meet and tell about your plans, the more connections you make for a possible partnership. In one scenario you might be able to bring a deal to your partner who then obtains the financing or pays cash in exchange for your small equity portion in the deal. Or perhaps you contribute a small portion of the down payment with your partner contributing the rest, and equity is split along that same ratio.

Something you have to consider when thinking about partnering is how the duties will be split. Is one person a shadow investor while the other does all the work? If so, how are profits shared? Or does one person do the financial part and the other handles the property management? These are all things to think about and should be explicitly spelled out beforehand to avoid potential issues with your partner.

2. **Owner financing** – Typically when an owner is selling a property it's because they no longer want to deal with it or because they need the money from the sale. There are, however, some owners that will entertain the idea of owner financing. In this situation the owner agrees to the sale of the property, transfers title to your name, but in essence becomes the bank. You will negotiate a sales price and monthly payment plus interest that you will pay to the seller of the property over a certain length of time, until the loan matures and you own the property outright. That monthly payment may even be less than what the owner currently nets in rental income, but if they're able to get away from the hassles of managing tenants, it may just be worth it to him or her. The risk for the owner is minimal in that if you as the buyer fail to make your monthly payment, the seller is able to once again take ownership of the property.

Owner financing isn't necessarily common, and you shouldn't rely on this as your only method to fund a deal. But it's certainly an option and never hurts to ask when negotiating. We'll look at this more in-depth in Part 3 of the book.

CHAPTER EIGHT - SOURCES FOR FINDING A DEAL

In a competitive market it is crucially important that when trying to identify potential properties you cast a net as far and wide as possible to ensure you are collecting the maximum number of properties to analyze. You don't want to wait for the deal to come to you. You have to go out and find it. Below are various resources for identifying potential properties for purchase. You should try to employ as many as makes sense to give you the upper hand on the rest of the buyers in the market. As has been the theme with this book, I will try to highlight both the pros and cons of each to allow you to make an informed decision on which options work best for your situation.

Deal Sources

MLS – The Multiple Listing Service, or MLS, is square one when looking for a property. Your only access to the MLS is through a realtor, unless you are a licensed realtor yourself. The MLS will produce a majority of the listings you analyze, and while it can be a good source, you have to keep in mind that all other buyers (your competition) are receiving the same listings. This makes for a feeding frenzy when a good listing comes up. Deals can still be had from the MLS, and in fact it's how I found my first deal, but it should not be the only source of properties you analyze. Your realtor can set the search parameters based on the criteria you have selected, and you will received automatically generated emails as soon as a new property that fits your criteria is listed. When these come up you need to act fast because you can be sure everyone else will too.

Wholesaler - One of the real estate investing strategies discussed earlier can also be used as a method for filtering through more deals, and that is wholesaling. Connecting with a wholesaler can bring you off-market opportunities that might not otherwise be available to your competition via the MLS. You'll pay a premium to the wholesaler for bringing you a deal, but the sale price will (or should) be less than what it would be on the open market. A word of caution though; you need to be careful in vetting the deals offered to you by a wholesaler until you've built rapport and likely have done a few deals together. Until this happens, you will likely be getting the bottom of the barrel offers that have already been turned down by the wholesaler's usual buyers. That being said, what may not be a good deal for one investor could still be a good first deal for you.

Short Sales/Foreclosures/REOs - A sad reality of owning real estate is that a percentage of the population is ultimately unable to keep up with their mortgage payments for a variety of reasons. When this happens the bank or lender will step in to begin the foreclosure process. This is done through a progression of options. We won't go in depth here, but it's good to understand the difference between the three.
   1. **Short Sale** – in a short sale a bank agrees to the sale of a property for less than what is owed on the mortgage. This is done to mitigate losses to the bank, and to prevent bankruptcy or foreclosure proceedings for the borrower. The homeowner still has their name on the title in this situation.
   2. **Foreclosure** – If an owner fails to make his or her mortgage payments, the lender can then choose to begin foreclosure proceedings. In this scenario the

lender takes title and attempts to sell the property via auction. The sale of the property must cover the balance of the loan in full.
3. **Real Estate Owned** – Real Estate Owned or REO occurs when the lender is unable to sell a foreclosure at auction. At this point the lender takes possession of the property and attempts to sell it with the use of real estate agents.

Each of these scenarios involve a lot of moving parts, have potential pitfalls and can make for a very long closing for a buyer. The benefit to the buyer is that the deal can sometimes be had at lower than market rates. All three can be found on the MLS, but foreclosures will only be purchased through an auction, whereas a short sale or REO can be purchased through a standard sale agreement.

HomePath – Similar to a bank owned foreclosure, a HomePath property is a foreclosed property owned by Fannie Mae, the government sponsored enterprise that purchases mortgages on the secondary market. And, like a bank owned foreclosure, a HomePath property might also be listed on the MLS. However, there are some unique advantages to HomePath properties. Typically, properties for sale via HomePath are only available to first time homebuyers or owner occupants. As such, this eliminates some your competition. Additionally, as an owner occupant you are able to purchase a HomePath property with as little as 3% down. On top of that, the mortgage insurance can be reduced once your equity in the property is at 10%, and can be eliminated altogether once your equity reaches 20%. One of the downsides to the program though is that you are dealing with a government entity, so along with added red tape is the less than flexible nature of Fannie Mae, as compared to a private seller. For instance, they will not accept an offer contingent on the sale of your current home if you have one. Other contingencies are considered on a case-by-case basis. All HomePath properties are sold in as-is condition, meaning you do not have the ability to negotiate the sale price based on issues that may arise during the inspection period, so you have to be sure of the value of the property before you enter into a contract.

Off Market Networking – As you get further along in your real estate investing career you will continue to come across more contractors, lenders, agents, other investors and so on. All of these people will become sources for potential leads. In your dealings with them, you should make them aware that you're always looking to buy (even when you aren't). You never know when a fantastic deal will fall into your lap, and even if you're not in a position to make a purchase you can perhaps build a relationship with the seller and agree to a mutually acceptable timeframe for the sale. Ahead of building a network of real estate professionals you should constantly be mentioning your desire to buy to family, friends, coworkers and the like. I had mentioned a similar strategy earlier when you are first learning about real estate investing and trying to get in touch with investors for the purpose of educating yourself. The same strategy can be applied when looking for a property to purchase. A family member might get you in touch with a coworker who has a second cousin who happened to inherit a property they don't want. Seems unlikely but I actually had similar opportunities presented to me. Now it's true that these opportunities might not come up every day or even every month, but the more you let people know you are looking to buy, the wider your reach becomes.

Mailing Lists - If you're looking to canvas an area with the announcement that you are in the market to purchase a property, a good way to do so is through a mailing list, sometimes called a "Yellow Letter Campaign" or more commonly known as direct mail marketing. There are multiple services online that will provide you with owner names & addresses, which will then generate and send the letter for you.

You'll be able to target a specific area, property type and various owner demographics that can get as specific as marital status or number of years owned. This can be an early foot in the door to the seller who hasn't listed his or her property yet, but perhaps has been considering it. This all comes at a price of course. Direct mail services can be expensive and, depending on the success rate, will likely require multiple rounds of mailing. On top of that, anyone else who is determined to find that off market deal can pay to access this same list and send letters to those same owners. Property owners can be bombarded with these mailings on a near daily basis. As a result, they become numb to the letters unless you catch them at the exact time they are looking to sell. And since there is no designated time for when any one particular owner might want to sell, you have to constantly stay in front of them with repeated mailings so that when that time does come, you are the person they think of first. Now consider the fact that even though it may seem like a significant amount of money to stay engaged in a direct mail campaign, the payoff could be huge in an off-market deal that is purchased below market value and without the influence of multiple offers.

Driving for Dollars – A method that's similar in scope to a direct mail campaign, is much less expensive but certainly more labor intensive, is something called "driving for dollars", or as was in the case of my second deal "walking for dollars". This method is performed by driving or walking your targeted area and looking for either for-sale-by-owner (FSBO) properties, or properties that appear to fit your specific criteria. If you drive to work, you might decide to take a slightly different route each day that takes you down a different street and allows you to see new properties each time. Or you might take a weekend drive snaking back and forth along neighborhood streets in your target area. One method I love to employ is to call the number on for-rent signs I see. When I see a for-rent sign it screams to me "mom-and-pop owner". I call the number and mention that I'm not looking to rent an apartment but instead am interested in buying the property. Even if the owner is not interested in selling at that time, I ask them to save my information for when that time comes, and also ask if I can stay in touch with them from time to time.

CHAPTER NINE - VIEWING PROPERTIES AND LEARNING WHAT TO LOOK FOR

Regardless of the method(s) you use to generate leads, one thing all will have in common is the need to view the property. There are experienced investors who can purchase properties sight-unseen, based solely on their ability to analyze the numbers, but as a new investor it is my recommendation that you never attempt to do this. The dangers are great if you don't know what you are doing. Viewing the property can happen initially online by browsing the listing pictures (if there are any) and eventually in person when you schedule a showing through your agent.

For simplicity's sake we'll assume that you have a buyer's profile with your agent on the MLS and had a property which matched your criteria that appears in your inbox. Depending on the quality of the listing agent, the listing may provide a good description and pictures, or it might not. When a listing contains only one photo, the exterior of the front of the building, buyer beware. More times than I care to count I would come across a listing with only one picture, confirm the financial aspects made sense, and schedule a showing only to walk through an absolute dump, wasting my time and my realtor's. If the listing agent only includes one photo, it's for good reason- the property is likely in bad shape. Now if you're strategy is to find a rehab project, a single photo listing could be a great indicator of just that. You can tell a lot from photos when you do find a listing that contains more than one. You can see if the current owner has taken care of the building, if the current tenants respect the property, and get a general feel for the layout of the rooms. One of the beautiful things about technology is the ability for you to "drive by" a property without leaving your computer screen by using Google Street View. You can guarantee that every time I looked at a listing, I was typing the address into Google to do a virtual drive-by of the property. It gives you just a little better feel for the location, proximity to other buildings, etc.

Beyond just the description and photos of the property, another major component to analyze is the rents, if they're listed. If they're not listed usually your agent will be able to get this information by calling the listing agent. Your previous studying of area rents, current sale prices and education in Gross Rent Multiplier will allow you to pretty quickly determine if the listing is a good deal at or around the list price. This is where having a good understanding of the numbers becomes invaluable. If you determine that the property could be a good deal, it's time to act fast. Remember, all of your competition has, in theory, received this same notification, is running the same numbers, and is ready to jump at the opportunity for a good deal. You want to get on the phone with your agent as soon as possible to schedule a showing as soon as one is available. During the search for my first property sometimes this would be the same day. I had the luxury of supervisors at work who were understanding of what it was I was doing and allowed for me to leave work at a moment's notice to go view a property. If you're unable to do so, ask your realtor to do it on your behalf. Ask them to do a live video feed to "walk" you through the property. This is a realtor you have chosen based on the fact that he too is a real estate investor, and as such you should be able to trust him if he views the property on your behalf and makes the recommendation of making an offer. Now you might say that's just too far outside of your comfort zone, and if that's the case then so be it. But keep in mind that when a good deal presents itself you have to strike while the iron is hot and do so before anyone else does.

As you view more and more properties, you will get a better feel for what it is you should actually be looking for. Your agent will also be able to provide help in this area. If you have a significant other, I also recommend brining him or her along too. It's amazing the different things each person will notice as you discuss your feelings on the property after doing a showing. It doesn't hurt to bring along a notebook as well. You want to be detailed about everything so that as you're running it all through your head, you're not solely relying on memory to help make your decision. Here's a handful of *major* items that you should get comfortable making note of as you begin going on showings.

1. **Neighborhood Makeup** – As you're arriving at the showing, pay close attention to the surrounding neighborhood. Presumably you should have a good idea of what the neighborhood is like, considering this particular property already fits your criteria, but each street can be a bit different so take note. Are most of the buildings in the area single family homes? Are most of them multi-family apartment buildings? This is important because if you find yourself in an area with a majority single family homes, it could indicate a higher percentage of owners, rather than renters, and might point to a weaker rental market for that particular area. Do other buildings along that street appear to be in good condition?
2. **Building Exterior** – Does the mortar between bricks appear to be crumbling in areas? Are there settlement cracks zigzagging along the mortar joints? Both are signs of the potential need to tuckpoint, the process of

removing and replacing damaged mortar. Is the siding pulling away in areas? Does the caulk around windows appear cracked or dried out? Both could be signs of potential water damage.

3. **Windows** – Once inside you'll be able to get a better view of the windows up close. Do they appear to be in good condition? Ask the listing agent when they were installed. If the agent doesn't know, ask to have that information provided. On a 3 to 4 unit building there could be a couple dozen windows, if not more. If they look to be in good shape, great! If not, it could be a bargaining chip if and when you get the property under contract.

4. **Mechanical System** – The heating system will most likely be one of the following: Gas Forced Air (furnace), Radiant Heat (boiler), or Electric Baseboard. There will usually be a sticker on the front of a furnace or boiler that indicates the model year, and possibly any maintenance performed over the subsequent years. If no sticker is present, again ask the listing agent for that information or to obtain it. It should be obvious that older units will be closer to the end of their useful life and should be factored into potential costs of maintaining the building. Is there also a central air conditioning system, or do the tenants use window air conditioners? How many gas meters are there? Is there one for each rental unit, plus a "building common" meter for laundry hot water or common area heating? These are all questions you'll want answered.

5. **Electrical Components** – This one is much more difficult to see unless there is a basement with an exposed ceiling. Older buildings might have electrical wiring known as knob-and-tube or cloth wrapped wiring. Both are outdated and no longer allowed per electrical code. Even if you can't see the wiring, it's still worth asking the question to the listing agent.

It's unlikely they will know the answer to this as well, unless there was a recent renovation. If the property was built later than the 1960's it's unlikely you'll have to worry about either of these anyways.

Another aspect of the electrical system to take note of is the electrical service coming into the building from the street. Find out how much amperage, or power, is being supplied to the building. You want to make sure the amperage being supplied will be sufficient at peak hours when air conditioners, tv's, microwaves, etc. are being run all at once. How many electrical panels are there? Is there one for each unit, plus a "building common" panel for exterior lighting, laundry, etc.? A good rule of thumb is a minimum of 50 Amps per panel per apartment.

6. **Plumbing System** – Similar to the electrical components, this one is tougher to determine without some exposed ceilings. Ask the listing agent if the water supply lines are copper, galvanized steel, or worse yet, lead. Galvanized steel water pipes corrode over time and cause pressure issues, and the harms of lead piping are obvious. Again, if the building was built after the 1960's it's unlikely to have galvanized or lead pipes.

If your knee-jerk reaction to all of this is: "I'm not an inspector! There's no way I can intelligently look at this stuff!" then I say "bologna". The things I've listed above can be determined and viewed by someone who has little to no experience with building components. There will come a time for you to hire a professional home inspector to get into the nitty-gritty of every little detail and issue with a property, and that will come once you have a property under contract. But ahead of that, you want to arm yourself with as much information and knowledge as possible so you're able to have a competent conversation with a listing agent or seller, and use that information to factor into an offer. This isn't something that requires you to go to a trade school in order to know what you're looking for. You just need to understand what it is and how it might affect your bottom line.

One thing you can be sure of is that you cannot take the seller's word on anything. Trust but verify. Remember, they're trying to sell you something so if they see an opportunity to make something seem better than it is, they might. It's not to say that all sellers have malicious intent. But with something of this magnitude you want to confirm what it is that you're getting in to. When I purchased my first building it was with the understanding that *all* the water supply lines were copper, as described by the owner. Indeed, this appeared to be the case; the exposed pipes to and from the water heaters were copper and the plumbing under the sinks that I could see were also copper. But that's just it; they were the pipes I could see. It wasn't until later, after I had purchased the building, that I opened some access panels to find that all the water lines within the walls were old, galvanized pipes. Not even my home inspector caught this or thought to look into it more during the inspection. The point here is that everything is not as it seems, and you need to do your due diligence. That might not be possible in some cases, but you should exhaust all options to get the information you want.

Considering the buildings components is only a partial view when considering what to look for in a property. Your tenants likely won't care, or know, if the pipes are copper or galvanized, for example. You need to also consider the building from the standpoint of a renter. You'll remember that part of our *Landlord Manifesto* is to not only purchase a multifamily building but to also occupy one of the units as a live-in landlord, so you'll be looking at your own new potential living space. But let's also look at it as if we're a renter who is being shown the apartment with the interest of renting the apartment. What is it that a renter looks for? What makes your property more desirable to live in than a comparable building? These are things you want to factor in, as it will help you down the road when you market a unit for rent.

1. **Accessibility** – One of my criteria for purchasing a property is that it is within a reasonable walking distance to public transit. That could mean a bus stop, subway or train station. In addition to that, I look for properties that have nearby access to a major highway. It should be obvious that you want to provide a place that makes it easy for a renter to get to and from work. This convenience will allow you to charge a slightly higher rent than what the exact same building could charge but is further away from these means of transportation.
2. **Safety** – This one is simple. If you wouldn't feel safe walking to and from that train station alone at night, then don't expect your tenants will be either.
3. **Commerce** – A renter is going to take into consideration the locations of the nearest grocery store, gym, restaurants, and other shopping. You should strive to find a property that is within a mile or two of all of these. The City of Chicago publishes all building permits and shows the location of each on an interactive map. Using something like this could allow you to find out if a new grocery store or restaurant is on its way to the area. If your city doesn't offer something like this a few phone calls or emails to the chamber of commerce could provide some valuable information.
4. **Unit Layout** – As you enter each unit, take note of the layout. Consider the location of the bedrooms as it relates to the entrance, living room or kitchen. Does the unit have a good "flow", or is it oddly shaped and sectioned off? It may all seem trivial, but this is a space someone will be calling home, and you want an apartment that is comfortable and

functional.

The key question to ask with each of these is "would I want to live there?", regardless of whether or not you actually end up living in that apartment or building. If I found myself answering that question with a "no", I would have strong hesitations about making an offer on the property.

There was one property I went to for a showing that was in one of the most desirable neighborhoods in Chicago. The pictures looked pretty good, and Bob Barker could confirm that The Price (Was) Right. The only hiccup appeared to be the location of the property from public transportation. It wasn't that public transit wasn't nearby. Rather, the elevated train ran directly through the backyard. "How bad could it be?", I thought prior to arriving at the showing. I realized how bad it could be, about every five minutes while I was there. One of the elevated "El" trains that Chicago is known for would come rattling by at full speed every five minutes or so, and I'm not exaggerating when I say that it seemed as if the building was shaking as the train passed. The noise was deafening. On top of that, the layout of the building was just odd. The owner tried to mitigate the noise problem by redoing the layout so that the bedrooms were at the front of the building, furthest away from the tracks. There was a lot of unusable space. The analytical part of me wanted to make an offer based on the price and location, but in my heart, I knew I could never live there and knew the process of finding tenants would be a nightmare. I passed on the deal.

That's an important takeaway from this section: you're looking at properties not only as the owner, considering building components and financial aspects of the deal, but also as a renter and the desirability of living there. Buildings that are a perfect match for everything you're looking for will be few and far in between, so you'll have to weigh both the pros and cons of each and always come back to the question of whether or not you'd want to live there. You might come across a property that you wouldn't consider living in, but it's a deal you can't pass up.

And that's perfectly fine. But at least you ask the question and identify the potential risks or difficulties you may have with owning the property.

CHAPTER TEN - STRUCTURING OFFERS

Take a deep breath... We've finally reached the fun part. Everything you have learned up to this point has set you up for success. You have a specific set of criteria which has steered you in a particular direction. You know how to analyze a property to determine if it is worth your time and further effort, and whether or not it makes sense financially. You've toured properties to get a better feel for the neighborhood and the quality of the building. And, finally, you've found one that is a candidate for taking that next step. It's time to make an offer.

The first offer you make can be a nerve-racking experience. After countless hours of researching, reading, and educating yourself there is still a sense of uncertainty with how to approach making what is likely the most significant purchase you've made in your life. Perhaps you don't know if you're making the right decision, or you may have hesitation wondering if a better deal may still be out there. The truth of the matter is this; most real estate investors will tell you that their very first deal was not much of a deal at all. They either over paid, bought a poorly performing property, or experienced a myriad of other issues. However, it's this first property that is the most important deal you'll make in your real estate investing journey. Your first purchase will allow you to learn and develop your skills as a landlord, and ultimately lead to further opportunities for growth. You need to get past any second guessing and trust in the time and effort you've invested in getting yourself to this point. Let's break down the major components of the offer and how you can tailor it to your situation.

Determining Price

After an exhaustive search that has brought you one dud after the next, you've finally found a property that not only meets your criteria but checks out financially, too. You've analyzed the gross rent multiplier as well as the cap rate and determined the list price is close to where it should be, based on the current rental rates. You'll first need to determine the price which you'll offer to the seller. Perhaps you've heard the phrase "a property is only worth what someone is willing to pay for it", and it's true. Just because a seller is asking for a certain price, doesn't necessarily mean you should offer it. That can work both ways; you might offer less, or even more than what the property is listed at. Remember this: list price is irrelevant. You have a to find a price that makes sense for you, regardless of what the seller is hoping to get for the sale.

Your research of the market might tell you that the seller is overly ambitious in their asking price and, based on the local GRM and cap rate, you offer a lower price. Or your research might indicate that the asking price is well below the value of the property and in an effort to outbid your competition you offer a price over asking. It's a double-edged sword, but this is where relying on data, not emotions, will help in making the right move. To further support your own research of value based on rents, your realtor will also perform a Comparable Market Analysis, or CMA. A CMA pulls data from other similar properties in the area to show recent list and sale prices. In putting together a CMA, your realtor will try to level the playing field by adding or deducting value to other recent sales to make them more closely match the property you're interested in. So, for example, if the property you are making an offer on has a two-car garage, but a recent sale in the area does not, your realtor might add $25,000 to the price of the recent sale to help make the comparison apples-to-apples. Or, if a different recent sale has three apartments with 2 beds and 2 baths each, and the property you're making an offer on has three apartments with 2 beds and 1 bath each, your realtor might deduct $10,000 per unit from the price of the recent sale. The CMA will provide a handful of properties that sold recently to show a range of sale prices for in comparison to what you will be offering. It's one more tool to bring yourself a sense of comfort with how much you ultimately decide to offer.

You've done your homework and have solid data on which to base your offer. You think surely you can present this information to the owner to justify exactly why you're offering what you're offering, and the owner will say "You're right! Sold!" Here's what is more likely to happen. Assuming this property is listed to the public and is not an arms-length, off market deal, the property will absolutely have competition. Competition to you means multiple offers for the seller. And in this situation, you are likely competing against buyers who are less educated than yourself. Now the price is based less on fundamental data, and more so on the state of the market. If it's a buyer's market where there are more properties available than there are interested buyers, you're in a good position to possibly purchase at a discount. However, if it's a seller's market, where competition is high and the number of available properties is low, you could find yourself in a bidding war. Your research is still valuable at that point, but in order to purchase the property you might have to go against what you've learned and concede a bit on price.

There are buyers out there who will not purchase a property unless it can be had for a certain percentage less than market value. Good luck and Godspeed to them I say. There is a time and place to be that selective for a purchase. But now, this early in your investing career, is not the time for it. That is not to say that you won't find a deal below market value, but if you wait for it to find you, or only make offers at a 20% discount, you may end up on the long road to nowhere. As mentioned before, your first purchase most likely will not be the one that makes you wealthy. Rather, it will likely be a deal that can best be described as "just fine". This might mean you barely break even, or even have a negative cash flow. But in my opinion, this is still better than sitting idly by and continuing to wait. Still strive to make a good, intelligent purchase, but recognize that it may not align with all the financial analyses. Only you can determine what price is going to work for your situation and what kind of return and performance you're willing to live with. I overpaid on my first property, when considering the fundamental data, but after running all the numbers I determined that I would still break even, and that's while occupying one of the apartments. In my mind the benefit was twofold:

1. I would live rent-free while my tenants covered the cost of my mortgage, thus being able to accelerate savings for the next purchase.
2. Once I purchased the next building, moved out and rented my unit, the first building would be cash positive to the tune of about $1,000 per month.

For me, in that situation, slightly overpaying made sense. For someone else, it might not. Perhaps you'd be comfortable at a negative cash flow, knowing that the amount you're contributing is still far less that what you would have been paying in rent. Or on the flipside, perhaps barely breaking even would not be acceptable for your situation. The long and short of it is you should first analyze the property in a "perfect world" scenario, so you know the true value of the property based on fundamental data. You need to then recognize what likelihood there is, if any, to have an offer accepted at the price. From there you can then determine the price at which you should offer based on likely competition and your willingness to accept the financial performance of the property at that price. Each person will arrive at that number for different reasons. If you base yours on carefully thought-out rationale, you won't find yourself kicking yourself later on. As the saying goes, "Don't wait to buy real estate. Buy real estate and wait."

With your heart set on a number, you now need the input of your lender. Let's say you find a property that you "have to have" and will pay any price to beat your competition. There will, of course, be restrictions to the amount you'll be able to pay. "A property is only worth what someone is willing to pay for it" is only true if the lender also agrees to lend on that amount. You've already been pre-approved by your lender up to a certain dollar amount. The bulk of the work in analyzing your financial situation, from the lender's perspective, has already been taken care of. With your offer price now established, your lender will want to analyze the specifics of the property you are prepared to make an offer on and at the price you are willing to pay. She'll look at the current rents and take the percentage of the total without the rental income from the apartment you'll be living in and use that to supplement your own personal gross monthly income. At the price you're offering, the down payment amount you're contributing and at the rate at which you're borrowing, she'll be able to determine your ability to make the mortgage payment each month and whether or not you can afford the property at the price you want to offer.

FHA Self-Sufficiency Test

If you've decided on utilizing an FHA loan to finance your purchase, there are certain requirements that must be met. The FHA requires that the rental income from a property is capable of covering the cost of the monthly principle, interest, taxes, and insurance (PITI) and determines so through a calculation called the self-sufficiency test. Your lender will determine the PITI based on the amount you want to offer, and the rental income of the property will be determined by an FHA certified appraiser. The appraiser will calculate rents based on current market rates, not actual in-place rents. Once the rent schedule is determined by the appraiser, the FHA allows 75% of the total rent (including the unit the borrower intends to occupy) to be counted toward the rental income, or in other words, a 25% vacancy factor.

Standard lending practices are similar in that typically only 75% of rental income will be counted toward your total net income to cover the loan, however FHA requirements differ in that the self-sufficiency test is standalone, meaning only the rental income, and not your additional personal income, is considered. If 75% of the rental income does not exceed the total PITI, then the purchase price must be lowered until it does. Further, the borrower must also show proof of three months of PITI reserves in addition to the down payment and all closing costs.

The self-sufficiency test is difficult to pass on a 4-unit property, and exceedingly more difficult on a 3-unit property. You need to be cognizant of this if your strategy includes FHA financing.

This is where having a "high horsepower" lender is beneficial. When you identify a property that you're ready to make an offer on, you'll want to notify your lender as soon as possible. Included with your offer to the seller should be your pre-approval letter from the lender that is specific to the address of the subject property. Working with a lender that has a large team will guarantee you get this within a matter of hours. As discussed previously, having that pre-approval letter included with your offer could be the difference between having your offer accepted or rejected.

Length of Closing

The length of closing is the time it takes from receiving the notice of an accepted offer to the point where the ink has dried on all documents and keys are finally turned over. A standard closing length is usually 30 to 45 days. There are a couple strategies to consider when determining the proposed length of closing. You might be able to entice a seller with a quick closing. This is entirely dependent on your lender's ability to process your loan application and get through the tedious underwriting process. Some lenders might be able to get this done in as little as two weeks. This could be a good strategy if you have a seller who is particularly eager to get out of the property fast. Another strategy could be to leave the date as "to be determined at a mutually agreeable date". This works well if you're current living situation is flexible, and the seller needs additional time to relinquish the property. Your realtor should be able to find out from the listing agent what situation the seller is in and if it's beneficial to offer a shorter or longer closing, or if it's a non-factor. In a competitive market, a favorable closing date is another piece of ammunition to increase your odds of an accepted offer.

Earnest Money Deposits

In an effort to show the seller that you are committed to following through with the purchase of the property, and effectively not waste their time, you will, on two separate occasions, deposit cash in the form of earnest money. These deposits are a guarantee to the seller that you will not walk away from the contract without just cause. Initial earnest money is deposited as soon as there is a signed contract. The second earnest money is deposited following the completion of attorney review. These deposits are credited towards your down payment during the closing. The amount of each deposit is at your discretion, with the second deposit typically being larger than the initial. A combined higher amount indicates to the seller a stronger willingness to make the deal happen and a confidence in your ability to close.

Contingencies

When making a purchase of this size it only makes sense to have safeguards in place to allow yourself a way to legally terminate the contract, if you must. These safeguards are known as contingencies, and without them you could be at risk of forfeiting the aforementioned earnest money. There are a handful of standard contingencies that are included with any offer, as well as some additional you may consider adding. We'll dive deeper into each once we have an accepted offer.

1. **Mortgage Contingency** – Simply put, the purchase of the property is contingent on the buyer's ability to obtain financing if not paying cash.

2. **Attorney Review** – During the attorney review period your attorney has the power to disapprove the contract under good faith.

3. **Inspection Contingency** – The results of your home inspection may constitute as reason to terminate the contract.

4. **Homeowner Insurance** – Similar to the mortgage contingency, the purchase of the property is contingent on the buyer's ability to obtain insurance

for the building, and the inability to do so could allow the buyer to terminate the contract.

5. **House Sale Contingency** – Not as common as the previous contingencies, the House Sale Contingency allows a buyer to back out of a contract if they are unable to sell their current home within a specified period of time.

6. **Zoning** – For a property that has a unit which might not have legal status, you might elect to make the purchase contingent on the zoning of the property, thus documenting the legality of the unit in question.

7. **Acceptance Timeline** – You might be able to influence the seller to select your offer if they think they might not get anything better in the coming days. Your offer could be contingent on the seller accepting within 24 hours, for example.

There are infinite possibilities to add contingencies to a contract, but each additional contingency must be carefully considered. While the first four listed here are considered standard and shouldn't be cause for hesitation with the seller, multiple other contingencies added might make your offer less appealing to a seller who has multiple other offers.

Hedge Your Bet

In a competitive market there are a few additional strategies you can use to further improve the likelihood of your offer being accepted. These should be considered on a case-by-case basis, and each presents potential additional risk to you as the buyer.

1. **Escalation Clause** – In order to outbid the competition, you may elect to add an escalation clause. Simply put, this clause raises your offer to a level that is higher than that of the highest offer

received by the seller. Let's look at an example.

A property is listed for sale at $500,000. Your research indicates the property is worth closer to $475,000, so you make your offer based on that. Your offer, however, includes an escalation clause of $1,000 over the highest offer, not to exceed $515,000.

- If no other offers come in above your initial offer of $475,000 then the seller is able to either accept or reject your offer at that value.
- If another offer comes in at $500,000 your offer is automatically increased to $501,000
- Or, if another offer had been made at $516,000 you offer stands at $475,000 as the escalation would increase your offer beyond your highest threshold.

As a buyer, the risk to you is that you lose negotiating power. The escalation clause precisely identifies your highest number to the seller. Furthermore, an escalation clause is not a guarantee of an accepted offer. For a variety of reasons, the seller may choose to select an offer that is still lower than yours.

2. **Waiving Contingencies** – In order to make your offer even more attractive to the seller, you may also decide to waive certain contingencies. Waiving any contingency can be a high-risk strategy, so you need to be absolutely certain of your decision to do so and discuss with your realtor. For example, you might waive your inspection contingency. In doing so, your ability to back out of the contract after your inspection reveals major issues with the property is forfeited. This is only recommended if you are confident in the condition of the property or if a "pre-inspection" has been performed prior

to making an offer. Alternatively, you might make an offer with a "general inspection contingency" in which you still have the ability to cancel a contract due to the results of the inspection, or otherwise agree to purchase the property without negotiating the cost of repairs.

Another contingency you might consider waiving is a portion of the financing contingency, that being the appraisal. Your ability to obtain a loan on the property is dependent on the property's ability to appraise for an amount that is greater than or equal to the value you are having financed. If you have rock solid data which supports the property appraising for a value higher than that which you are borrowing, this could be an option. Waiving this portion of the financing contingency comes with the risk that the appraiser does not see eye to eye with your own research. And if you were to find yourself in this situation you could end up losing your earnest money or be required to come up with the difference in cash between the appraised value and the offered value.

Waiving any contingency should only be done after careful consideration and extensive research and discussions have taken place with both your realtor and lender. It should be viewed not as a last-ditch effort, but as a confidence in your knowledge of the property.

3. **"Cash Offer"** – One last strategy that you might consider is a "cash offer with right to mortgage". When competing for an accepted offer on my first purchase, I was often frustrated to find out I lost a property to an all-cash offer. It amazed me that there were people who had that much cash available to make a purchase of that size without obtaining a loan. It wasn't until much later that I found out an all-cash offer is not always what it seems. While

there certainly are people who can and do make all-cash purchases, you can also use this strategy to your advantage by making a cash offer with the right to a mortgage. In doing so you are hedging your confidence in being able to obtain financing for the property. The way this differs from a typical, non-cash offer is that if, during the closing process, you are unable to qualify for financing, you forfeit your earnest money. This again signals to the seller your confidence in being able to close. This strategy got me into a little bit of a pickle with the purchase of my personal residence. During attorney review, the sellers requested proof of funds for the all-cash offer we made. Of course, my wife and I didn't have the amount needed to be able to make a purchase with cash but were completely confident in our ability to obtain financing. Not the seller's realtor, nor the seller's attorney nor the sellers themselves seemed to understand the cash with right to mortgage offer that we made. They were confused as to why we were waiting for final underwriting approval from our lender. In some instances, you may need your realtor to provide a thorough explanation to the seller's realtor of what this type of offer is and the benefits it provides the seller.

Letter to the Seller

The final component of your offer is your attempt to make a connection with the seller on a personal basis. This is done with a letter to the seller. Some might say this is nothing but a wasted effort, but you might find that the seller is able to identify with you and perhaps see a bit of himself in you as well.

Your letter should describe who you are, what it is you like about the property, and precisely why you want to purchase it. And it needs to be genuine at that. Tell the seller about yourself and your plans to own and manage multiple apartment buildings. Describe the amount of work you've put in to getting to this point. Acknowledge the seller's ability to manage this building and your hopes to be able to accomplish the same. Don't fawn over the seller. Anyone can recognize the difference between disingenuous praise and a heartfelt compliment. Point out specific aspects of the property you particularly like, such as an architectural feature or your appreciation of the renovations the seller has completed. Often times a property is a deeply personal belonging to the seller, so describe how you plan to care for the building long into the future.

I've heard story after story about a seller selecting an offer that may not have been the highest but contained a personal letter in which the seller was able to connect with the buyer. And from what I was told, this was exactly the case on the purchase of my first property. Supposedly there was another offer higher than my own, but the seller owned multiple multi-family buildings and was able to relate with what I was trying to do. It's not a guarantee of an accepted offer, as I wrote 7 or 8 of these before going under contract, but it is a way to possibly provide yourself a leg up on other offers. I've provided an example personal letter in the Appendix. Take a look and see what aspects you might be able to use in a letter of your own.

Strategy for An Accepted Offer

1. Determine your offer price based on logic and data. Recognize the state of the market and decide if you need to stray from the fundamentals.

2. Include a preapproval letter specific to the property you're offering on.

3. Propose a closing date that is beneficial to the seller.

4. Indicate a confidence in your ability to close with a high earnest money deposit.

5. Review standard contingencies and add others if

necessary.

6. Consider methods to get a leg up on the competition.
7. Include a personal letter to the seller.

Negotiation

There are three possible outcomes after submitting your offer: acceptance, rejection, or a counteroffer. Short of acceptance, the next best thing is a counteroffer. A counteroffer opens the door to negotiating, and this is a good thing. While the acceptance of your offer is the ultimate goal, the outright acceptance of your initial offer right away could leave you feeling as though you grossly overpaid.

A counteroffer is a chance for the buyer and seller to find common ground. You may find that the seller is willing to haggle on price and will engage in a back-and-forth of sorts until a mutually agreeable number is met. However, the psychology of negotiating is such that the number the seller is fixated on could be something they're mentally unable to compromise with. As a result, you must find a different way to get what you want, while still satisfying the seller's need to sell at a certain price. The important thing for you to know is that *price isn't everything*. Rather than strictly negotiating price, you should consider also negotiating terms. Even if the seller does not counter with a new price, the opportunity for a deal is not dead.

Let's consider a few scenarios where the seller counters at a price that is still beyond the maximum amount you are willing to pay. Negotiating some of the following terms might still allow you to land a deal that is favorable to you, while also meeting the seller's wishes.

Closing Costs – If a negotiation has come to a stalemate within 3-5% of the ultimate price at which both parties will accept, try negotiating to have the seller cover some or all of the closing costs. Typical closings costs are around 3-5% of the purchase price. Accepting the seller's higher counteroffer but

> **What is a closing cost?** Closing costs are essentially the cost of doing business for purchasing real estate. They are comprised of services and fees that have contributed toward finalizing the purchase. There are many, but below are just a few:
> - Attorney fee
> - Environmental report
> - Prepaid homeowner's insurance
> - Title insurance
> - Lender/application fee
> - Various taxes
> - Prepaid mortgage interest

getting them to agree to pay for closing costs could be a net zero change to get through an impasse. Let's look at an example.

A property is listed for sale at $485,000. You offer $450,000, to which the seller counters at $475,000 as their take-it-or-leave-it price. Your think the property could still be a good deal up to $460,000 but already know the seller won't accept the offer. So, you respond by stating you will accept their counter of $475,000 if they agree to pay for $15,000 of your closing costs. The seller gets the value they proposed, and you still save the $15,000 in closing costs to purchase the property at the value you believe it's worth.

Rate Buy Down – One method for capturing a discount on price over a longer period of time is by paying a premium for a lower interest rate. This is done by paying a fee know as a "point" to the lender at closing. As part of you negotiation you might propose that the point premium is paid by the seller. This strategy is only beneficial to you as the purchaser *if you plan to hold the property for an extended period of time*, as the benefit is in the form of less total interest paid and a lowered monthly payment over the life of the loan. A mortgage point is 1% of the value of the loan, and purchasing a point typically lowers the interest rate by $1/8^{th}$ of a percentage. Let's take a look at an example.

You're in negotiations with the seller of a $500,000 property. Your initial offer was $460,000 to which the seller countered at $485,000. You see this as an opportunity to negotiate terms to your advantage while giving the seller more than his counteroffer price. The second counteroffer you present is $495,000 with the condition that the seller pays two mortgage points. Let's compare how the numbers shake out:

> **OPTION 1**
> Acceptance of seller counteroffer at $485,000
> -95% LTV loan amount: $460,750
> -Added cost: $0
> -Interest rate: 4.75%
> -Total interest paid over 30 years: $404,506

> **OPTION 2**
> $495,000 second counteroffer, 2 points purchased
> -95% LTV loan amount: $470,250
> -Cost to seller: $9,405 (2% of loan value)
> -New interest rate: 4.5%
> -Total interest paid over 30 years: $387,518

As you can see, the savings on the interest over the life of the loan is $16,988. While it's not the discount you initially sought, the lower amount of total interest paid effectively saves you an additional $6,988 beyond the seller's initial counteroffer, at no net cost to the seller. Furthermore, I've used a more conservative figure of .125% per point in this example. You may find that your lender offers up to .25% per point, in which case the savings in interest over the life of the loan in this example would be over $41,000. Still, you must weigh whether or not capturing those savings over the course of 30 years is worth it in the long run, or if financing a loan which is $10,000 less in total value makes more sense.

Flexible Acceptance Structure – If other negotiation attempts have failed you might resort to structuring a deal with added flexibility. Perhaps the seller is overly ambitious with their valuation of the property and is asking far beyond what the market is willing to pay. The property is listed for sale at $550,000. You offer $450,000 based on supporting data. The seller barely budges an inch and counters at $540,000 knowing full-well that you're miles apart in price. The strategy here is to once again counter at a price slightly higher than your initial offer, but establish that if your new offer is accepted the seller is allowed to continue to market the property and accept a higher offer if received within 30 days. If the seller receives a higher offer, they can accept it and terminate your purchase agreement. If not, they must come to terms with the true value of the property and proceed with the purchase agreement in place. In essence you're telling the seller that the price you're offering is the best they're going to get, and you're so confident in that amount you're willing to let the deal go if another higher offer comes in. The risk is on the seller in that if they do not accept your counteroffer, they may end up with no deal at all. This strategy may not work in a hot market or if your timeline doesn't allow it.

When negotiating with a seller, it is important to understand that a counteroffer constitutes a rejection of the offer previously made. While that may seem obvious, I point that out because once a counteroffer has been made, the offer that was previously on the table becomes null and void. So, for example, if you offer $550,000 on a property, to which the seller counters at $600,000 and you say "thanks, but no thanks", the seller cannot then accept your previous offer of $550k. In that case you would have to resubmit an offer of $550k to make it valid.

CHAPTER ELEVEN - ACCEPTANCE OF OFFER

"Congratulations, your offer has been accepted!"

At long last, after all this time researching, viewing properties, and negotiating with sellers, you hear the words you've been waiting to hear. It took me 9 months, 8 offers, 23 showings and countless other properties analyzed online to finally hear those words for my first purchase. Those six words start the clock on your closing timeline, and it seems ironically appropriate that such a lengthy process can culminate into a whirlwind of events that finishes in as short as a few weeks. When I look back at each of the properties I offered on, I'm thankful that most of those offers did not get accepted. The offer that did eventually get accepted was on the building that is perhaps the very best out of the entire bunch. It's funny how things work out.

There's one building in particular that stands out in my mind. It was a 4 unit building that needed A LOT of work. A lot of work that I would likely never have had the time or cash to be able to accomplish at that point. I was so gung-ho and excited about the potential for reno

vating the building that I brought my parents to a second showing. My dad, who has the ability to look past the current state of affairs and see what a property could look like after renovation, simply said "Oh my God…". He was pretty much speechless after that and just shook his head. My mom, on the other hand, simply cried. She could not stand the thought of me getting in over my head and taking on such a monumental project. And it would have been monumental, indeed. Thankfully I used my better judgement (and the influence of seeing my parents' reaction) to walk away from that property before ever making an offer.

My reason behind telling you this story is that although at times the process can seem never ending, overwhelming or fruitless, things have a way of working themselves out in the end. I was a phone call away from calling off my search before having my offer accepted. You never know what is right around the corner. The well-known story about how Thomas Edison tried 10,000 times before perfecting the incandescent lightbulb is an obvious comparison to make. Without a doubt Edison believed each of those iterations was going to be the one that worked, and yet he didn't quit after thousands didn't work. Each offer you submit has the potential to be your next deal, so don't get discouraged; your patience will be rewarded. But for now, let's get back to our accepted offer. The clock is ticking…

With the acceptance of your offer comes the depositing of

> Those 9 months of actively searching for and offering on properties prior to having an offer accepted ended up costing me more than just time. One of the methods I employed to help partially fund my down payment was to withdraw money from my IRA as a first-time homebuyer. I withdrew the $10,000 limit allowed by the IRS and parked it in a checking account so it was readily accessible. I certainly did not anticipate the process of getting a property under contract to take so long.
>
> The IRS stipulates that any funds withdrawn for this purpose must be utilized within 120 days from the date of distribution to the date a purchase contract being signed. Failure to adhere to this rule results in the distribution being taxed at ordinary income tax rates, as well as a 10% early withdrawal penalty.
>
> Unfortunately for me the process was much longer than the 120-day period stipulated by the IRS. It wasn't until tax season the following year that I realized my mistake. Simply put, it was a $3,800 learning experience.

your initial earnest money. You'll remember from before that this initial amount is less than what the second earnest money amount will be. You'll also remember that the sum of both will be used as part of your down payment should you get to that point. Your earnest money is only at risk if you did not put proper contingencies in place. This money is typically deposited and held with one of three parties: the seller's agent, the seller's attorney, or a title company.

It cannot be stressed enough that prior to wiring money you must call the recipient to confirm the wire instructions, verifying the name of the banking institution the money will going to, the routing number and the account number. Wire fraud is becoming increasingly more common. Criminals will hack the email account of the closing officer, real estate agent or attorney and send wire instructions for their account, rather than the account information of the correct parties. When contacting the party who will be receiving the wire, be sure to retrieve the contact information from a Google search, rather than the instructions you received, this way ensuring you're not calling the fraudster themselves.

Disclosures and Inspection

Depending on your state, sometimes you might receive seller disclosures prior to having an accepted offer. Disclosures are a seller's way of telling you of any defects they are or are not aware of in the property. However, most of the time these disclosures are not provided until a signed contract has been executed. This can be viewed in either a positive or negative light. Information that comes from a disclosure statement might give you reason to ask the seller to further reduce the price. However, it might also lead to something that gives you reason to walk away from the deal entirely. Common disclosures include the following:
- Existence of lead paint, asbestos, mold or radon (a harmful gas)
- Known structural issues
- Property line infringements

- Renovations performed and whether or not it was with a permit
- Unsafe conditions

These are only a handful of disclosures. There are a variety of others. Take a look at the property disclosure example provided in the Appendix. Knowing common disclosures ahead of time might even help you sniff out problems while still in the property search process.

A seller stating that they "are not aware" of any of these issues does not mean that the issue does not exist. However unlikely it may be that the seller does not actually know these things are wrong with the property, they can essentially plead ignorance. Legally it gets them off the hook if a problem were to come up after closing on the property. An important phrase on the document is that the disclosure "is not a substitute for any inspections or warranties that the prospective buyer or seller may wish to obtain or negotiate." As such, you will perform your own inspection of the property to confirm these disclosures and potentially find other issues not previously known.

When hiring a home inspector, you should first and foremost confirm they are licensed and insured within the state you are purchasing. Your inspector should _not_ be your uncle Bill who has bought a couple houses before and knows a thing or two about maintenance. Don't try to save a few hundred dollars on something that could end up costing you tens of thousands of dollars down the road. Your real estate agent should be able to provide one or two inspectors you can reach out to. See if they have referrals and by all means call to see how their experience was with the inspector. Reach out to family or friends to see who they have hired in the past. You don't want to get stuck with just one option as there's no guarantee that any one inspector can fit an inspection into their schedule on your tight closing timeline. Your contract will typically state that an inspection, if desired, must be performed within 10 business days of the acceptance of the offer. Ideally, you will have already identified one or two inspectors prior to going under contract on a purchase.

Once you have an inspector selected and have scheduled a date for the inspection, I highly recommend you are present for the entire duration of the inspection. An inspector will notice things that you would never even consider looking for, and he'll provide invaluable information for you as the potential future owner of the property. Follow him around and ask questions. Find out what it is he's looking for, why it's important and whether or not it falls within the normal range for the age of the building that's being inspected. Below is a list of some of the more important aspects of an inspection you should ensure your inspector is covering. It is far from a comprehensive list, rather some of the highlights that could reveal hidden problems:

- Water damage – a good inspector will use an infrared viewing "gun" to scan the ceilings of the top floor to determine if there are any current leaks, or if there may have been some in the past
- Gas leaks – your inspector will use a gas "sniffer" to determine if any pipe fittings are not securely tightened to prevent gas leaks
- Mechanical systems – regardless of what time of year it is, your inspector will want to start up both the heating and cooling systems to determine if they are providing adequate heating and cooling output. This is done with a laser that reads the temperature coming from HVAC vents or radiators.
- Age of roof – your inspector will take a climb up to the roof and you should do the same. While there he'll attempt to gently pull back some of the roofing to determine how many layers there are and provide an estimate as to the age.
- Condition of foundation – your inspector will walk the perimeter of the building from the outside or within the basement if there is one. He may find that there are settlement cracks in the foundation and whether or not they appear to be new or active, or if they are

typical for the age of the building and likely dormant. Buildings do settle over time, so don't be afraid if he determines that there are cracks in the foundation. It's only an issue if it has caused uneven settlement or if the cracks are still active.
- Electrical systems – although your inspector won't be able to see within the walls and conduit to determine the type of electrical wiring in place, he will be able to tell you if there is adequate amperage servicing the property, if the circuits are properly grounded and if ground-fault-circuit-interrupters (GFCI's) are in place where required.
- Other areas of inspection include smoke detectors, plumbing systems, windows, façade, bathroom & ceiling fans, among many more.

In his report your inspector will typically not provide an estimate as to the cost of repairing or replacing any particular building component, but he can provide insight as to how much longer the useful life is and when you might have to make those repairs. For example, he might determine that a water heater is 10 years old when the typical life span is 7-10 years, thus noting the exposure for possible replacement in the near future.

So long as your contract to purchase the building is not as-is, the results of your inspection could provide you with reason to further negotiate price or terms with the seller. You are not required to disclose the entire inspection report to the seller, but if there are items that you wish to negotiate you will need to provide the evidence specific to those items from the inspection to the seller. Let's take a look at an example in which the inspection determines that the roof needs to be replaced, a very significant undertaking.

> After viewing the roof up close, your inspector determines that there are multiple layers, indicating continued deferred maintenance, possible code violations

and therefor the need to do a complete roof replacement. You get a quick opinion from a contractor and determine the work could cost around $15,000 or more. You're left with a few options to negotiate with the seller in order to be compensated for this defect.

- Ask for a seller's credit – You might ask that the seller provide a credit for the cost to replace the roof and therefore the sale price would be reduced by $15,000.

- Ask for closing cost assistance – As was discussed earlier in the negotiation phase, the seller might be psychologically attached to their selling price so you might be able to get them to pay for some of or all of your closing costs. If the seller isn't open to this idea, you could potentially offer to increase the sales price by the amount that the seller would cover in closing costs. By doing so you reduce your out-of-pocket expenses and in turn roll those costs into your loan. The seller provides that cash upfront but receives it back in the form of a higher sales price. Depending on the loan type you use the seller is typically allowed to contribute up to 9% of the sales price.

- Ask for the seller to perform repairs – the seller may be more prone to paying for the repairs themselves rather than reducing the sale price of the property or contributing to your closing costs. In doing so you get the repair you asked for and the seller still gets the price they desire. You could take it one step further and offer that the seller places the funds in escrow for you to receive after the closing. The benefit to the seller is that they don't have to deal with the hassle of hiring a contractor to do the work, and the benefit to you is that you have control of who is doing the work and possibly bidding the work out to find the best price.

Of course, the seller has the option to say "no" to any of these offers and chose not to engage in further negotiations. With something as significant as a roof replacement it would be unlikely, as any other buyer would almost certainly find the same issue and ask for some form of credit as well. However, smaller requests for repairs in a competitive market might be dismissed by a seller who knows they have the upper hand.

Attorney Review

The acceptance of your offer started the clock on not only your inspection timeline, but also the timeline for attorney review. While you and your inspector are taking a look at the nuts and bolts of the property, your attorney and the seller's attorney are dotting i's and crossing t's. Attorney review is the period of time that the two attorneys representing each the buyer and seller can propose clarification of or modifications to the contract.

Each party has the ability to, within 5 days after the date of initial acceptance, either approve the contract, disapprove the contract (as long as disapproval is not solely based on price), or propose modifications. In the case of proposed modifications, the attorney review period is extended by a specific duration (usually 5 additional days) in order to allow time for each party to review. Proposed modifications can range from an extension of the closing period to adjustments of contingencies. There are infinite possibilities for modifications you might request. Included in the Appendix is the modification letter from my attorney that was sent to the seller's attorney during the review period of the closing of my first property. What you'll see is that more than anything the line items are confirmations of information not previously mentioned in the contract or disclosures. You'll also see the handwritten notes in response to each item by the seller's attorney. This can be a back-and-forth process, as was the case for me in the following example, until both parties agree in writing to each item. If there is an item that one party is unable to agree upon, that item can simply be removed from the proposed modifications, or that party has the option to terminate the contract per your attorney review contingency.

As you will see in the letter from my attorney, one of the modifications listed was that the real estate taxes be prorated at 110% (line item 20). In Chicago, as is the case with most localities, real estate taxes are paid in arrears, meaning that taxes for the current tax year are not paid until the following year. In the case of the sale of a property, that means the new owner will be paying for the taxes during the time in which the previous owner possessed the property. In order to account for this, one of the items paid by the seller at closing and placed into your escrow are property taxes for the current tax year.

As we are all too aware, taxes tend to go up year over year. Not knowing exactly what the taxes will be for the current tax year until the tax bill is issued the following year, your attorney will propose that the current tax rates be prorated at an amount more than the current taxes to reflect the fact that they are almost definitely going up.

Initially, my attorney proposed that taxes be prorated at 110% of the most recent tax amount. Without getting into the specifics behind the meaning of each portion, here is how the numbers worked out:

Most recent assessed value:	$39,514
Most recent state equalization factor:	2.7253
Most recent local tax rate (Chicago):	6.833%
Most recent tax bill:	$7,358 (product of the above three)
Proposed proration:	110%
Proposed tax paid by seller:	$8,094

The seller's attorney countered by offering no proration

(100% of the most recent tax bill), which I would not accept. After further discussions between the attorneys, they were able to eventually agree on a 105% proration. Following the same math from above, the amount paid into escrow by the seller for taxes was $7,726. Unfortunately, as I would find out about a year later, the total property tax bill that year ended up being $7,941. So, it was close, but about $200 short of actual.

The proposed modifications, including any means of compensation for repairs determined by the inspection, are listed in a document supplemental to the contract known in legal terms as a Rider. Once all items have been confirmed by the seller and all proposed modifications have been either accepted or removed from the contract Rider, attorney review period can be closed. Once closed, these modifications become a binding part of the contract and no further modifications can be made. At this point, you will then deposit your second earnest money with the same party as is holding the initial earnest money. You are now one step closer to finalizing the purchase.

Lender Appraisal

All the while during the inspection period and attorney review period your lender is doing her legwork to fulfill the obligations of the lending institution. As you recall, the saying "a house is worth whatever someone is willing to pay for it" is only applicable if the house also appraises for that value (or if the buyer pays cash). In order to mitigate their risk in lending you money, your lender will order an appraisal of the property to ensure it appraises at or above the purchase price. The cost of the appraisal is paid for by the buyer, though many lenders will offer a closing credit to cover the cost of the appraisal. (If it's not offered, ask!)

When appraising the property, the appraiser will perform one of two methods to observe the condition of the property: a drive-by appraisal or a full appraisal. As the name suggests, a drive-by appraisal involves observing the building from the exterior, taking a few pictures and not entering the apartments. The other method, a full appraisal, involves the appraiser entering every room in the property. Clearly a full appraisal is a much more accurate way to depict the condition of the property and therefor allows for the appraiser to be more accurate in their valuation. Typically, your lender will decide which method they want the appraiser to perform, but you can ask for a drive-by appraisal if desired. I wouldn't recommend asking for a drive-by appraisal, as it will almost always result in a more conservative (lower) appraisal valuation, but there could be some strategy in wanting one. If the property you intend to purchase is one that is in very poor condition and needs a gut-rehab, it could make sense to order a drive-by appraisal. The effect is that you essentially shield the appraiser from seeing the dismal conditions inside and prevent a considerably lower appraisal. This strategy is specific to this situation, so unless you're planning a gut rehab it doesn't make sense to push for a drive-by appraisal.

After observing the property and making notes on its condition, the appraiser will get to work on determining its value. There are a couple different approaches used by appraisers when determining the value of a residential property. Let's take a look at each.

1. Sales Comparison Approach

Similar to when you were trying to determine a price to offer on the property and your real estate agent performed a Comparable Market Analysis, the appraiser will investigate multiple recent sales of comparable properties in the area. The appraiser will gather data regarding not only sales price, but also number of units, total square footage, number of rooms, type of construction, among many other factors. In order to tighten the spread on the comparison, the appraiser will actually make adjustments up or down on the value of the comparable properties. For instance, if the subject property has a basement, and 2 of the 3 comparable properties also have a basement, an adjustment will be made to the third property to *increase* the value to reflect what the value would be if it did have a basement. Or, if the 3 comparable properties each have central air conditioning, but the subject property does not, the value of the comparable properties will be *decreased* in value to reflect the value of the central air conditioning. This is done in attempt to make the comparisons closer to apples-to-apples, since it would be nearly impossible to find another building that has the exact same specs as the subject property, let alone 3 or more.

With the revised comparable property values the appraiser can then back into a revised
- price per square foot
- price per unit
- price per room
- price per bedroom

The appraiser will then do his or her voodoo magic to assign a value for each of those 4 metrics to determine 4 different valuations of the subject property. This will produce a range of potential property values. With all of that information in hand, the appraiser will then assign an opinion of the value of the property thus concluding the Sales Comparison Approach.

2. Income Approach

When gathering data on comparable sales in the area, the appraiser will also gather data on comparable rentals in the area. The rental comparisons are like-kind in that they have the same number of bedrooms & bathrooms, as well as a similar square footage area. That information is used to determine the rents likely to be achieved at the subject property (current in-place leases are not considered which could be a good or bad thing), and therefore a gross monthly rent amount. The appraiser will then use the Gross Rent Multiplier that we know and love to determine the value of the property based on income.

With both approaches considered, understand that in residential real estate much more emphasis is placed on the Sales Comparison Approach over the Income Approach, as it much more accurately reflects the nature of buyers and sellers in current market conditions. Part of the appraiser's report is a study of the condition of the market. He or she will categorize comparable sales and days on market into three buckets:
- prior 7-12 months
- prior 4-6 months
- prior 3 months to current

This will portray the trends for the area and if, in general, prices are increasing, stable, or decreasing, as well as if properties are selling at a faster or slower rate.

Once the report is issued by the appraiser hopefully you have reason to celebrate with a value that is higher (hopefully much higher) than that of the purchase price. If not, you may need to go back to the drawing board to negotiate a new price with the seller, or terminate the contract entirely as is allowed by your Financing Contingency.

Insurability

I'm going to put it out there right now that this section is a snoozer. The subject of insurance is not going to be the most exciting topic in this book, but it is a necessary topic and one that may help answer some questions that never seem to be explained in a classroom setting or on the path to adulthood. That being said, I wouldn't blame you if you decide to skip this section entirely, but if you do manage to trudge through it, I promise it'll be the last you read of it.

Concurrent with the home inspection and the lender's appraisal is your task to *ensure* the property can be *insured*. What does that mean, exactly? Your lender will want to make sure that the property is insurable so that if something catastrophic happens, it's not solely the responsibility of the homeowner to pay for repairs. Remember, many of these requirements are put in place to protect the lender in the event of a default. The appraisal sets a baseline for what the property could potentially be sold for if the owner is unable to make mortgage payments and defaults on the loan. Similarly, insurance provides a level of comfort to the lender so that if, for example, a property is destroyed by a tornado, the owner doesn't walk away from the mortgage requirements and leave the lender holding the bag on a worthless property.

Different lenders will have different requirements for "how much" insurance you need to buy. In general, most lenders will require that you purchase a policy that covers the cost of the loan. Certain areas of the country, however, will require that additional coverages be taken out, such as flood insurance in New Orleans, or hurricane insurance in many parts of Florida, for example. Your lender will stipulate what coverages you need so you know what it is you're shopping for.

Like so many other aspects of a property purchase, you will want to have options when it comes to selecting an insurance agent. Pricing will vary from company to company, as will their ability to provide certain coverages. You need to find an insurance agent that not only provides a good price but also adequate coverage to protect your investment. Now is not the time to select a bargain-barrel insurance company. You do not want to get to the final steps of mortgage underwriting only to have your loan denied based on insurability, so shop around and choose wisely.

There are multiple factors that are considered by your agent when determining the cost of your insurance:
- Age of property
- Construction type
- Geographical location
- Neighborhood crime rate
- Specialty features (pool, fireplace, etc.)
- Additional coverages (sewer backup, flood, etc.)

When discussing insurance, there are a couple of terms you should be familiar with that are the most frequently brought up. The first is "premium". Your annual premium is the total yearly cost of the insurance policy. When financing a property and paying a monthly mortgage, the annual premium will be divided into 12 monthly premiums and paid for as a portion of your mortgage payment.

The other term you should be familiar with is "deductible". The amount of your deductible is the amount you will have to come out of pocket before insurance kicks in to help. For example, you might have a $3,000 deductible. A hailstorm causes $2,500 in damages. In this instance you have not reached your deductible amount and therefor will not receive help to pay for the damages from your insurer. In another example, a windstorm destroys your roof and causes $20,000 in damages. You pay the first $3,000 (your deductible amount) and your insurer covers the remaining $17,000. The amount of your deductible is on a sliding scale and is at your discretion (with some limits set by your lender). A higher deductible (more out of pocket costs for damages) results in a lower annual premium. Conversely, a lower deductible (less out of pocket costs for damages) results in a higher annual premium. You need to decide which option is more suitable to your tolerance for risk and ability to pay.

In the Appendix you'll find an example of a quote I received for the homeowner's insurance on my first property. It is worth noting that the following are considerations of a *homeowner's* policy specifically, as the strategy of the *Landlord Manifesto* is to occupy the building as a live-in landlord. If your intent is to purchase a property you will not be living in, you will need to purchase a "landlord's" policy, as you will be unable to get a homeowner's policy without living in the property. There are differences between the two in terms of what coverages you can obtain, and the cost of each, so for the purpose of this book we will focus only on the homeowner's policy.

There is a lot to understand on an insurance Declaration Page, so let's break down each component so you know what it is you're paying for, and what the policy is protecting. Not all quotes will look the exact same, but they will have the same basic components and language. As long as you understand each you will have no problem navigating quotes from various agencies.

In this example the quote is organized in two major sections. On the left are the Coverages, or the items that are being insured. On the right are the policy Limits and Premiums. The "Limit" column shows the value of coverage for that line item, and the "Premium" shows the portion of your annual premium that pays for that amount of coverage.

Dwelling

Far and away the most expensive line item on your insurance quote will be that of the cost of the structure itself. On a homeowner's policy, you will typically be offered two options: Replacement Cost or Actual Cash Value. When given an option, you will always want to select Replacement Cost. As the name implies, Replacement Cost is the value to replace the entire loss *in today's dollars*. Contrast that with Actual Cash Value, which is the cost to replace the structure, less depreciation. Let's take a look at an example to help illustrate better:

You and your identical twin each purchase a property across the street from each other, coincidentally both for $500,000. The structures are the same construction, same number of units and are similar in all other aspects. How weird! After 5 years of ownership the unthinkable happens and a fire burns both the buildings to the ground. What are the odds?! You each initiate a claim with your insurance agents to begin the tedious process of being compensated for your loss.

Replacement Cost
Lucky for you, your policy coverage is 100%

Replacement Cost. In determining your settlement, your agent concludes that the cost to completely rebuild the structure, in today's dollars, will cost $625,000 and, as such, a settlement is offered at that value. This amount will allow you to pay a contractor to rebuild a structure that is equal to or better than the previous structure, and you end up in the same position you were in prior to the loss.

Actual Cash Value

Unfortunately for your identical twin, in order to save a few dollars on his monthly premium, he chose to cover the property with an Actual Cash Value policy. In determining the settlement, his agent has a couple methods at his fingertips. He might conclude that the value of the property, prior to the loss, was $585,000 at fair market value and offers that amount as a settlement. Or he may determine the Replacement Cost is $625,000 and deduct 5 years' worth of depreciation, resulting in a settlement of $600,000. In either scenario, your twin must come out of pocket for the balance required to rebuild at $625,000.

Increased Dwelling

Most insurers will include an additional amount over and above the standard Dwelling coverage. That amount is the Increased Dwelling. Simply put, the increased dwelling is an additional 20% on top of the Dwelling Coverage A to guarantee the replacement cost can be met

Dwelling Extension

Also included in your policy coverage will be structures on the property, not physically attached to the building, such as a garage or a shed. The limit amount shown is the value to replace those items in the event of damage.

Personal Property

When you purchase a homeowner's policy you are not only protecting the structure itself, but also your personal belongings inside the property. This might include furniture, electronics, clothing and other items. Your agent might ask what kind of furnishings you have to determine this value, otherwise it can be somewhat arbitrary. It is very important to note that this coverage is <u>not</u> extended to your tenants. If a fire damages your tenant's personal property, your insurance will not cover the cost to replace those items. More on this later.

Personal Liability

In today's lawsuit-happy society, the importance of personal liability coverage cannot be overlooked. Personal liability coverage protects you against claims made against you as the property owner for bodily injury or property damage that occurs on your property. It can also help pay for attorney defense costs and court costs. If a reckless tenant stumbles home drunk and proceeds to fall off a balcony and break his legs, he might turn around and sue you for being a negligent landlord and not providing adequate protections from his drunkenness. It's important to have coverage against such a scenario. Some insurers are able to offer more coverage than others, and if you find that you're unable to obtain what you feel is suitable coverage, you may want to consider getting an umbrella policy to provide even further protection.

Medical Payments

Similar in scope to the personal liability coverage, the medical payments coverage helps pay for medical expenses for someone on your property, with your permission, who is accidentally injured. Important to note is that this coverage does not pay for you or your own family's medical expenses.

Credit Card / Forgery

In the event you are the victim of credit card fraud or forgery, this endorsement can help pay for those losses.

Damage to Property of Others

As the owner of a building with tenants, if you are directly involved in the damage to someone else's property, this will help cover the cost of those damages. For instance, if you are cleaning gutters and the ladder slides off and falls on top of a tenant's car, this endorsement will help pay for the repairs to the car.

Loss of Use

Next to the dwelling coverage, this is probably the most important coverage you can have as a landlord. In the event of an incident that severely damages your building, loss of use coverage is designed to compensate you for not only for the lost rental income that would be earned during normal operation, but also for the cost to place your tenants in another temporary living situation, such as a hotel or entirely different apartment. Loss of use is enacted during the period of which the property is considered uninhabitable and until the repairs have been completed, though there are limits to the total dollar amount and length of time.

Credits

Each agency will have their own method for offering policy discounts based on other policies you have with them (bundling) and property improvements such as a home security system.

Policy Options and Endorsements

Without getting too into the weeds, this section offers further coverages for miscellaneous items within your property such as jewelry. However, there are two line items on my declarations page that are worth discussing further.

> Building Ordinance or Law – if you own an older structure that gets damaged and subsequent inspections by local authorities determine that outdated electrical systems (that may not have been part of the original damage) must be entirely replaced due to current code violations, this endorsement covers the cost of these repairs.

Back-Up Dwelling – this endorsement, though not always necessary, was of particular importance to me on this building because there is an apartment unit in the basement. Back-up dwelling coverage insures the damage of property caused by sewer backup into the building (not flood water).

You can breathe a sigh of relief now; we're done with the insurance section. Congratulations, you're now certified insurance-literate. That was the main goal of this portion, so you could understand what it is you're paying for. Admittedly it's not the most exciting material, but without having a good grasp of it you might end up paying for more than you need or have less coverage than you ought to obtain.

You may need a reminder that we're still in the process of getting to the closing; you have an accepted offer, you've performed a home inspection, the attorneys have reviewed each line of the contract and have come to mutually agreeable terms, your lender has performed the appraisal of the property, and you now have evidence of insurability from your insurance agent. You are now only a step away from signing on the dotted line.

CHAPTER TWELVE - CLOSING

The culmination of all of yours and others' effort comes down to about an hour of signing documents. It's over in the blink of an eye and it's easy for a lot of information to go over your head unless you take the time to carefully read every single word, of every single line, of every single document. In the interest of yours and others' time, this is not realistic. Your attorney will be with you at the closing, and he will give you a high-level overview of each document and why you're signing it to keep moving things along. Rest assured that most of the documents you sign will be standard documents required by the Real Estate Settlement Procedures Act (RESPA) and Housing and Urban Development (HUD), and that you're not signing your life away in the process. I'll attempt to do the same here and provide a high-level overview of a few of the major components of the closing process.

On the day of closing, you will typically meet with your attorney at the office of the title company, though it could also be at the office of either the buyer's or seller's attorney. Present in the room will be yourself, your attorney, a representative from the title company who is also a public notary, sometimes the seller's attorney, and possibly even the seller (the latter two being less common as the seller will typically have pre-signed all documents).

As you get settled in for the process you will have hopefully already heard three very important words from your lender: "Clear to close". The notification of clear to close means that you have satisfied all requirements of the final underwriting of your loan, and that your loan has been funded by the lender. These requirements include a final credit check, confirming the appraisal is at or above the purchase price, evidence of insurability, proof of funds for down payment, among many more. The purchase of the property hangs in the balance of the mysterious underwriter (not to be mistaken with the undertaker). I always thought of the underwriter as a nameless, faceless person in the shadows with the power to ultimately approve or deny your ability to purchase the property. You will never have any direct contact with this person and can only hope he or she gives you the nod of approval.

That approval may happen in advance of the closing, or as was the case in my first purchase, on the day of the closing. If you remember early on in this book, I had inadvertently paid off a student loan in the days leading up to my closing. No longer having that "good debt" on my credit report caused my credit score to drop, and as a result I had to pay a slightly higher down payment in order to satisfy the lender's requirements. This all of course affected the underwriting process and caused enough delay that we were waiting around in the closing office for nearly an hour before anything began in earnest. It was a nerve-racking 60 minutes of fiddling around on my phone waiting to hear those three words. Finally, the transaction was given the clear to close, and with funding in place we could begin.

Leading up to closing day you will have been provided a final loan closing disclosure by your lender. By law, your lender is required to provide this no less than three days prior to closing. A closing disclosure outlines all costs you will have in the transaction. These costs can fluctuate slightly depending on a variety of factors and timing, and that's why the closing disclosure will have been provided as an *estimate* once you put the property under contract, and then finalized in the days prior to closing. The finalized closing disclosure will be provided to detail the loan including payment information, closing costs, and cash to close. Let's take a look at two prominent sections of the closing disclosure:

Loan Terms & Information

The details of your loan will be spelled out to summarize the amount you're borrowing, the interest rate you're paying to borrow that money, and the estimated total monthly payment including taxes and insurance.

Closing Costs

Closing costs consist of a myriad of items that affect the bottom line. Typically closing costs amount to approximately 3-5% of the loan total (not the sale price). There are a variety of items that contribute to your total closing costs, including:

- Loan fees – including application and origination
- Appraisal fees
- Title fees
- State, County and Locality transfer taxes (similar to sales tax)
- Prepaids – one year homeowner's insurance, mortgage insurance (if applicable), 6 months of property taxes (depending on how your locality bills taxes), and prepaid mortgage interest which is the amount of interest that accrues between the closing date and the end of that first month.
- Attorney fee
- Multiple fees associated with chain of title

The following are some of the most consequential documents which you will be signing at closing. Of course, your attorney will provide a detailed description of each, but it's good to have a general understanding prior to getting to that point.

Promissory Note – Simply put, the promissory note is a promise to repay the amount borrowed, including interest. Of particular interest, you should be aware of two sections:

- Prepayment Penalty – Your loan may stipulate that if you make an additional payment toward principal or pay off the loan in full prior to the end of the term, the lender may be entitled to a premium beyond the mortgage interest rate. This is important to know because if your plan is to refinance you must also factor in the cost of the prepayment penalty.

- Recourse vs. Non-Recourse – The promissory note will define the extent to which the lender can pursue assets in the event of a default. A recourse loan allows the lender to attempt to collect other assets in addition to the mortgaged property, such as a personal residence, cash savings or wage garnishment. A non-recourse loan limits the lender to seize only the mortgaged property and nothing else.

Warranty Deed – The warranty deed is the instrument used to transfer title from one party, the Grantor, to the other party, the Grantee (i.e., seller to buyer). It is also a guarantee that the Grantor is the owner of the property described in the deed and has the right to transfer that property.

Assignment of Rents – The assignment of rents is another failsafe for the lender in the event of a default on the loan. In essence, you are granting your lender the ability to collect rents from tenants should you become delinquent on your mortgage payments, fall into bankruptcy, or otherwise not uphold the terms of the mortgage agreement.

Assignment of Leases – The assignment of leases is the method by which the current in-place leases at the property are assigned over to the purchaser. So, although the leases were signed by the seller at an earlier date, following the sale of the property the leases remain valid and enforceable by the purchaser. You will receive an assignment for each of the apartments at the property.

Finalized Survey – The purpose of a survey is to record the exact property dimensions and precise location relative to specific landmarks. Most commonly you will see the legal property location description in a format known as "metes and bounds" which reads like a treasure map. The survey will also determine if there are any property line infringements.

Master Statement – The master statement is the final accounting for both parties. It will itemize every credit and debit to show the final net balance due *to* the seller, and the final net balance due *from* the buyer.

> Don't overlook the importance of reviewing each line on the master statement. On my most recent closing, the line crediting my side for the total earnest money deposited was short by $25,000. Someone had forgotten to include my second earnest money check, and neither attorney caught it until I brought it to their attention. I'm not sure if it would have been realized before completing closing, but without that revision my cash to close was $25,000 higher than it should have been as a result. Always double check.

- Debit vs. Credit – Both yourself and the seller have costs on each side of the balance sheet. A debit can be thought of as cost owed, whereas a credit can be thought of as an amount gained or previously paid.
- Cash To Close - This is the amount due from yourself after all debits and credits have been reconciled.

PART THREE: LANDLORDING

Following the closing on your newly purchased property you might not feel any different, and the rest of your day might continue on as it normally would. But what you have just done cannot be easily undone. You can't go back to the seller with a receipt and kindly ask to return your purchase. You now have responsibilities that will affect your day-to-day life for a long time to come. There will be trying times ahead that will make you question your very decision to get into this in the first place. Always remember, however, why you chose to do this. What you have done is taken the first major step towards achieving your "Why". The purchase of this first property will hopefully lead to the subsequent purchase of multiple properties, allowing you to ultimately accomplish what it is you set out to do in the very beginning.

But let's not get ahead of ourselves. Before becoming a real estate tycoon, you need to first learn what it is you're doing with this initial property. It's not as easy as just collecting rent and sitting on a mound of cash like Scrooge McDuck. All the books ever written on real estate, this one included, will never be enough to prepare you for every scenario or every circumstance. The most effective way to learn is going to be on-the-job training. The following chapters are going to supplement that training to allow you to be as successful as possible. Let's learn how to be a landlord.

CHAPTER THIRTEEN – EARLY DAYS

Over the course of the multiple showings, building inspection, appraisal and the rest, it will have become apparent to the tenants that the building is in the process of being sold. The previous owner may have sent a notification to each of the tenants describing that a new owner would be contacting them soon. You should reach out to each tenant via email as soon as possible and follow up with an in-person introduction to meet these people face to face. Although not necessary, it doesn't hurt to have multiple copies of a signed letter from the seller stating that you are the new owner and to now direct all correspondence to you. You can request copies to be provided to you at closing.

If you are following the overall strategy as prescribed, you will be moving into this building as an owner-occupant. You'll want to meet your new neighbors and assure them you're just a regular guy or gal who goes to work each day like they do and won't be banging on their doors collecting rent (hopefully). I haven't been in the position of a renter who lives in the same building as his landlord, but I have to imagine it's not the most comfortable feeling in the world, at least not at first. You want to convey to them that you're not there to make their lives miserable. Quite the opposite in fact. I like to talk up the fact that if there's ever an issue, I'm there to get it resolved right away. You'll find yourself at times doing more than necessary to keep your tenants happy, but the way I look at it is that this is a service industry, no different than a waiter tending to guests at a restaurant, and you want to keep those guests (tenants) happy. That being said, you do not want to be walked on. You must be firm but fair in dealing with tenants and follow the golden rule of treating others how you'd like to be treated. Your tenants should feel comfortable in approaching you when they run into you in the laundry room or at the front door to the building.

Undoubtedly there is a slight awkwardness about living around your tenants. After all, they're giving you a substantial portion of their monthly income for the privilege of living amongst the person they are making wealthy, right? That's certainly how it feels at least. In time you'll get over this, but it takes some getting used to. If you take on the mindset of "I'm just another tenant" you'll have no problems with this. But if instead you are the overbearing, nosey landlord, then you're in for some difficult times ahead. I keep interactions with tenants cordial and brief. A simple "how's it going" or "how has your weekend been" goes a long way in affirming to them that you're "just another tenant". Contrast that with an interaction that pries into their personal space, and you'll soon find you are instead the "weird landlord that lives in the building and makes tenants want to move out".

Tenants may take it upon themselves to dive deeper into conversation, and there's no harm in getting involved in that. You should be friendly with your tenants, but you should not *be friends with* your tenants. For instance, I have a tenant who works at a brewery and is a genuinely cool guy. Occasionally he'll even drop off a six-pack of his newest brew at my doorstep for me to try. He's invited me to the brewery to hang out and have beers, and had he not been my tenant I would have done so. But you do need to draw a line in the sand somewhere. It's important to distinguish these people as tenants rather than friends. My reasoning behind this is it is far easier to enforce policies with tenants than it would be with friends. Otherwise, you'll find yourself bending the rules and making exceptions. Along these same lines you should never rent to family and friends. It may sound harsh but it's necessary.

In the initial days of communicating with these or any new tenants, you'll want to "train" them, as is so effectively described in Mike Butler's book *Landlording on Auto Pilot.* Mike describes how you need to set precedents with your tenants so they know what is and is not acceptable in terms of living in your building. One precedent I like to set right away is the appropriate chain of communication regarding matters at the building. Presumably you are still working a full-time job at this point, and you can't respond to every request at the drop of a dime. The following chain prevents allows you to prioritize your responses and can lessen the amount of stress you take on. It will also serve as a means of being notified of incidents that do require your immediate attention.

High Concern - Emergency Situation (i.e. fire, gas leak, etc.)
- Immediately call 911
- Follow up with a call to your landlord (you)

If I see a tenant calling me, I know I need to excuse myself from whatever it is I am doing and take that call.

Moderate Concern (i.e. oven not working, sink is dripping, etc.)
- Text your landlord

In this situation I'm able to quickly look at a text, respond right then, and begin to determine what is necessary to resolve the issue.

Low Concern (i.e. wanting to paint a room, purchasing a pet, etc.)
- Email your landlord

In this situation I don't have to burden my mind immediately with whatever it is the tenant is reaching out about, and I can respond at my leisure in a reasonable timeframe.

> Create a somewhat professional email account. Rather than just (your name)@gmail, come up with a "company" name and email address like XYZrentals@gmail. This gives you just a touch more professionalism, plus it separates business matters from personal matters.

Without setting this communication precedent you may find yourself continuously taking calls for the most trivial concerns that can absolutely wait for your response. In order to enforce this, you may even need to respond to a call or text with the requirement that the tenant first email you their concern before you'll provide a response to it. Eventually they'll get the picture and follow procedure.

With any building you purchase there will be certain acquisition costs beyond what you already budgeted for in terms of any repairs that might be required. These are the standard items you will find yourself purchasing with every building to get things started on the right foot. I've listed a few below but as you do this longer, you'll know the things you need to buy right away in order to make your life easier.

1. Keys – Depending on the previous owner and their level of organization you may get a box full of keys, or you may get nothing at all. You'll need to first sort through what you have, determine what is necessary and what gets tossed, and proceed to make copies of those keys you keep. It's even possible you may need to temporarily borrow tenants' keys in order to make sure you have your own copies. Once organized with multiple copies and labeled key tags you'll want to buy yourself a lockable key organizer and mount it in a secure location.

2. Lock-Out Boxes – Along the same lines as the first item, you'll also want to purchase combination lock boxes for each unit and the building itself. On multiple occasions prior to getting these myself I would have tenants calling me at the most inopportune time to

let them into the building because they lost their key. There should be one lock box on the exterior of building with a common key that allows entry into the building. Once inside the building there should then be one more lock box for each apartment, that way if a tenant gets locked out, they don't then also have keys to the rest of the units. Rather than you having to go let the locked-out tenant in, you can simply provide them a code to retrieve the building key and another code to retrieve the lock out key for their unit. Just don't forget to get those back.

3. Rent Drop Box – As was described as one of the methods for collecting rent, you'll want to provide a lockable drop box in a common area for tenants to deposit rent.

4. Lightbulbs – Do yourself a favor a get a big box of lightbulbs. I require tenants to supply and replace lights within their units, but bulbs are constantly burning out in common areas or on the building exterior, and they're also helpful to have at unit turnover.

5. Dryer Vents – What you will find is that people rarely, if ever replace the flexible vent leading from a dryer to the outside. You will then also find that these flexible vents are caked full of lint from years of running the dryer. For 15 bucks or so not only will you reduce the fire hazard associated with a clogged dryer vent, but you will also improve the efficiency of the dryer as well.

6. Fire Safety – Speaking of fire hazards, you should purchase a fire extinguisher for each apartment and one for a common space like the laundry room. Additionally, replace any old or non-functioning

smoke/CO detectors in apartments and ensure there is one in common spaces as well.

Collecting Rent

One of the most obvious of your new duties as landlord will be that of collecting rent. Similar to what was described before in terms of keeping your tenants happy, you will want to provide them with multiple means for paying rent so that they are able to choose a method that is most convenient to them. Allowing a method that is convenient to your tenants ensures that you will get paid in a timely fashion, so in essence you are looking out for your own interests here. I allow for three methods in which tenants can pay rent:

1. Cash or check in a locked rent drop box located somewhere in a common, secure area within the building.
2. Bank Transfer – this includes methods such as Zelle bank-to-bank transfers or scheduled automatic ACH transfers.
3. Cash App Transfer – in today's ever-evolving tech world there are constantly new methods of person-to-person monetary transfers through the use of phone applications. At the time of writing this book I currently use Venmo as an easy way for tenants to pay rent from their phone.

There is third party software that you can purchase that allow a tenant to make a payment online, but be mindful that there will be a fee for you to use such a service and with the other options listed it might not make sense to enlist this option so early on in your landlording career.

There are a couple ground rules to collecting rent, and these ground rules need to be spelled out in the lease (we'll get into lease writing specifics in a bit). This is where being "firm but fair" is paramount, particularly the "firm" aspect. Once these ground rules are set you must stick to them.

1. Rent is due on the 1st of the month, and I allow a grace period of 5 days. If on the 5th of the month I see that rent has not been electronically transferred or there is no check in the lock box, I send an email to the tenant stating the following:

"*(Tenant)*, rent was due on the 1st. As of this morning rent has still not been received. Please submit your rent payment no later than 5:00 PM this evening. Failure to do so will result in eviction proceedings being filed against you."

This will get a tenant to respond rather quickly. Some landlords will recommend a hardline stance of rent being due on the 1st and is late on the 2nd. However, I can understand that there may be unforeseen circumstances, or a tenant just has a slip of mind. Furthermore, your mortgage holder also allows a grace period, usually as much as 15 days. What I do is schedule my mortgage payment to be made on the 10th to ensure I have all rent collected and checks have cleared prior to my mortgage payment being made. If you get a grace period with your mortgage payment, it's only fair to allow the same to your tenants.

> Open a new checking account specifically for all transactions related to the building. This will be used for depositing rent, paying your mortgage, and all miscellaneous expenses. You want to keep everything separate from your personal expenses so it's easier come tax time.

2. Never accept a partial or split payment. Acceptance of a partial rent payment (with the expectation that the balance will be delivered shortly thereafter) can be viewed as an outright acceptance of a lesser

amount of rent than is actually due for that month. (In Chicago this is upheld with a city ordinance that prevents landlords from evicting tenants if partial rent payment has been accepted in lieu of a full amount.) You must explicitly state this to your tenants and if a tenant ever submits a partial payment immediately reach out to the tenant in writing and state that you have <u>not</u> accepted the amount paid and return the funds if possible until such time that a full payment is possible. This precedent is particularly important if you have friends living together as roommates and who want to each send their respective portion of rent. <u>Do not allow this</u>. In this scenario one person is to pay the entire rent amount. The burden is then on that person to track down his or her roommate to collect the other half of the rent.

Something to take into consideration when deciding which payment methods to allow is the use of money orders from currency exchanges or similar check-into-cash type institutions. Whatever the reason may be, there are people who still choose to not have personal checking accounts with a bank. They instead turn to these currency exchange type services to issue money orders in lieu of using cash or other methods to pay rent. Generally speaking, this is a safe and reasonable way to accept rent from a tenant. The only time I've had an issue stemmed from a problem caused by my own bank. I attempted to deposit the money order into my bank's ATM, but the machine "ate" the money order. After an internal investigation it was determined that the money order was "nowhere to be found" and it became my responsibility to work it out with the payor (my tenant). Under normal circumstances a tenant might have just contacted their bank to put a stop-payment on their personal check and reissue a new one. Given that this was a money order, that was not possible. Instead, the currency exchange required a 30-day waiting period before they would allow the money order to be cancelled and then reissued, which of course cost $30 for the service, plus an additional $10 for a notarized affidavit. I share this story simply as a precautionary tale to help potentially avoid unnecessary hassles.

CHAPTER FOURTEEN - MARKETING AN APARTMENT

The leasing process is something that can take up a lot of your time if not done wisely. It is also the single most important process you will have as a landlord. That bears repeating; the leasing process is the single most important process you will have as a landlord. Without a solid system in place, you can throw everything else out the window. A poor leasing process will result in vacant units or, perhaps worse, nightmare tenants who don't respect the property or don't pay rent. We're going to lay out a set of criteria for potential tenants in this section, and if you follow the process described you'll put yourself in an excellent position to avoid all those troubles.

If at all possible, I try to coincide my lease start dates all around the same time of year. I do this for multiple reasons. First being that I know each year when my "busy season" is for leasing units. Rather than constantly have my mind occupied with getting units leased throughout the year, I like to condense it all within a 3–4-month time frame and knock them all out at once. The rest of the year I can focus on other aspects of the business. Another reason is the seasonality of moving. According to the US Census Bureau, approximately 40 million Americans move each year, and 64% do so between May and September*. You want to be able to capitalize on the peak demand during these months, and therefor benefit from higher rents and greater competition for reliable tenants. Another related benefit of having leases start around the same time is it allows you multiple units to show to perspective tenants (although early on hopefully you don't find yourself with multiple units available for lease).

> We've been working under the assumption that the building you purchased is completely occupied. Along with inheriting the leases and rent payments, you're also inheriting the problems that may arise as a result of not having been to one to have vetted these people. If you inherit tenants hopefully you get lucky and the tenants are in fact good people who respect the property and pay rent on time. However if you find yourself with a disaster of a tenant who has a significant duration remaining on the lease, you may again need to get creative and persuade them to leave. This might mean you offer to pay for their moving expenses or simply offer cash to move out by a certain date. Either way, the small amount of money you need to spend is much less than the hassle of keeping this person as a tenant in your building.

Advertising

Advertising your unit for rent is your first opportunity to show off the features of the apartment. It's the "foot in the door" for a prospective tenant in determining whether or not they could see themselves living there. Knowing that, you want to portray the unit in the best light possible, both literally and figuratively. The first step prior to advertising a unit for lease is taking high quality photos of the unit. When I say high quality photos I'm not simply talking about pictures from your phone. While the quality of the image itself from a phone may be good, what is not good is the frame width. Have you ever noticed how much less of a subject appears on your phone camera than what appears to the human eye from the same distance? Without getting too technical it has to do with focal length. The human eye has a much smaller (wider) focal length than does a phone camera. Additionally, your phone will constrain the image to an aspect ratio suited for the shape of the screen. Instead, what I recommend you do is invest in a decent DSLR camera and wide-angle lens, or a wide-angle lens attachment for your phone. What you will find is that the images capture so much more of a small, enclosed space, such as a bedroom or bathroom, and allow for an image that is more consistent with what the human eye sees in person. Let's compare the two. The following images were taken standing in the same spot, the one on the first with a phone and the second with a DSLR fitted with a wide-angle lens. Notice the difference? The second image allows the viewer to see much more of the space.

High-quality, wide-angle photos go a long way in portraying a unit to appear as large as possible. It should also go without saying that the unit should be clean and organized prior to taking the pictures. You don't want to show off the mess that current tenants live in. If tenants are currently occupying the unit when you need to take pictures kindly ask them to tidy up before stopping by for pictures (some people have a different definition of "clean".... Good luck).

Regarding lighting, it should be obvious that you shouldn't take the pictures at night. Take the pictures at a time of day when natural sunlight is at its highest. Open the blinds and turn on all the lights. Lastly, do not use the camera flash when taking pictures. This tends to cast a harsh, white light on objects and produces glare, reflections and shadows that make the space feel smaller than it is.

The next step in the advertising process is to get information out to the public. The following are the methods I use to advertise the unit for rent, most of which are free of cost:

- Zillow – pushes your listing out to three different websites, Trulia, HotPads and Zillow's own rental page. This is the only service that charges a fee, but is still very affordable at $9.99 per week.
- Apartments.com
- Zumper, which also pushes the listing out to Padmapper (Zumper is only available in certain markets)
- Craigslist – I tend to fall back on Craigslist as a last resort if interest in the unit seems to be low. I usually find that the quality of prospective tenants who come to me from Craigslist tend to be lower than that of the previously mentioned methods. This is purely anecdotal, though. You may find you have the opposite experience.
- Lastly is a "For Rent" sign. There are varying opinions on the use of these signs and the degree of their effectiveness. My personal preference is to not use them for two reasons; one is that I just don't like the look of them. The signs don't portray a professional image, and that appearance

can be damning. Second is they don't provide the same kind of information that an online listing with photos can. In fact, I've seen For-Rent signs that provide a phone number and that's it. What good can that do? As a result, you'll get needless calls from people wanting to find out more about the unit and you'll end up in a phone conversation trying to describe the features when they could have gotten all they wanted from the online ad. That being said, if it works as nothing else than a lead generator and you refer them to the online listing for more, then it did its purpose. Like I said, this is personal preference. See what works for you.

For the online options I create an identical listing and post it on each website, ensuring a wide net is cast to advertise to as many potential renters as possible. Before doing so you must of course describe the unit and its features. You'll remember early on when you were initially searching for a building to buy, one of the criteria was the desirability of living in the building, not only as the owner-occupant but from the perspective of a tenant as well. The overarching question was "would I want to live here?". Here is where that comes back into play. You need to find a way to make your listing stand out compared to all the other listings with similar bed/bath counts and rental price in your area. An enticing description can be the difference between a potential renter requesting more information about your apartment or moving on to your competition's listing. By no means should you be deceitful in describing the unit features, but there are certain choices of words that are better than others.

Let's imagine I have an older landlord friend named Joe. Joe is a good landlord and takes care of his properties. But Joe doesn't put much effort into describing his rental properties online. He always says "What does it matter? I just need to get people in the door and they'll see for themselves that I have a nice apartment for rent!" Coincidentally Joe and I each have an apartment available for rent in the same neighborhood. The units have identical layouts and features, and both are listed at the same asking price. How weird! Joe and I share best practices and in doing so both advertise our units for rent on the same websites. Let's look at each of our descriptions for what is essentially a carbon copy of the same apartment.

JOE'S RENTAL

Apartment for rent. Two bedrooms, one bathroom. 1,000 square feet. Five rooms total. Available for rent August 1st.

MY RENTAL

Logan Square sunny second floor apartment. Two beds, one bathroom.

-Hardwood floors throughout.
-Spacious bedrooms will both fit a queen-sized bed.
-Central heat and air conditioning.
-Separate living and dining rooms with vintage built-ins add charm.
-Fenced-in back yard with patio waiting for your grill!
-Coin laundry located in building.
-Train station within walking distance.
-Available for rent August 1st.

See the difference? Sure, Joe's listing provides basic information about the unit; just enough to let you know it's not a cardboard box. As a renter how could you possibly picture yourself in the unit with so little information? It is true that the pictures provide for additional description themselves, but some details could be overlooked, and you want to highlight all the best features of the apartment in the description. You want the potential tenant to focus on all the reasons why this is the right spot for them. In contrast to Joe's listing, my listing paints a picture of an apartment that can be visualized even without the help of photos. There are various elements to the listing that will help it stand out in a crowded field. Let's break it down.

- Neighborhood location – You'll notice these are the first words in the listing. Although it might be obvious if the online listing is viewed in a map-view, you want to reinforce where the apartment is physically located. This helps your potential renter place him or herself in the city relative to where they work, which often times is a huge deciding factor on where to move. A potential renter may have a certain neighborhood already picked out in their head but might not necessarily know street names and numbers by location. Stating the neighborhood reaffirms to your potential renter that they're looking exactly where they want to be.
- Descriptive wording – Beyond stating to the potential renter the number of bedrooms and bathrooms, you want to go on describing the apartment in ways that evoke excitement. Mention all the best features the apartment has to offer. A few examples I've utilized:
  - Bright and sunny could easily be swapped out with "large windows throughout" or "drenched in afternoon sunlight". Use inviting words to capture the reader's attention.
  - In the case of this apartment, which was built over 100 years ago, I don't want to advertise the fact that the building is old (read "worn down"). Instead, I use words like "vintage" and "charm" that put a positive spin on the apartment's features.
  - When describing the bedrooms, I use the word "spacious" as a positive descriptor. You could also use "roomy" or "airy". The important part is that I

give the reader a solid reference point in the queen size bed. Most people can visualize the size of a queen size bed as opposed to trying to think about what would fit in a 12'x12' space.
  - Miscellaneous descriptive adjectives to consider: cozy, quiet, comfy, high ceilings, renovated, private, character, beautiful, expansive, etc.

- Building and surrounding area – Continue on to describe other features about the building, whether it be a patio or garage parking. Furthermore, you should mention one or two benefits of the surrounding area, such as nearby public transportation or a grocery store down the street.

- Available date – This is one thing our friend Joe got right, and you could make the argument that this should be the first piece of information you provide. You will find that in a lot of your listing responses you'll get interested renters who are wanting a move-in date earlier than the apartment is available. This is helps weed those people out, though not always entirely. We'll go over another method to help in this area later. You'll want to give yourself plenty of time to advertise and show the unit to potential renters. I recommend you list your unit for rent no less than 2 months in advance of the available date. Anything shorter than that and you could find yourself going down to the wire to get the placed rented, which is a stressful experience. More than two months and you'll find it difficult to attract anyone who is searching for an apartment that far in advance. Two months seems to be the happy medium.

A few more notes on the description. You'll notice another difference between Joe's listing and mine is the use (or non-use) of square foot sizing. Joe tells his readers that the apartment is 1,000 square feet in size, while I elect not to provide that information. Why is that? Am I being misleading? Quite the opposite. Similar to the example about bedroom sizing and providing the queen size bed as a reference point, I find that often time people do not have a realistic understanding of how big or how small a space actually is by simply reading a square foot number.

Stating that an apartment is "X" square feet can lead to a negative reception by the reader either before or after the reader actually sees the space in person, if they even get to that point. The reader might have a preconceived notion that 1,000 square feet is cramped (an adjective I don't suggest you use) and might immediately move on to the next listing. Place that same person in the apartment and they might be astonished as to how *roomy* 1,000 square feet actually feels. The opposite could also be true by overshooting expectations. The reader of your advertisement might walk into a showing and say to themselves "there's no way this tiny apartment is 1,000 square feet!". With that in mind I simply choose to forgo providing this information and let the potential renter decide for themselves if the space is large enough without me telling them so.

Lastly, there's one more tool you can and should utilize to further depict the layout of the unit and that is a floor plan. Providing your advertisement readers a floor plan helps visualize the space in its entirety, rather than the reader trying to piece together pictures like a puzzle and figure out which hallway leads to what room, and so on. There are various online tools you can use to draw a floor plan for free, and it's surprisingly easy to do without any experience. There are even apps that will automatically take measurements of your rooms and generate a layout for you. I suggest you utilize one of these methods to provide your readers a floor plan.

Remember, you're trying to make your advertisement appear better than all the other similar listings in the area. This is the sales aspect of your duties as a landlord. The product you're selling is the apartment, and the leads are every person that makes his or her way to your advertisement. You only need to convert one of those leads into a customer, and the more leads you bring in the better are your odds of converting.

Application Requirements

Another component of the listing description that deserves its own section are the requirements which prospective tenants must meet in order to be considered as a potential tenant. These requirements set a baseline for who you will allow to live in your investment. The requirements are in place to protect the physical property, your ability to collect rent, and the safety of neighboring tenants.

1. Minimum credit score – the minimum credit requirement for all of my units is 650. This tends to be a middle of the road credit rating that allows for a maximum amount of people to apply, while still effectively filtering out people who have had less than desirable credit histories. This can vary by area. I have a brother who owns rentals in a far less populated area and where that population is more prone to lower credit scores. He sets his minimum at 550 and is still able to find quality tenants. I have the benefit of a larger renter pool so I'm able to seek a slightly higher credit rating. Yours may be higher or lower.
2. Minimum monthly income – In order to ensure the tenant or tenants are capable of paying what you are asking for rent you'll want to make sure their total combined income is at least 3 times that of the monthly rental amount. This is closely tied to the old adage of not spending more than 33% of your monthly income on housing. As the rental amount of your unit goes higher, so too does the necessary income amount of your prospective tenants. You don't want a tenant who has to choose whether to purchase groceries or pay the rent. A minimum monthly income of 3x the

rent will prevent this from ever being a scenario.
3. Prior histories
    a. No prior evictions – This one is simple and to the point. You may have heard commercials for retirement account investments which state "past performance is no guarantee of future results..." and while this may be true for the trading of mutual funds, people are creatures of habit, and a prior eviction tends to be a good warning of that person's nature as a renter. I don't want the added risk, so I simply don't rent to people who have been evicted before.
    b. No prior bankruptcies – A person's ability to manage their finances is of utmost importance to you as a landlord. Nothing is more indicative of a mismanaging of finances than a bankruptcy. While I understand that mistakes happen in life or events occur that may have been outside someone's control, but why should you as a landlord put your financial wellbeing at risk because of someone else's mistakes or misfortunes? It may sound harsh, but the renting of real estate is not a charity, and you must keep your own best interests in mind.
    c. Criminal background – This requirement plays into the safety of not only yourself but that of the neighboring tenants as well. You want to make sure your property is a safe place for all tenants and even the broader neighborhood at large. Traffic violations are one thing, however violent crimes may be a reason to disqualify. You need to check your local landlord-tenant ordinance before implementing criminal background

requirements, or any other requirement for that matter. In Chicago, landlords are not allowed to disqualify on the basis of prior convictions alone. If the applicant is otherwise qualified, the landlord is required to perform and "individualized assessment" of the applicant's criminal history prior to denying them for housing. Be sure to understand what is permitted in your market.

These requirements are fairly standard in the real estate world. You might tweak them to allow a little more flexibility in who you rent to, but one thing you should not be flexible on is the enforcing of your requirements. Once you set them do not waver from them and do not make exceptions. They are in place for a reason, and they serve no purpose if not strictly adhered to. Furthermore, if you deny a person from renting your unit based on one of your requirements and then subsequently rent to someone else who also does not meet that requirement, you could find yourself in potential legal trouble, however unlikely that may be, but again it's not worth the risk. Establish your requirements and stick to them.

Pricing

When it comes to assigning a monthly rental amount to your available apartment, I have found that there is no exact science for determining the "correct" amount. There are many variables that go into determining the price. Certain intangible variables will provide you little ability to control. Time of year plays huge into this equation. You can typically expect to receive a higher rent amount in the summer than you would for the exact same apartment in which the lease begins during the winter. But even that is subject to regional influences based on weather. Supply & demand is another factor. It could be that there has been a construction boom in your area and more and more apartments are becoming available, thus driving down the median rent.

Tangible variables such as unit features are easier to identify and can cause your rental amount to be higher or lower.

In your first few years of landlording, before you have sufficient experience under your belt, you may not have a good feel for how much rent you should be charging in your area. The rent charged by the previous owner is a good place to start, but you need to do your research to determine if those are fair market rates. The best insight to determine your own rental amount is to see what your competition is charging for a similar unit. What I do is go on any one of the websites on which I list my own rentals and do a search in my area for a comparable unit to see the range in rent prices. This gives me a high-water mark and a low water mark; it's my big picture view of comparable rentals in the area. From there I begin to focus in further in attempt to find rentals that are more similar to my own. If I see a unit that doesn't have central air conditioning but mine does, I know that mine can *likely* support a higher rent amount. If I go on to find another rental that has central A/C and a dishwasher, but my rental does not have a dishwasher, I know my rental is less *likely* to get a rent amount as high. I continue to do this until I feel I have found 3-4 closely comparable rental properties in my area. Now, instead of just throwing darts at random rent prices, you at least have some data that is based on real, local values.

The reason I emphasize "likely" is because you might find that the amount you ultimately rent your unit for might be vastly different from the competition on which you based your listing. On any given day you might have someone come across your rental who is willing to pay much more than what the rest of the area is asking for a comparable unit. It could be that the person absolutely falls in love with your unit or location, or it might be someone who is running out of time to find a new home and is willing to pay a premium to get a place fast. It goes without saying that the higher and higher you price your rental, the less likely this is to happen.

And of course, the opposite can be true, too. You might price your rental at what you feel is a reasonable rate for the size, features and location, and compared to your competition. But for whatever reason, the unit might sit on the market unable to attract someone to sign a lease at the listed rental amount. I've had this happen before and it's nearly impossible to pinpoint an exact reason. I had tenants in a unit who had decided to move on. Their rental amount for the previous year was $1,425/month. When I began advertising the unit for rent, I increased the rental amount by the standard 3% year-over-year increase ($1,465). The listing seemed to generate a lot of interest, however after about a month on the market and multiple showings I couldn't get anyone to sign. I reduced the price back to the original amount of $1,425 yet still I couldn't get anyone willing to sign the lease. This continued until I finally got the apartment rented at $1,300/month. A unit that I had rented for $1,425/month for the previous year could not command the same amount the following year, even with improvements done to the unit. I wasn't sure what to chalk it up to other than "it happens". I could have chosen to be stubborn and refused to reduce the rental amount lower than what I had achieved in the previous year, but at some point you have to analyze how much time you have remaining until that unit becomes vacant and when to cut your losses and get the unit occupied by reducing the price. For example, if you're asking $1,200/month and are finding it difficult to get the unit rented, I argue that it's better to reduce the price to $1,000/month (thus forgoing $1,200 in annual rental revenue) and have the unit 100% occupied for the year, than to continue advertising at $1,200, let it sit vacant for a month and *hope* you get the unit rented before the next vacant month comes around. In this example the net loss to reduce the rent by $100/month is the same as the unit sitting vacant for 1 month, but you need to analyze it for your situation to see which makes most sense. Of course, you could be stubborn and not budge on price, but at what cost? I made this mistake once, and only once, because it was an expensive mistake. This was the only instance in which I've had a unit vacant, and it was for a month. It's not pleasurable to have an apartment sit empty with no rent coming in. The lesson here is that there is never a "correct" rental amount. Instead, base your rental amount on what the area is *likely* to support, and you will put yourself in a good position to achieve a reasonable rental amount with a confidence that it is *likely* to become occupied in your desired timeframe.

I like to price my apartments right at or just below the fair market rate for the area. I don't try to squeeze every last drop out of the monthly rate just for a few dollars more. My preference is to have an abundance of people interested in an affordable apartment, that way I can choose only the best people who fit my criteria for renting. Not only does pricing your apartment this way yield more qualified applicants, but it also increases the likelihood that the tenants will continue to stay at the apartment, reducing turnover expenses and the hassles of going through the leasing process altogether. The alternative, trying to achieve a much higher rent price, will likely yield far fewer prospective renters and, as a result, could force you into selecting a renter who may not be the best fit.

Pre-Screening

With your listing published for the world to view you can now sit back and wait for the inquiries to flow in, hopefully early and often. It will soon become very apparent if you priced your rental at a price the market can sustain, or if you were overly ambitious in your hope for a high rent. If you start getting inquiries like crazy, it's indicative of a few things. First, that the effort you put into advertising your unit is effective. Well done! It also means that you priced it right, or even possibly too far below the market rate for the area (you might reconsider a higher asking price). If inquiries are few and far in between it might mean that you overpriced the rent, or it might just be early on and interested renters aren't yet searching for the date your apartment is available.

However, let's assume you priced the unit competitively and you're at about the 2-month timeframe prior to the unit becoming available. Interested renters are now reaching out to you for more information and to setup showings. Prior to doing so, however, you first need to get more information from this person before you go any further. Potential renters can be very demanding of your time. Likewise, you also need to be demanding of information from them. I'd like you to meet another friend of mine. This friend goes by the initials PSQ. PSQ serves as the first line of defense in preventing me from wasting my time. Rather than going through the effort myself, PSQ helps me by getting additional information about interested renters and does so in a way that allows those people to volunteer as much or as little information as they choose. PSQ doesn't charge me or the interested renter anything for this service. What a great friend! I'd like to introduce you to my friend PSQ, otherwise known as the Pre-Screening Questionnaire.

When an interested renter reaches out to me for more information, the very first thing I do is respond to them thanking them for their interest. I then also introduce them to the PSQ. The pre-screening questionnaire is a way for you to ascertain more information than what might already be presented to you in their inquiry and certainly prior to meeting this person, in person. The primary goal of the pre-screening questionnaire is to vet whether or not this person meets your qualifications for living in the unit *before* you spend any more time engaged in dialogue or performing a showing. It also gives you a general sense of who the person is and a little bit more about them. It's a series of a dozen or so questions that takes no more than a few minutes for the respondent to complete. Sometimes you might send the PSQ to someone and never hear back from them again. If that's the case, then it did exactly what it's intended to do; weed out undesirable people. If someone is not willing to take a few minutes to answer some simple questions about themselves, it tells me that they are either trying to hide something or are just too lazy to do so. In either case, that's not the type of person I want renting my unit. Good riddance. However, the majority of people will make the effort to fill out the form and send it back. From there you can then decide if it makes sense to go any further or politely let the person know otherwise.

The pre-screening questionnaire is broken up into 4 different categories: About You, Previous Housing, Employment Information, and Credit / Criminal History. I've provided a template in the Appendix, but let's examine each a little further to discuss why they're important.

1. About You – This section is the general information gathering section. Contact information, current address, etc. This is pretty straightforward. Also included though is a part about pets. Depending on your policies you may or may not allow pets. Either way you'll want to know what pets this person has, if any. Notice the question is not "do you have any pets?". Instead, the question of "what kind of pets do you have" forces the person out of a potential yes / no response and into a more descriptive response. It might provide you with some additional general information about the person, or it might provide you a reason to pass on this person due to a no pets policy.

2. Previous Housing – The Previous Housing section is intended to give you some insight into this person's past rental experiences. The "why are you moving" question puts the spotlight on the reason that brought them to you in the first place. The response could be as simple as "moving in with boyfriend" which would not be reason for alarm. Or you might get a response stating "landlord evicting me" which of course raises all the red flags (I've actually received this response). Typically, the reason is nothing unusual, but it's still good information to have.

Asking someone how long they've been at their

current residence is also good information to have. If someone has managed to stay at a single residence for an extended period of time (more than one year) it *typically* suggests a decent tenant. Clearly another landlord has allowed this person to stay in their property and continued renting to them. That other landlord may have different standards than you do, so you still need to analyze carefully. You might also have someone who is moving out from their parents for the first time. And while 18 years at home is a long time, mom and dad might not necessarily be willing and happy landlords.

Date of desired move is your secondary check of the respondent's acknowledgement of the "available date" provided in your listing. You'll be surprised at how often people will reach out to you for more information on the apartment and subsequently provide you with a desired move in date well before, or after, the apartment is available, even though the available date is stated in the listing. You can easily dismiss a person that does not have a desired move in date that falls in line with your available date.

3. Employment information is vital in providing you assurance in this person's ability to pay rent and pay it on time. Occupation is supplemental information. The next two questions are the meat and potatoes of this section. Time at current job shows stability. A person who has been at their job for a longer period of time is less likely to get fired or leave, which equates to income security and dependability of rental payments. You still want to hedge against the possibility of not receiving rent, so asking this person what may affect their ability to pay rent is a fair question to ask. This question is extremely broad, but it designed to make the respondent stop and think for a minute. Answers can vary from "nothing"

to "loss of job" to something as blunt as "death". I've seen them all.

If the respondent is a non-working fulltime student, they will obviously not meet your minimum income requirement, as their monthly income is $0. In this case you will often times see the person volunteer the information that they will have a parent cosigner, which can be an acceptable means of meeting the income requirement. But what if the respondent is a someone who left their career to pursue a graduate degree and is doing so fulltime? Most likely they are not reaching out to their elderly parents to cosign a lease. In this situation you can ask for a certified bank statement showing the person has bank savings in excess of 2x what the annual rent amount will be. For example, if the monthly rent is $1,000, you'll want to see savings of at least $24,000 in the bank to ensure that this person is able to pay you rent in addition to all their other expenses whilst living off savings.

4. The Credit / Criminal History section is a precursor to the eventual background checking process that will be performed if the respondent gets to that point. It is also an affirmation of the qualifications portion previously discussed. The reason for having it on the pre-screening questionnaire is twofold. First and foremost, what I've found is that if a person has ever been evicted from an apartment or convicted of a felony, they are highly unlikely to fill out the form and send it back. I say this because in all the inquiries I've ever received I have never once had a person admit to either of these things. They simply just don't send the form back. The second reason for having this section is to see if the person is truthful. It's possible that I have, in fact, had a convicted felon respond to the questionnaire and state they are not such, but even if they were to lie about either of the first two

questions it would get uncovered when performing the background check.

Asking about a person's credit provides you another avenue to potentially pass on a respondent based on your minimum credit requirement. Sometimes rather than providing a number, people will simply state "poor", "good", "excellent" or something along those lines. When I get a response stating "poor" or anything less than 650 I remind the person of my minimum requirement and leave it at that. Not mentioning a cosigner is intentional. A person with poor credit will usually have a history of untimely payments and you do not want to be another one of their creditor's holding out your hand waiting for payment. If the respondent replies asking if you'll accept a cosigner I will at that point reply stating that a cosigner is acceptable, but I will not jump to offering that option straight away.

The PSQ is going to be your best friend throughout the leasing process. It will save you valuable time and help ensure you attract the right person for your apartment who meets all your requirements. Searching for "the right person" must be very carefully structured. The Fair Housing Act of 1968 was written into law to provide a basis for which protected classes may not be discriminated against in their obtaining of housing. According to the US Department of Housing and Urban Development, the Act "protects people from discrimination when they are renting or buying a home, getting a mortgage, seeking housing assistance, or engaging in other housing-related activities." The Fair Housing Act of 1968 has a long history, and the passage of the Act is largely credited from the culmination of events that took place in my hometown of Chicago.

In 1966 Dr. Martin Luther King, Jr., who had been successful in his fight against the Jim Crow segregation laws and his quest for the Civil Rights Act of 1964, brought the movement he had started in the Deep South to the Midwest. According to a Chicago Magazine article from July 2016, "his crusade, called the Chicago Freedom Movement, would confront a less overt but equally insidious injustice: namely, the discriminatory and duplicitous real estate practices, such as steering, redlining, and panic peddling, that kept blacks boxed inside big-city ghettos." Dr. King was quoted as saying "If we can break the system in Chicago, it can be broken any place in the country." Discriminatory practices by real estate agents and landlords alike segregated Chicago such that the black population was forced into select, overcrowded areas of the city. Economic exploitation, hinged on racism, brought about ghettos that were a breeding ground for horrendous living situations, not too dissimilar to the conditions Lizzie Maggie would have seen decades earlier in the New York tenements. Throughout the summer of 1966 King staged non-violent marches and rallies that brought national attention to Chicago and exposed the city for its discriminatory practices against racial minorities, particularly African Americans.

Much of what was emphasized in King's Chicago Freedom Movement was embodied in the eventual passage of the Civil Rights Act of 1968, which included Title VIII, known as the Fair Housing Act. The Fair Housing Act, and later amendments, sought to prevent discrimination against various classes of persons, including:

- Race
- Color
- National Origin
- Religion
- Sex
- Familial Status
- Disability

It is important to recognize where we've come from to understand where we are now, and this history lesson, albeit brief in length, underlines the basis for why we have fair housing laws. As a landlord you want to be sure your criteria for renters adheres to these requirements, not just because it's the law but because it's the right thing to do. It's hard to imagine that the kind of discrimination which existed in King's era still exists today, but the sad reality is that it does. None of the above classes prevent a person from being a good renter, and that should be the only thing that really matters when it comes down to it.

The Fair Housing Act prevents discrimination to what are considered "protected classes". While it is illegal to discriminate renting to a person on the basis of one of the protected classes, it is not illegal to deny a person housing based on various "non-protected classes". The list runs the gamut, and is technically infinite, but a few of the more common non-protected classes include smokers, convicted felons or sex offenders. Credit and income, which were previously discussed in our requirements section, also fall into the category of non-protected classes. If you felt so inclined you could deny a person housing because they have tattoos, because of their political affiliation, or because their favorite color is orange. None of these things are considered a protected class. While I admit that I'm being purposefully outlandish in a few of these classes, I do so to emphasize the point that you could potentially have innumerable requirements for being accepted as a tenant to your building, however unadvisable that may be. The more stringent your requirements are, the smaller the population is that will fit within your boundaries, and therefore the less likely you are to find a tenant.

When you receive inquires for your rental you will find that you get all types of people from all sorts of backgrounds. A common concern for new real estate investors, though unfounded, is the possibility of renting to a tenant who receives subsidized housing, colloquially known as a Section-8 Tenant. Referring again to the Department of Housing and Urban Development, the federal housing choice voucher program is designed to provide assistance to "very low-income families, the elderly, and the disabled to afford decent, safe, and sanitary housing in the private market." There is a certain negative stigma that is associated with those who receive subsidized housing. I've often been asked the question "what if you *have to* rent to a Section-8 Tenant?!" but it's not that simple. First and foremost, your property must be Section-8 qualified. If your property is not qualified, then you're not able to rent to people who receive the voucher. It may be your choice to not rent to Section-8 tenants, for whatever reason, and if you don't seek qualification for your property then there is no "have to".

The negative association people have to Section-8 tenants in relation to their being undesirable tenants is not completely baseless, but I believe this is mostly anecdotal and tends to be the exception rather than the rule. It is true that some Section-8 tenants can turn out to be bad people, but the same can be said of any person who does not receive subsidized housing, too. And that is why we have our minimum requirements and our background screening process. Just because a person receives subsidized housing does not prevent you from implementing the same requirements you would for any other person. Special exception must be made for the income requirement, but if together with the subsidized portion of their rent they still meet or exceed your requirement, then that person still qualifies. However, if the applicant does not meet one of your other requirements you are able to deny that person. Again, there is no "have to". That is why I say the concern is unfounded.

The percentage of rental properties that are Section-8 qualified is significantly less than those which are not. I have one property that is Section-8 qualified and what I have found is that once a Section-8 tenant comes across a good apartment that is qualified for the program they will do everything they can to be a good tenant so they are allowed to remain in that apartment, as they know searching for another can be a lengthy process and competition among other Section-8 tenants is high. This leads to them being some of my very best tenants who take care of the apartment as if it's their own home. Add to that the fact that you are guaranteed the government subsidized portion of their rent every month and suddenly Section-8 becomes more and more attractive. I know one landlord in my area who owns over 800 units who strictly rents to Section-8 tenants. It can be a very profitable business strategy and almost always ensures you will have no vacancy. As a matter of fact, the combined total between my Section-8 tenant's portion of the rent and the subsidized portion is the highest rent I receive out of all of my units.

Conducting Showings

Following the publishing of your rental online and receiving the returned, completed prescreening questionnaires you can now begin to schedule showings for those interested renters who meet your defined qualifications. Some people will ask to set up a showing at a specific day and time, others will simply ask when they can set up a showing. One of the challenging aspects of being a landlord while also working a full-time job is that you are typically not available during your normal working hours. This limits the time frame in which you yourself can show the unit. Now, if you so choose to you, could potentially pay someone to show the unit for you, however I don't think this is necessary nor do I think it's wise. I like to meet the potential renter myself and be able to answer whatever questions they may have. You can tell a lot about a person by the way they carry themselves, if they show up on time, and how they interact with you. Even with a full-time job I have still been successful in performing every showing myself, and doing so on my own time.

When someone asks to setup a showing at a specific time, or if they leave it open ended, I politely let them know that weekday showings are only available at 6:00 PM, and on weekends the time slots are more flexible. I choose 6:00 PM for a couple reasons. One, it allows me time to get home from work and prepare for the showing. If you get out of work at 5:00 PM and it takes you 30 minutes to get home on a normal day, give yourself a little extra time for the unexpected. What you don't want is to find yourself sitting in traffic frantically trying to get to the unit on time. The other reason I choose 6:00 PM, and not too much later, is that while I recognize doing a showing during the day would be the least intrusive for the current occupants, it obviously is not an option for me while at work. So, I select a time that will be minimally intrusive to the current tenants and try to respect the fact that they don't want strangers walking around their unit as they are winding down their day. A showing typically only takes 10 minutes, so I am out of their way fairly quickly. On weekends I allow for a more flexible time schedule between the hours of 10:30 AM and 4:00 PM.

> Whenever possible, try to schedule group showings. The benefit is twofold. First, it cuts down on the number of showings you have to perform, and the amount of time spent doing so. Second, having multiple groups show up to a showing drives up competition. I always emphasize the fact that the unit has received a lot of interest, and having multiple people show up further reinforces that. It may cause someone to pull the trigger on applying rather than waiting to see what else is available and risk losing your unit to someone else.

With this information provided to the interested renter I ask them to let me know which day and time is *convenient* for them. The phrasing of this, though very subtle, I believe is very important. A day and time that is "convenient to" the interested tenant triggers an emotional response which places the importance on that person's time, rather than your own, when in actuality you are allowing the person to schedule it on a time that is most convenient to *yourself*. Just think of the opposite response; you tell the person the next showing is on Wednesday at 6:00 PM, period. It leaves them with zero options and the person is immediately trying to determine if they can fit it into their schedule. With multiple options it gives the interested tenant some room to juggle their own schedule and find a day that works best for them.

Once a day and time has been determined be sure to email the current tenants of the upcoming showing. You need to do this for each and every showing so there are no surprises when you come knocking at the door. Assuming the unit is not vacant, the condition of the unit is obviously "lived in". Similar to when I email the current tenants when I need to take pictures of the unit for the listing, at the start of showings I ask that the current tenants kindly tidy up prior to each showing. What I've found is that people will usually comply with this. If you have been fair and decent in your treating of them, they will usually reciprocate by cleaning up before each showing. I think people understand you're trying to get the unit rented and they don't want to hinder that. And I think people generally don't want to be seen as slobs by other people. Either way, it makes a world of a difference to show a clean apartment versus one that is a mess.

The Showing Process

On the morning of the showing, I always send a reminder email to the interested renter to confirm both the showing time and that they still plan on coming. I provide my phone number and ask them to call or text when they have arrived in front of the building, and also ask that they call or text if they are running late for whatever reason. It should go without saying that you want to carry yourself in a professional manner. That means dressing the part of a real estate professional. I'm not suggesting you have to wear a tie, but you should consider something other than shorts and sandals. Along with your attire another useful tool you should consider getting yourself is a leather-bound document folder, the type you might take to a job interview. The folder serves two purposes. First, it adds to your professional "look". When an interested renter sees you approaching, they are more likely to associate you as the landlord/owner/manager. The other purpose of the folder is to hold the additional information you will be providing to the interested renters at the showing.

> One of the advantages to being a live-in landlord is that you're already at the showing location. There is no getting in the car to travel to the location. This might seem like a minor convenience but consider this: each time you have a unit for rent you may end up doing dozens of showings. If you're not living in the building, or very close by, that means dozens of trips and time spent traveling back and forth.

After introducing myself to the interested renters and

thanking them for coming, I provide each person with an informational handout titled "Application Requirements". I've provided a template in the Appendix. The handout summarizes some of the unit features described in the online listing, including who pays for what utilities and the date when the unit is available for rent. The handout also re-emphasizes the minimum requirements for renters. Along with the online listing this is now the second opportunity for the interested renter to acknowledge your requirements so that there's no "I didn't know" or "you didn't mention that". This is important because you don't want to get through a background screening only to find out the person doesn't meet the requirements. With this additional information in hand, you can now lead the interested renters in to begin the showing.

You may have heard the phrase "being able to walk and chew gum at the same time". It's meant to describe two things that are not mutually exclusive and can easily be done at the same time. Well in my case, it could have been "walk and provide information about the unit at the same time." I'm not the type of person that normally gets nervous or self-conscious during a conversation, but let me tell you that in the first few showings I performed I was a wreck. I was so concerned about whether or not the interested renter would like the unit and worried about whether or not I was saying the right thing that I probably would have been better off saying nothing at all. I tripped on my words and struggled to answer simple questions. I would start to sweat and become self-aware of how poorly it was going and that only exacerbated the problem. So, in time I developed a strategy to help myself through these situations to provide information in an efficient and effective manner. I developed a showing "script".

Some people can hold a conversation with a wall and a showing script will be wholly unnecessary. They are the type of person who has the ability to speak confidently in any situation. But if you're the type of person who is more of the listener than the talker, this method might prove effective for you. After those first few bombed showings I decided I was going to start going through a structured talking points script so I could put myself at ease, make other people comfortable during the showing and provide the necessary information. The following is an outline of how I structured the showings. You can tweak yours as needed, but by creating a script of your own you ensure you cover all aspects of the showing every time, and you do so in a timely manner.

"Hi, [interested renter], I'm W.R., good to meet you. Thanks for coming out today"

Provide each person a handout with highlights of the apartment and minimum requirements for applying.

Lead interested renters to the apartment. Provide a brief overview of the unit: "2 beds, 1 bath. Central heat and AC. Available August 1st."

Turn on all lights and tell interested renters to feel free to look around and ask any questions they may have. Give the interested renters space.

After some time, casually walk through the apartment and mention a few other features, just to show the interested renters you are still engaged. Let them know to take their time and to let you know when they're satisfied.

Lead the interested renters out the rear of the apartment and show them the common laundry room.

Exit the building and begin walking back to the front. Provide details of the neighborhood including locations of nearby grocery stores, available transit options, and parking.

Let the interested renters know to think it over and call or email with any questions. Describe the application process in the event they are interested in going forward.

As you're reading this you're probably thinking, "He can't be serious? Does he actually need to lay this all out for himself in order to do a showing?" And I admit, thinking about it now, it seems ridiculous. But it's because I created this for myself that I'm able to do the same showing "script" each and every time I perform a showing. I know the exact flow and stick to it each time. It makes for a better experience all around. When I do showings now, I don't actually walk through these steps in my head. Instead, it has just become muscle memory. Even if you don't need to create this to be able to interact with people, it helps to have a game plan so you can cover all parts of the showing and it doesn't end up being unnecessarily long or risk leaving out important information.

Prior to the start of any showings, you will have had to run through a scenario in your head that is unique to a live-in landlord: will you tell the interested renter that you live in the building? This is a very important question to ask of yourself and I believe is critical information you need to share with the interested tenant. They are going to find out eventually anyway, so why wait? If your concern is that by telling the interested renter that you live in the building will scare them off, you may be right. But if that's the case then how is it fair to that person to not disclose that information until after they have paid for the background screening, or worse, once they've begun to move in? As I begin to wrap up the showing and lead the person back to the front of the building, I casually begin to tell them (if they haven't figured it out already) that I not only own the building but that I also live in one of the units, too. Sometimes this is met by a response that is an attempt to disguise their disappointment. You can usually see it in their face. But how can you blame them? To be honest, if I were in that position, I would think it would be pretty strange to live in the same building as my landlord and would definitely have second thoughts. During this conversation what I attempt to do is reassure the person that I am just "another tenant" who goes to work every day just like they do and won't be knocking on their door at all hours. I simply say the only time they will see me is if they need something fixed, or maybe when I'm doing laundry. In fact, I try to sell it as a benefit. I tell them if anything is ever wrong, I am right there to fix it almost immediately. Sometimes this seems to ease their concerns. Other times, when I think I have a person who is very interested in moving forward with the application, I never hear from them again. I've likely lost a number of good tenants by telling them I live in the building. This is just another challenge of being a live-in landlord. In time, once you move out, this will no longer be an issue. But it's something you need to deal with in the short term. Withholding that information from a prospective tenant is hardly a good way to get started on a positive note with someone who might be living in your building. You should be upfront and honest in everything you do with your tenants, and it starts with letting them know you will be living a door or two away from them.

One of the inevitable misfortunes of doing showings is the reality of showing no-shows. Early on, a showing no-show would really get to me. I had made the effort to tell the current tenants about the showing, had coordinated my schedule to be at the unit to show it, and what do I get in response? Nothing! No call, text, or email to let me know the person wouldn't be able to make it. I would think to myself, fuming, "how can this person not have the courtesy to at least reach out and let me know they wouldn't be able to make it?!". What I failed to recognize until later is that some people are just not like you or me. Some people live in their own world, and it never occurs to them that it might be important to cancel a showing out of respect for your time. If someone misses a scheduled showing without having notified me, and then reaches out later apologizing and requesting another showing date, I will typically take the higher road and schedule another showing with that person. There was one time, however, that an interested renter missed two scheduled showings, both times without notifying me. She then tried to schedule a third. I kindly told her I don't accept tenants who don't respect my time. This was met with an email response from her that berated me for my arrogance. I chose not to respond and let the issue fizzle out. You'll deal with plenty of people like this in your real estate journey. Best to just let it roll off your back and take the high road.

CHAPTER FIFTEEN - LEASING A UNIT

After 32 email inquiries, 17 pre-screening questionnaire responses and 12 showings (with 2 no-shows) you have found the 1 person who is interested in taking the next step in renting your apartment. You've done so with time to spare and without having to reduce the advertised rental rate. It has all gone exactly as planned thus far. So, what's the next step to keep this momentum going? It's time to put on your Sherlock Holmes hat.

Background Checks

Presumably you've had a showing that went well, and a perspective tenant has decided this could be the place for them. They let you know they want to go forward with signing a lease. Prior to doing so, however, you'll want to do a bit of P.I. work in finding out who this person actually is, and whether or not they are a legitimate candidate for living in your property. The pre-screening questionnaire is a great first step in sifting through those people who do not meet your basic requirements. It prevents you from wasting time performing showings for people who would otherwise not meet the standards you have set to be a renter in your apartment. That being said, however, what is to stop someone from misleading you in their responses on the pre-screening questionnaire? Other than perhaps a sense of guilt, the answer is nothing. So as thorough landlords we must do our due diligence and investigate further. It's not to say that most people are liars, but you are potentially engaging into a contract with a person for an extended period of time so it's in your best interest to confirm the information they provided to you. Trust but verify.

Prior to drafting a lease for signature, you will want to perform a thorough background, credit and criminal history check. You'll remember that on two different occasions (on the online listing and on the informational handout at the showing) you stated your minimum requirements for being approved as a renter in your apartment. It is here in the background check that you will verify the information provided to you by the interested tenant on the pre-screening questionnaire. While there are a multitude of companies that perform this service, the one in particular that I like and recommend is Smart Move by TransUnion. First and foremost, there is name recognition with TransUnion being one of the three credit reporting bureaus. You are asking someone to submit to an inquiry into their background and you want to assure them that it is a) reputable and b) accurate. The name alone goes a long way in assuring the interested renter of both. The interested renter wants the report to be accurate for their own sake, but for your part you of course want to make sure it's accurate as well. I am much more confident that the results produced by a nationally recognized bureau are of a higher degree of accuracy than that of a smaller, lesser-known company. Regarding cost, TransUnion provides you with the option to pay for the screening yourself or to have the interested renter foot the bill. I always elect to have the interested renter pay to have the service performed. The fee, though reasonably priced, could add up to a lot over the course of multiple showings. In addition, it is one further level of assurance that if the interested renter is willing to come out of pocket to have their background checked that they were likely being truthful in their initial responses.

As mentioned, TransUnion Smart Move is just one of many options when deciding on a background screening service.

Whichever service provider you chose, any quality background check will include each of the following:

> You should remind the interested renter that the background check results in a "soft inquiry" and does not impact their credit score.

- Credit score and history
- Criminal history
- Previous evictions

Other useful information that may also be provided includes an analysis of the person's stated income and how it compares to national averages for that industry. Even with this information it may still behoove you to confirm this information with the interested renter's employer.

As you are aware, my minimum requirement for credit score is a modest 650. The credit portion of the background check does not stop there, however. Meeting or exceeding that score is only the first step. An in-depth analysis of any and all creditors is also required. Again, any worthwhile background screening service will provide this information. You don't need to be a financial advisor to recognize when things are amiss. There are two indicators that can signal potential problems: a pattern of missed payments, and/or multiple credit lines with very high balances as a percentage of the credit limits. If a person has a history of missing credit card or loan payments, why would you think it would be any different for them paying their rent in a timely fashion? One or two late payments is not something that should raise serious concern, but consistent past-due payments should sound the alarm for a person who is likely to treat their housing obligation in the same way. Similarly, a person with multiple credit accounts with high balances should also draw scrutiny. You'll remember much earlier on when we discussed the mortgage pre-approval process that there is both good debt and bad debt. An interested renter who has a large student loan balance (with a history of timely payments) is a lot different than an interested renter with a high balance on multiple revolving credit lines. Just because a person has student loan debt does not in any way indicate that person's ability to pay their loans, or you for that matter. Typically, multiple credit card lines with high balances indicates a person who is struggling to stay on top of their finances. An in-depth analysis of open credit lines and loans will allow you to see how much that person has committed themselves to paying each month, and to determine how much will be remaining to also meet their obligation to pay rent. You do <u>not</u> want to be left holding the bag when that person has no more money that month to pay all of their creditors.

A bit more on the actual credit score number. I've had multiple instances when interested renters stated what they "thought" their credit score was on the pre-screening questionnaire, but also stated they hadn't checked it in a while. And of course, it's those people who, when going through the background screening process, don't end up meeting the minimum requirement. But there's no need to shut the door on them right then and there. You do need to recognize that sometimes people get themselves into a situation, whether that be divorce, medical problems or others, which can have an impact on their previously good credit score. In fact, their payment history and credit balances may indicate an otherwise stellar applicant. But we have minimum requirements for a reason and can't "move the goalpost" for some applicants and not others. If you find an interested renter who doesn't quite meet your minimum credit requirement you can always offer the option of a co-signer. This can also be offered to a person who has no credit history. When utilizing a co-signer, the same minimum requirements apply to that person as do the person who is actually intending on living in the unit; the co-signer will have to submit to the full background, credit and criminal history check. The co-signer simply offers you further surety that rent will be paid, and if not, provides you with another avenue to legally go after the amount owed. Although I've never been in the situation myself of having to utilize a co-signer for an apartment I've lived in, I would think that the act of getting someone else to vouch for me would make me damn sure that I paid rent and it never came down to a landlord seeking anything from that co-signer. From that perspective I think it's generally a safe bet to rent to someone with a less than stellar credit score but who is able to obtain a co-signer. This must still be analyzed on a case-by-case basis, of course. For instance, if someone had an absolutely atrocious credit score with a history of missed payments, I would not offer that person the option of a co-signer for the simple reason that I see it as likely that the person will miss rental payments and I will then have to deal with the hassle of attempting to collect it from the co-signer. It's a situation I'd like to avoid if possible.

While I would say that a vast majority of applicants will end up checking out, not every applicant is going to be desirable. You'll find that some people are just not what they chalked themselves up to be. Perhaps the background check brings to light that an applicant is a convicted felon, or you get someone who does have that atrocious credit score mentioned previously. Whatever the reason, you determine you will not be going forward with leasing to this person. At this point there is some red tape involved, and you could find yourself in legal trouble if you do not follow the proper protocol.

Let's take a few steps back, though. To understand this better we must first define a few things. The entire process of gathering background information on a person it is what is considered obtaining a "consumer report". The Federal Trade Commission defines a consumer report as "information about a person's credit characteristics, rental history, or criminal history." This information is typically obtained from a credit reporting agency, or CRA. Using the information provided in a consumer report to make a decision on an applicant must comply with the Fair Credit Reporting Act, or FCRA. I'll spare you the time and boredom of reading the 115 page document and summarize by saying the FCRA covers a variety of topics including the permissible purposes of obtaining a consumer report, compliance with the procedures of obtaining the report, and many more topics, including, of course, taking unfavorable action against a person as a result of information contained

within a consumer report. Although it is all important, it's that last part that we will focus on. This unfavorable action is what the FTC considers an "Adverse Action". As it relates to a potential tenant, the FTC defines an Adverse Action as "any action by a landlord that is unfavorable to the interests of a rental applicant or tenant." The FTC further clarifies with some examples:
- Denying an application
- Requiring a co-signer on a lease
- Requiring a deposit that would not be required for another applicant
- Requiring a larger deposit than might be required for another applicant
- Raising the rent to a higher amount than for another applicant

Our unfavorable action, in this case, would be denying an application. It is your duty and legal responsibility as a landlord to notify the applicant of this decision. I prefer an email notification so there is an electronic paper trail of compliance with the FCRA, though it can also be provided orally or as a mailed document. The notification simply explains the decision you made and the applicant's right to obtain the consumer report from the CRA. The notification does *not* need to provide the specific reason for the denial of the application. However, it does need to provide the following information:
- the name, address, and phone number of the consumer reporting company that supplied the report
- a statement that the company that supplied the report did not make the decision to take the unfavorable action and can't give specific reasons for it
- a notice of the person's right to dispute the accuracy or completeness of any information the consumer reporting company furnished, and to get a free report from the company if the person asks for it within 60 days

I've provided a template in the Appendix for you to use and

modify as necessary.

The simple truth is that most people in this position are entirely unaware of their right to obtain the consumer report that was performed on them. And I am fairly confident in saying that, although required by law, most landlords probably do not provide an adverse action letter; they simply deny the applicant and move on. You don't want to be caught in a situation with an applicant who is well aware of their rights and sues for discrimination because you didn't take the time to send a letter. You need to tread lightly, though. Sending a letter like this can cause an emotional reaction from an applicant who is devastated by the fact that they have been denied the ability to rent an apartment. I had one person who, after receiving the notice, sent me multiple emails and left voicemails crying, fraught with disappointment, wanting a specific reason as to why they were denied. It is best to remain vague in these circumstances and again refer the person to the credit reporting agency in order to obtain a copy of the consumer report for themselves. All of this is to say that hopefully you never even get to this point with an applicant and the first applicant you have is the person you end up leasing to. You will at some point in your real estate career have to deny someone, so it is best to know how to do it correctly.

Creating a Lease Agreement

In any contract, the purpose could be dramatically reduced to a one sentence agreement between two or more parties. For our purposes, an apartment lease could simply read "I will rent this apartment to you for $1,000 per month for 12 months." It engages two parties into an agreement, states a monetary consideration, and defines a duration. We know, of course, that no rental agreement, or any contract for that matter, is so simple. Perhaps the very first contract ever written was this short, but with each problem that arose in time, a clause or additional sentence was added, and thus contracts became long, tedious, cumbersome things. Ours, as you'll see, will be no different.

When engaging into a rental contract for your apartment, you'll want one that protects you as a property owner and landlord. In a city like Chicago especially, where the laws are written heavily favoring tenants' rights, it becomes even more imperative to have a rock-solid lease that shields you from all angles. That is not to suggest that tenants should not have certain rights, not by any means. But you need to protect yourself and your investment from duplicitous tenants who are out to take advantage of you. The best contract is one that is signed and then never pulled out again.

Sometimes it makes sense to do something yourself, and sometimes it pays to pay someone else to do something for you. Regarding creating a rental contract, you should not overlook the importance of hiring an attorney to do this for you. Even if you're able to find a rental contract template online, you should still consider hiring a real estate attorney knowledgeable in the practice of your specific area to review the document and make edits. I have been lucky in being able to utilize a contract that was made available to landlords in the Chicago area by the Chicago Association of Realtors, and their process in producing the lease presumably involved rigorous editing by attorneys and real estate professionals alike.

> Reach out to your local Realtors Association to find out if they have a lease template you can use for your own rentals.

At risk of stating the obvious, a rental contract should contain the following at a minimum:
- Address of the leased premises
- Monthly rental rate
- Duration of the lease, including start date and end date with a specified time of day
- Items within the unit owned and provided by the landlord (i.e. appliances)
- Utilities included in the rental amount, if any

- The names of people who are authorized to live in the unit
- Printed names, signatures and dates

Addenda

ADDENDUM ITEM	REASONING
Smoking inside the building is prohibited.	Smoke will end up permeating the walls, ceilings, carpet, etc. and cause higher turnover costs.
No more than 8 occupants at a time in the unit or on the premises.	Simple safety concern, especially with smaller apartments.
No fish tanks or other aquariums.	Avoids the obvious potential water damage.
Candles are strictly prohibited.	Fire hazard, simply put.
Grills cannot be used on the porch and cannot be within 5 feet of the building when in use.	Also a fire hazard.
Tenants must keep unit generally clean and regularly remove trash. The unit has received a preventative bug treatment. If bugs or pests are discovered as a result of Tenant living conditions, the cost of remediation will be at Tenant's own expense.	People can be messy. This is your avenue to pass along cost for a pest service if it was caused by the tenant.
A move-in inspection will be completed by both Tenant and Landlord at the start of the lease.	This notes the condition of the unit upon move in. More on this soon.
Listing the unit for temporary stays on websites such as Air Bnb, VRBO, and similar websites is strictly prohibited. Failure to adhere to this may result in immediate termination of the Lease.	This prevents people living in the unit who were not approved to do so, regardless of the length of stay.
The use of Draino, Liquid Plumber, or similar products can cause severe damage to pipes and is strictly prohibited.	If you've heard that Draino can "melt" pipes, it's true, as I can speak from experience.
Seasonal replacement of the heating/air conditioning filter is the responsibility of the Tenant. Failure to do so will increase cost of utility bills and increase risk of damage to equipment.	I stock each unit with (4) new air filters so the tenants have a one-year supply and can replace them without hassle.
At expiration of the Lease, Tenant must return unit in broom-clean condition.	I don't expect units to be spotless upon move-out, however I do expect them to be empty of all items and left in a reasonably clean condition.
Tenant acknowledges that rent is subject to increase at expiration of the Lease. Market conditions determine the adjustment of rent. An adjustment of 2-4% is typical.	I add this item simply as a reminder that rent tends to go up year-over-year. This helps justify a rent increase by providing a "I told you to expect this" clause.
Should the Lease not be extended, Tenant agrees to allow for showings as early as 60 days prior to termination of the Lease, or earlier as agreed upon. Tenant also agrees that showings will typically take place at 6:00 PM on weekdays, and during generally acceptable hours on weekends, or as agreed upon otherwise.	This item is added to set a precedent for performing showings nearing the end of a tenant's lease. Given that I work a fulltime job and an unable to perform showings during the day, when tenants are typically away from the unit at work, I want to have it in writing that I will most likely be doing showings while tenants are home.

The above are the standard items that will provide you with a baseline contract. Everything else added to it could be considered supplemental. Your contract will continue to grow out of experience or misfortune. It is an ever-changing document. With each new tenant I have, I tend to find one more thing to consider adding to my lease. These are the specifics that apply to my situation that I would not have otherwise found in a template or boilerplate contract. The way

I capture these items is to attach them as an addendum to the rental agreement. With each passing year the list grows or gets revised. Some of the items are related to safety concerns, others are intended to protect the physical property. Some have come out of experience, others are preemptive to avoid the potential experience. Below is the list of items currently included on my addendum, along with the reasoning behind each.

Facts and Figures about Pet Ownership
- The United States Census Bureau found in the 2017 American Housing Survey that 49% of Americans own a pet of some type.
- The American Veterinarian Medical Association found this same dataset to be nearly 57% of Americans.
- While the Census Bureau did not distinguish between pet types, the AVMA found that of those who own pets, 38% own dogs and 25% own cats, comprising far and away the largest percentages of any pet type.
- The American Society for the Prevention of Cruelty to Animals estimates that the annual first year cost for either a dog or cat ranges from $1,000 - $2,000, not including the initial purchase of the animal.
- The American Kennel Club estimates that ongoing costs of grooming, feeding, veterinary visits, etc. are around $1,000 per year depending on pet size.

People love their pets, and they are willing to spend significant sums of money to care for them. They will tell you of course that the cost of pet ownership is priceless. Which brings me to the point of this portion, and fits nicely into the continuation of creating a rental agreement: should you allow pets? I think the question is an easy one to answer.

By disallowing pets, you are effectively eliminating 50% of the potential rental population right off the bat. And yet so many landlords are unwilling to allow pets of any kind. Some chose to only disallow dogs. Doing so eliminates roughly 20% of the potential rental population. The better question to ask, instead, should be "why *disallow* pets?" Some landlords may site destruction of property and noise disturbances, among other reasons, as rationale for not allowing pets (specifically dogs). And while those may be legitimate concerns, is it really worth decreasing your ability to find a good tenant? By allowing pets it is my belief that you have a significant leg up on your rental competition. Given that so many apartments do not allow pets, I believe that once a pet owner finds a good apartment that *does* allow pets, they are more likely to take even better care of the unit out of concern of finding another similar quality/priced unit that also allows pets in the future. It took me awhile to come to this realization. At first, I did not allow dogs. But in time I began to realize how many people I was turning away when they asked if my apartments allowed dogs. My concerns just didn't warrant the discrimination. And besides, all of my rentals are furnished with durable materials like hardwood floors and tile, so what is it really that will be destroyed other than the tenant's own belongings?

As we have seen, pet owners spare no expense when it comes to caring for their pets. Herein lies the opportunity for you as a landlord. Not only does allowing pets broaden your renter pool, but it also allows you to charge a slightly higher rent, or a monthly pet fee. At a minimum the monthly fee on a per annum basis should cover the cost of any additional cleaning that may be needed as a result of allowing a pet. This is really only applicable to cat and dog owners, but it can and should be charged for pets of any kind. Part of your normal operating expenses will be that of move-out cleaning, so the pet fee serves to simply supplement the cost of that. On top of covering your cleaning expenses, you may choose to charge more just to profit a little more on a monthly basis. I see nothing wrong with this; people love their pets and are happy to pay the cost of ownership. A pet fee is just one more of those costs.

Ultimately, you'll have to decide on whether or not you allow pets, or which pets you may specifically disallow, if any. Choose wisely though, as you may be putting yourself at a disadvantage by doing so.

Other Considerations Prior to Tenant Move-In

Move-In Fee or Security Deposit?

The choice to charge a move-in fee or collect a security deposit is a decision that would have been made prior to you advertising the unit for rent. With a signed lease in place, now is the time for you to exercise whichever option you chose. But which one is the "right" choice? Well, it depends on your appetite for risk, or perhaps your ability to find decent people. Both options have their pros and cons. Let's take a look at each.

Move-In Fee

The move in fee is a one-time, non-refundable payment from the tenant. Some of the benefits include that you're able to use the money at your discretion for things such as hiring a cleaner, purchasing turnover supplies like paint, or just setting it aside as part of your reserve funds. Charging a move-in fee also allows for a lower "entry cost" to tenants. Rather than having to come up with the cash for both a security deposit and first month's rent, the tenant's upfront costs are much lower, which could potentially broaden your renter pool. That said, there are some drawbacks to collecting a move-in fee which are addressed by instead requiring a security deposit.

Security Deposit

A security deposit is traditionally in the amount of one month's rent, collected up front in addition to the first month's rent. Unlike the move-in fee, a security deposit *is* refundable. In some states, there are statutes that require the funds be placed in a separate interest-bearing account. The purpose of collecting a security deposit rather than a move-in fee is that it provides some insurance against the possibility of unpaid rent, tenant-caused damage to the unit or for cleaning at the end of a lease. Any use of funds from a security deposit must be carefully documented with receipts, reasons behind using the funds, and with prompt notification to the tenant. It is also generally accepted that the tenant should be allowed the chance to remedy the problem, if so desired. For example, if a tenant breaks a window and it very clearly was their fault, they should first be given the opportunity to shop around for quotes to have it replaced before you do so yourself (keeping in mind that any repair must be approved through you). Having a security deposit held over the heads of tenants will generally guarantee the apartment will be left in a clean condition upon move out.

So, with all that in mind, which option should you chose? The safer bet without a doubt is to collect a security deposit. And you might ask why anyone would consider the alternative. I, for one, however, prefer a move-in fee to a security deposit. From my standpoint there is far too much red tape to navigate in collecting, tracking and refunding a security deposit. This of course puts me at a higher risk of costly repairs out of my own pocket, but I believe this is drastically mitigated in the way you choose tenants and how you deal with people. Regarding the example above about the broken window, if that were to occur without a security deposit in place, I would have a frank conversation with the tenant that they caused the damage and that they *should* pay for it. It's my belief that if you have been fair in dealing with the tenants throughout the course of their lease that, like most decent people, they will pay for the repair. However, that might not always work out. You could find that they refuse to pay for the damage, in which case you don't have the security deposit to fall back on. The biggest reason I like collecting a move-in fee rather than a security deposit is that it provides me cash up front for unit turnover. When a tenant moves out, I use part of the move-in fee from the incoming tenant to hire cleaners to clean the unit prior to the new tenants coming in.

> There is a third option that combines the best of a move-in fee and security deposit, and that is to require the renter to purchase a surety bond. A surety bond is like an insurance policy against damage to your apartment. You, as the obligee, will specify the damage limit, say $1,000, and the principal, who in this case is the renter, will pay the surety company a percentage of that amount as a non-refundable premium, typically 15-20% or $150-200 in this example.
>
> In the event of damage to the apartment, the obligee will file a claim with the surety, and, if approved, get reimbursed for the damages up to the limit amount. The surety will then seek reimbursement from the principal for the amount paid out to the obligee. A surety bond provides tenants a low upfront cost option, while also providing landlords the comfort of knowing they can get reimbursed for damages.

I did a showing once for two people who seemed very interested in leasing a unit. As I was wrapping up the showing I summarized the lease requirements, the rental amount and reiterated that there would be a move in fee if they decided to go forward. One of the guys was very candid in asking the question, "why don't you charge a security deposit, and what would prevent me from destroying the place right before I move out?" I actually appreciated the question. My honest response to him was that nothing prevented him from destroying the place. I went on to say, however, that I do my best to rent to good people who care for the apartment as if it were their own home. The truth is that's your biggest insurance against costly damages. Sure, having a security deposit in place can pay for damages caused to the unit, but what about the mental cost of dealing with bad tenants, the hassles of scheduling contractors to do repairs or the constant worry about someone who might skip rent? I'd rather rely on finding good people who won't cause these problems in the first place. (By the way, I ended up renting to them and they were in fact great tenants.)

    The current cost of my move-in fee is $375, which is typical for my area. Of that $375 I spend about $150 on cleaners and maybe $50 on supplies, but typically I already have stock paint and supplies and can put the balance into my reserve account to save for other purposes. On that note, I will reiterate a comment I made earlier about when it pays to pay someone else to do something. In the first year or so of landlording, I would personally clean all my apartments prior to new tenants moving in, just to save a buck. I would snap on a pair of rubber gloves, pull out the old mop and bucket, turn on Bachman-Turner Overdrive's *Takin' Care of Business* and go to work cleaning. I would stay up late the night before (or early morning of) between old tenants moving out and new tenants moving in. I began to wonder why I was going through the trouble, but the final straw was when I enlisted my girlfriend (now wife) on a particularly uncleanly apartment, and I watched her scrub the inside of an oven as I cleaned out a toilet. I thought, "what the hell am I doing..." Since then, I have found a lovely woman who, with her assistant, comes armed to the teeth with cleaning supplies and leaves the place spotless a couple hours later for an unbelievable reasonable price. It honestly feels like the best money I can spend because the new tenants come into a place that is shining and smells like a lemon grove. Do yourself a favor and pay for someone else to clean your apartments. You'll be thanking yourself.

    On the flipside, something I still choose to do myself (for the time being) is paint touchup. For most people, painting is either something you hate, or you really hate. I actually don't mind it. The extent of painting for a unit turnover is typically scuff marks from furniture or areas where you have to patch drywall, so in my mind it doesn't make sense to hire someone to come in and do something you could do yourself fairly quickly and cheaply.

After that long-winded tangent it's probably easy to forget that we were discussing the choice of either charging a move-in fee or collecting a security deposit. Which one you choose doesn't matter so much as when you collect it. I make it crystal clear to all tenants that upon the lease being fully executed by both parties, the move-in fee / security deposit is required within 24 hours, or the lease is voided. Getting the tenant to commit monetarily will assure you that they are not going to walk away from the lease and end up renting some other apartment, leaving you scrambling to find someone else.

Renters' Insurance

Another item required from the tenants at lease signing is proof of renters' insurance at the leased address. The reason why I require renters' insurance, and the same reason I explain it to tenants why it is required, is for *their* protection. The homeowner's policy covering your property does not extend to tenants and their possessions. I tell the tenants that if, God forbid, a fire started in the unit below theirs and burned all their possessions, my property insurance would not cover one penny of the items they lost. When thinking about it in those terms, tenants typically don't even think twice about this. Not to mention that the policy for a one-year period can generally be purchased for less the $150.

Along with the address of the leased unit, I also have the tenants list me as an "additional interested party" which includes my contact information. The reason for this is that the insurance agency will notify all parties (not just the tenant) of any changes or cancellations in coverage, something you would definitely want to be made aware of. In my experience, listing the landlord as an additional interest has no effect on the cost of the policy, so it's good practice to remind the tenants of this so they don't think you're requiring them to pay for anything extra.

It's important to note that being listed as an "additional interest" is different from an "additional insured". Each are exactly as they sound. An additional interest is a party that doesn't require the coverage but does benefit from knowing that coverage is in a place and if there are any changes. On the other hand, an additional insured party *is* afforded policy coverage and has the ability to make a claim. This typically has added cost to the policy purchaser. Although it sounds like it could be a good thing to be listed as an additional insured, in actuality it could prevent you from making a claim and recouping cost. A renter's insurance policy extends coverage to third parties, however if you are listed as an additional insured, you are no longer a third party but are instead a policy owner. Let's say your tenant deep fried a turkey for Thanksgiving and burned down the apartment in the process. Your property insurer (and you as the claimant) would first attempt to collect the loss against the company providing the renter's insurance policy (and the renter as the defendant). However, if you are listed as an additional interest, there is now a conflict of interest. You would be both the claimant and the defendant, and you can't file a claim against yourself.

Tenant Move-In Checklist

The process of a tenant moving out is inherently linked to the process of that same person moving in. With the exception of normal wear and tear, I expect the unit to be in the same condition that it was prior to the tenant moving in. Therefore, diligent documentation of the condition of the unit is critical in establishing the baseline for what the tenant received upon move-in. This is done with a move-in checklist that is completed by both the tenant *and* you.

The move-in checklist is a document that captures the current state of each and every room in the unit, and all components within that room. This doesn't have to be anything fancy and can easily be created in Microsoft Excel. There are generic components like Floors, Walls, Ceilings, Windows, etc. that will appear in each room, and there are more specific components such as Refrigerator, Oven, Toilet, etc. that will only appear where applicable. The checklist allows the tenant to go room by room and select one of three options for the condition of each component: Poor, Fair or Good. There is also an area to provide further comment on each component. So, for example, the section for a bedroom looks like this:

Bedroom	CONDITON			COMMENTS
	POOR	FAIR	GOOD	
Floor				
Walls				
Ceiling				
Window				
Ceiling Fan				

The process for completing the move-in checklist is to first go through the unit yourself and provide any comments you deem necessary or helpful in documenting the current state of the unit. Below is a list of items I always make note of:
- New air filter installed on XX/XX/XXX
- Fire extinguisher is fully charged
- New batteries installed in smoke alarm(s)
- Unit has been sprayed for seasonal preventative bug maintenance
- Unit professionally cleaned on XX/XX/XXXX
- Other items such as "bathroom renovated April 2019" or "new kitchen appliances"

These are the things you want to make note of, but the tenant will either be unaware of or will likely not think to mention. After you've had a chance to provide your comments you can then pass the checklist off to your new tenant. I instruct the tenants to complete the checklist prior to moving *anything* in so that there's no chance of them documenting damage they themselves caused during the moving process. I also let the tenants know it's in their best interest to be as detailed as possible. It's important that the tenant is the person selecting the "condition" of each room, not you.

Once the tenant has completed the checklist, signed & dated with their comments, you then have the opportunity to fix anything they might have noted. For example, if they mentioned that the bathtub is draining slowly, I would take the necessary steps to fix this and then make note of the fix in red next to their comment. Other items, such as a window blind with a broken blade, might be of minor concern and require no further comment or replacing. Depending on additional fixes required, this process might take a few days. Once all the fixes are completed and noted in red, I then sign and date the document myself and send a copy to the tenants for their record.

The purpose behind all of this, of course, is so that the condition of every aspect of the unit upon move-in is agreed to by both parties in writing. If a repair is needed later during the lease period, or upon the tenant moving out, the checklist provides you a means of verifying that the component being repaired was not received by the tenant in the broken condition.

"Tenets for your Tenants"

Home ownership comes with the ever-present responsibility of upkeep and maintenance, and in real estate investing that responsibility is multiplied by however many units you own and manage. Renters, as you might expect, will never take quite as good of care of the unit as you would yourself, regardless of how diligent you are in selecting people who might portray those ideals. So, in attempt to help protect my investments I try to play defense on some of the things I have seen as "repeat offenders" when it comes to maintenance, and I get it out in front of my tenants as reminders of things they should be doing as part of their routine as responsible tenants. To provide this constant reminder of the things I want the tenants to be doing, I print out a poster titled "Helpful Hints for a Happy Apartment", set it in a frame and hang it somewhere in the unit that's out of the way but where it will still be seen regularly. And since the poster might not necessarily match with the tenants' taste in home décor, I make certain that I secure it to the wall in a fashion such that they can't take it down and hide it away.

The items on the list are born out of things that I have

seen as repeat offenders in terms of maintenance issues or things that could potentially cause issues. I try to phrase it in a way that portrays a way for the tenants to make their living experience more comfortable with less problems, but in reality, the poster is self-serving to reduce the number of maintenance requests I receive, and also to prevent costly repairs. Some of the items, such as air filter replacement and the insistence of not using Draino for clogged drains, is mentioned in the previously discussed lease Addendum, but months into a lease period it may be easy for a tenant to forget. The things that are constantly on your mind as a landlord are not the same things that are on the mind of a tenant, so what better way to keep the tenants aware of those things than for them to see it every time they go into their kitchen pantry? Although I don't actually expect that tenants are reading the poster every time they pass, I do believe that the occasional glance at it, even in passing, will engrain certain habits into their day to day lives that will help you in the long run.

CHAPTER SIXTEEN – EXPENSES OF REAL ESTATE OWNERSHIP

The reader will remember way back in the beginning of this book we discussed the different "Whats" available to achieve your "Why" in life. We went on to discuss the various reasons why I believe real estate is the most effective method for achieving your goals, and one of those reasons was real estate's ability to produce a positive cash flow. Similar to a stock dividend, the cash flow from real estate could allow for compounding gains in the form of further investment, or it could allow you to pay yourself as a way to reap the rewards of your hard work. The determination of being cash flow positive, where you have more money at the end of the month than you do expenses, or cash flow negative, where you are spending more than you are taking in, hinges on one thing: effective management of expenses. Watched with an attentive eye, your investments could produce a comfortable, positive cash flow and allow for the property to be self-sustaining. But mismanaged, your expenses could run wild, putting you into the red every month and requiring you to come out of pocket. In this section we're going to cover the basics on expenses, as well as methods for you to minimize your costs and how to spend wisely to ensure long term sustainability.

Types of Expenses

With any business, whether it's a coffee shop or real estate investing, there are two expense *types*, and those are Operating Expenses and Capital Expenses. Each has their place on your balance sheet, and each requires careful management to ensure you are stretching your dollar as far as possible. Let's first get a basic understanding of each expense type, and then discuss strategies to minimize costs to therefor maximize profit.

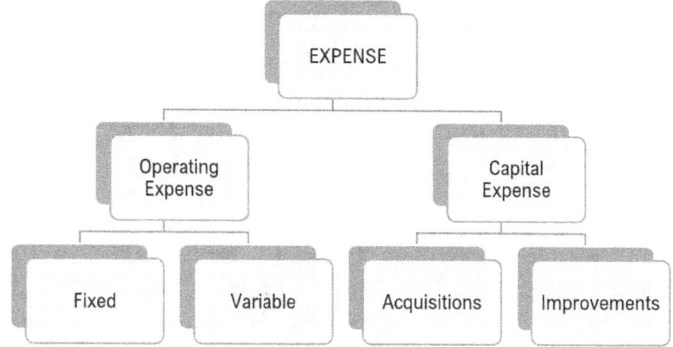

Operating Expenses (OPEX) – As the name implies, an operating expense is the cost of running your business, or in other words "keeping the lights on". Within this category of expenses are the subcategories of *fixed* or *variable* operating expenses. Operating expenses are captured on the balance sheet in the same year in which they are incurred. Below are some common examples of operating expenses we might see as real estate investors:

Fixed
- Loan principal and interest (assuming a fixed rate)
- Property taxes (within the current year, as taxes do of course change)
- Insurance
- Management costs (if third party management is utilized)

Variable

- Utilities (water, gas, electric)
- Maintenance
- Repairs
- Vacancy (this is not an expense so much as it is a loss of revenue, but categorized as an expense)

As a real estate investor, it is in your best interest, and frankly your duty, to ensure your operating expenses are as low as possible without allowing the quality of your product to suffer, that is, the quality of living for tenants within your property. That's important to note because it is those landlords who allow quality to suffer in an effort to increase profitability, who *earn* the stigma of being a "slum-lord". As we will learn, there are effective ways to minimize costs, but it should never be to the detriment of quality. As a rule of thumb, you can expect operating expenses to amount to approximately 50% of your gross revenue, *prior to any loan costs*. The reader will recall when we were analyzing properties in Chapter 4, we called this the 50% Rule. For every dollar of rent you bring in you can expect to spend fifty cents in order to "keep the lights on", before even accounting for the cost of the mortgage and interest. If that seems like a lot, you're right- it is! So, as you will see, it is imperative to effectively manage these costs to prevent yourself from bleeding out.

Capital Expenses (CAPEX) – Simply put, a capital expenditure can be viewed as an expense that will have long-term effects on your balance sheet. Whereas an operating expense is recognized in the current accounting period, a capital expense has a *useful life* beyond the current accounting period and therefor has tax benefits in both the current year as well as subsequent years. This is the biggest difference between the two, and we'll get into the tax implications later on. Capital expenses typically have a (relatively) high initial cost, and therefor are not something that occur on a regular basis.

Acquisitions

- Additional rental properties

Improvements
- Bathroom / kitchen renovation, etc.
- New equipment such as HVAC, water heater, etc.
- Building addition

For our purposes, at this point in time anyways, we will focus on the improvements portion of CAPEX. While it may be part of the overall goal to grow your real estate investing business, it may not be possible early on to earmark a portion of your revenue as savings toward future purchases. So, for the time being, we'll simply discuss the subcategory of improvements. Some improvements to your property not only have the potential to increase the value of your property, but they can also potentially allow for increased rental revenue. However other improvements, while necessary, may not lead to increased revenue or value. Take a roof, for example. A necessary building component, but not one that will allow you to charge more rent than your competition. It is also something that has a useful life and will, in time, need to be replaced. As such, part of your rental revenue needs to be budgeted for such capital expenditures.

Typically, real estate investors figure anywhere from 5 – 10% of their rental revenue for capex. That is not to say that every month you will be spending 5-10% of your rental revenue on these improvements, but rather you are contributing to a reserve fund for the inevitable "rainy day". Each month the reserve is built up a little bit more so that when the time comes for a major improvement, the funds are there to do so. As such, capex savings can be a tempting expense to ignore by not contributing to the reserve. But being consistent with contributions (if feasible) will be reason to thank yourself when a major, unexpected expense arises.

Tracking Expenses

Vital to the health of any business is knowing and understanding its expenses. Regardless of the type of expense, each transaction influences the business's bottom line. It is important to make the distinction that your involvement in real estate is not a hobby, but a business. Knowing your expenses without understanding them is useless. Understanding your expenses comes from diligently tracking them to identify patterns, trends and areas for improvement. And tracking your expenses can only come from a persistent, dedicated effort, otherwise you will find yourself playing catchup and relying on memory.

Once or twice a month I set aside time to sit down and track expenses. I go through every transaction I made for the month. What I have done is built a simple spreadsheet that allows for a description of the expense, a category of what type of expense it is, and a formula to reconcile with the bank account balance. This is another simple spreadsheet, but the data that it provides can be powerful. Essential to the usefulness of the spreadsheet is the requirement of the user to retain receipts. As you will find out with owning real estate, you are constantly making miscellaneous purchases as part of your ongoing operating expenses. It is easy to simply throw out a receipt after making a purchase; it is not easy to remember what a specific transaction was intended for weeks later. So, my recommendation with utilizing an expense tracking spreadsheet like this is to save each and every receipt, setting it aside until the time comes for you to sit down and reconcile, whether that's weekly, monthly (as I do) or at whichever interval you choose.

Over time you will begin to be able to determine average monthly costs for variable expenses, such as utilities, and identify trends, such as a tenant that is causing particularly costly maintenance. Your tax professional will be thanking you too, as it will allow him or her to appropriately bucket theses costs come tax season. This same spreadsheet is of course used to also track rental revenue, and other sources of revenue such as laundry, parking, and move-in fees. Hard as it may be to believe, there will come a time when you may be using a spreadsheet like this to verify you have indeed received all rent that is due for the month (I say this because there was a time when I forgot to cash a rent check and didn't realize it until I sat down to do my expense & income tracking). Ultimately, tracking your expenses is going to tell you whether you are cash flow positive or cash flow negative. Without tracking expenses, you are essentially driving in the dark without headlights. If you are cash flow positive, you want to know how to increase your income as much as possible. And if you're cash flow negative, you want to be able to figure out ways to turn that around, and quickly. So, the question becomes; how can we minimize expenses?

Methods to Minimize Operating Expenses

Improving your cashflow is a delicate balance of maximizing cost effectiveness while still maintaining a responsible level of management. Cutting costs at the expense of losing good tenants is not a sustainable solution. As previously mentioned, real estate is a business. You are in this to provide financial gains, not just for fun. With that in mind, we need to find ways to improve the bottom line without allowing quality to suffer. Consider a manufacturer making a widget, who needs to reduce component costs, increase efficiency, and still provide the high-quality product customers have come to expect. Translated into real estate terms, we need to reduce cost exposures, increase tenant holdover, and continue to provide desirable apartments for rent. We know that our two operating expense types are fixed and variable, the former having little to no effect on quality of living, and the latter having a significant impact. Let's examine each to determine some ways to minimize our expenses, and thus maximize our cashflow.

Fixed Operating Expense Reduction

Unless you are paying for management services, your fixed operating expenses are typically the "behind the scenes" costs that don't have an impact on the quality of apartments you provide for rent. There is, however, ample opportunity to reduce these costs when it makes sense. We'll assume that if you are following the theme of this book then you are self-managing and do not have management fees to consider. That leaves us with loan borrowing costs, property taxes and insurance as the three major fixed operating expenses that we can target for reduced cost.

When talking about loan borrowing costs, we are talking about the interest rate you are paying on the money you are borrowing from your lender. For the first 10-15 years of the loan (depending on interest rate and amortization), your interest cost will typically be the single highest portion of the mortgage payment. Even a modest savings on this expense could save you big over an extended period of time. The point at which the principal payment amount becomes greater than the interest payment amount is called the inflection point, and you want to get there as soon as possible so as to decrease the total amount of interest paid over the life of the loan. One way to do this is to make extra payments applied directly toward principal, which effectively shortens the life of the loan and reduces total interest paid. But what if you simply want to reduce your interest expense, without committing available capital to additional principal payments? In order to do that you would need to decrease the interest *rate*. This is where considering a refinance of your loan makes sense. In today's volatile financial environment, there's constant talk about the Federal Interest Rate changing, or fears about the availability of money thus effecting the ability of borrowers to get a loan. It's nearly impossible to accurately predict what conditions will be like in 6-12 months, let alone 30 years, so you need to block out the noise and take a look to see if refinancing makes sense for your particular situation at that particular time. One needs to be careful though, because the savings made in interest can be easily wiped away by closing cost expenses. Seek out lenders who not only offer a cut to your current interest rate but can also refinance with no closing costs. They do exist. Let's look at an interest rate comparison to illustrate the potential for expense reduction.

Current loan details – 12 months after start of loan
Original Loan amount: $500,000
Term: 30 years
Interest rate: **4.75%**

Monthly principal: $657
Monthly interest: $1,951
Interest paid over lifetime of loan: $438,965

Refinanced loan details: - 12 months after start of loan
New Loan amount: $492,283 (note the new loan amount is the balance you have paid down)
Term: 30 years (also worth noting, the term length "restarts")
Interest rate: **4.25%**

Monthly principal: $678
Monthly interest: $1,744
Interest paid over lifetime of loan: $379,542

As you can see, a half point reduction in interest rate results in a savings of $186 dollars per month, and while that may not seem like much, that is a total reduction of over $59,000 in interest paid over the life of the loan. The temptation for many people is to refinance every time interest rates drop. But you will notice that the loan term in the example above did not change, and unless you are able to refinance into a shorter term without negatively affecting your ability to cashflow due to the higher principal payments, it usually does not make sense to continually refinance (not to mention closing costs, if applied). Doing so will continue to extend the date at which you pay off the loan in full, not to mention there are typically closing costs associated with a refinance as well.

The next fixed operating expense that allows an opportunity to minimize expenses is property taxes. In Chicago, properties are reassessed every three years, meaning the tax assessor's office analyzes the property and decides how much the taxes should go up (very rarely ever *down*). Over the course of those three years, the taxes are fixed, but when reassessment rears its ugly head there is an opportunity to reduce the burden. The opportunity presented is the ability to dispute how the property should be valued, and therefor the amount of tax burden imposed. While you can do the legwork to dispute the assessment yourself, in my opinion it is best left to the professionals. There are law firms that are built on doing nothing but property tax appeals. They know the ins and outs of property tax laws, and methods to reduce your tax burden to the greatest extent possible. It doesn't come without a cost of course, but most of these firms will have a percentage-based fee contingent the savings they earn you, so the more they save for you, the more they earn. It's in their own best interest to reduce your tax liability as much as possible.

The final method for reducing a fixed operating expense is by soliciting quotes for homeowner's insurance. Like lenders, insurance agents are in constant competition with each other to acquire the business of homeowners. And unlike refinancing, this can be done as often as you like (though it might prove to be more of a hassle than worth it at times). You can use this competitive environment to your advantage to shop around for an agent who is hungry for business and can offer you similar coverage for a lower price. After some time owning a property, you may also find that certain coverages previously thought needed, may no longer be necessary, such as flood protection or other optional coverages.

Variable Operating Expense Reduction

Operating expenses are generally unavoidable, so the key is trying to minimize the frequency and severity of them. Reducing cost for variable operating expenses is ultimately a game played with superior defense. What I mean by that is there are typically more opportunities to save money down the road than there are upfront savings, though upfront savings can still be had too. With that in mind, the following are some ideas of how to reduce your operating expenses. Some are upfront savings you can realize in the present, and others aim to avoid much larger operating expenses in the future.

COST REDUCTION METHOD	ADDITIONAL CONSIDERATIONS
Utility sub-metering	Push the costs of utilities on to your tenants
Preventative maintenance: replacing air filters regularly, purchasing hair strainers to prevent drain backups, ensuring bathroom/kitchen fixtures are not leaking, the list goes on. All of these items are far less expensive than hiring someone to fix damaged building components.	Buy filters in bulk, enough for a 1-year supply per unit. I like "Tub Shroom" brand strainers, they're inexpensive and effective. During lease turnover check faucets, toilets and tubs for slow drips and tighten valves
Purchase your repair & maintenance items while the big-box home improvement stores are having their national sales	A little-known trick is that you can actually get competing stores to match whatever discount is being offered by the other. For instance, Menards will advertise their "11% off everything" sale, and although Home Depot does not advertise it, they will match the 11% off during that same period
When possible and practical, perform repairs & maintenance yourself	You always need to consider your abilities and the time-value of money
When hiring a contractor to do repairs or maintenance, always get multiple quotes	Pricing can fluctuate drastically from one contractor to the next. Always be sure you're hiring a reputable contractor none the less
Minimize tenant turnover	Retaining current tenants avoids turnover costs such as cleaning and touch-up.
Minimize vacancy periods	If a tenant does decide to move out, ensure you have a lease agreement in place immediately following the current lease to avoid any vacancy.

❈ ❈ ❈

The Youtube Handyman

I'll be frank in saying that if you plan to self-manage your rentals then you better be comfortable with hand-tools, unless you want to pay a premium to have someone else fix something every time a repair is needed. I have come to realize that having these skills is *figuratively* invaluable, but I've *literally* saved thousands of dollars by doing a lot of work on my own. I also recognize that not everyone is equipped with the tools or know-how to perform maintenance and repairs on their own, and that's ok, so long as you're willing to learn. While these skills are by no means necessary to be successful, when starting out they will help you save money and learn the ins and outs of your property. Not to mention when a handyman charges you $100 per hour in the future you understand why it is you pay such a high price for their skills.

With the purchase of your first property should also come the purchase of a set of hand-tools, assuming you don't have a collection already. And if you do, it's the perfect time to expand that collection and purchase more. I would argue that you could purchase a collection of tools to equip yourself for almost all repairs or maintenance you might encounter, all for under $1,000. That may seem like a lot of money to spend but consider that tools generally last a lifetime and compared to the purchase price of a property, it's a relatively small but worthwhile investment. But if you're like some, and don't know a hammer from a saw, how could you possibly know what to even purchase? One approach might be to do it like they do in the show "Supermarket Sweep" where the contestant runs around with a shopping cart and dumps as much as they can into the cart. Alternatively, what I've done is created a list of the essential tools that might be used on a regular basis (as opposed to specialty tools that are used much less infrequently). This list is far from all-inclusive but will give you a good starting point.

Toolbox	Claw hammer
Needle-nose pliers	Standard pliers
Tongue and groove pliers	Vice-grip locking pliers
6-in-1 screwdriver	Adjustable wrenches (small and large)
Utility knife and blades	Pipe wrenches (small 10" and large 18")
30' tape measure	Combination wire cutter and stripper
Allen wrench set	Socket wrench set
Small pry-bar	Drill bits, various sizes, both wood and metal
Wood chisel	Steel-wire brush
Tin snips	Hacksaw
Sink basket wrench	Stud finder
Electric outlet tester	Drain snake
Caulk gun	Paint roller, brushes, and supplies

Various accessories: duct tape, electrical tape, painter's tape, plumber's tape, pipe thread sealant, variety pack wire nuts, plumber's putty, drywall screws, WD-40

Cordless 18v power tool combination set: drill, circular saw, reciprocating saw, flashlight. This will be the single most expensive item, but don't buy cheap. Dewalt makes high quality tools that last a long time.

With this new weapons cache there is no project you can't tackle. But again, what if the problem you encounter is something you have no idea how to fix? What do you do then? Even being as handy as I am, I can't tell you how many times I have consulted Youtube for "How-To's" on various home repairs. I swear there is a video for every imaginable repair you might grapple with. The great thing about watching the videos is you can pause, re-watch and play along as you are doing the repair. Often times the host of the video will explain the procedure in common sense terms, along with the proper safety precautions to take, and does a great job at making an otherwise daunting fix, much less so.

My last recommendation for becoming a self-sufficient handy man or woman of your own, is to learn firsthand from the professionals. Sometimes you'll encounter a repair that seems far beyond your capabilities or level of comfort, no matter how many Youtube videos you watch. It's then that you call a professional to do the fix for you. But the money you pay should not only be for the work they perform. Whenever I hire a contractor to do work at my properties, whether it's a plumber, electrician or otherwise, I will oftentimes stand at their side for portions of the procedure (depending on how long or involved it is) and closely watch what it is they're doing, while also asking them questions about the procedure throughout. What I have found is that if you take an interest in what it is they are doing, the contractor will generally be more than willing to help you understand the procedure, and in the process (perhaps unknowingly) equip you with the knowledge of how to tackle the problem should it arise again in the future. Granted not all repairs are something you can or should be doing, but early on if you're still learning and paying someone to perform relatively simple maintenance, it's a great opportunity to learn and build confidence by watching someone else do it first.

※ ※ ※

The Mental Cost of Self-Management

All of this talk about maintenance and repairs is the perfect segue to discuss the ever important, and omnipresent realty of self-management during the fledgling years of your real estate journey. As novice real estate investors, not having enough units to justify the need for a property management company, we must take on the responsibility of managing ourselves. It saves money and provides invaluable experience, "learning on the job" as we have referred to it. But this is no revelation; we've been implementing self-management all along our journey. As we finish discussing costs in the form of operating expenses and capital expenses, there is one more very real, albeit unseen, cost of self-managing your properties, and that is the mental cost.

I'm often asked by friends how difficult it is to be a landlord, or whether or not I think they'd be capable of doing it as well. My straightforward answer to them is usually "It's not difficult, you just have to be willing to put up with a lot of bullshit". Finding work-life balance can be difficult enough as it is, and adding the responsibility of managing real estate on top of that makes it that much more difficult. Managing on your own means that you're always "on-call". Always. You'll have to find ways to fit the property management into a day already busy with your regular job, and that can be a very difficult thing to do. Sometimes managing your rentals will be on autopilot, without so much as a hiccup. And other times there will be a deluge of problems, one after the next, that will make you question why you ever got into this in the first place. I'll give you an example. There was a particularly exhausting span of 48 hours in which I had *all* of the following happen to me:

- Furnace gave out and required a new gas manifold.
- High winds during a storm blew over a wooden fence
- Dishwasher began leaking water all over a kitchen floor
- Refrigerator stopped cooling
- Microwave stopped working

It wasn't just a one-two punch. It was a one-two-three-four-five punch, and I was ready to throw in the towel. Thankfully this all happened on a weekend so I could manage it immediately.

There will be other times where you will lose sleep over issues you're dealing with, like finding a new tenant before the end of a lease period or worrying about sewers backing up during a major storm. I'll share another story with you, one in which caused me to lose many nights of sleep. You may recall earlier on when we discussed the process of going to showings and we started to learn what to look for in a property. One of the things I had mentioned was to inspect for rodent droppings. I wish I knew then what I know now because it could have alleviated a lot of stress. Had I inspected for rodent droppings on my first property purchase I may have realized there was a rat infestation within the walls and mechanical chases of the basement unit, which of course allowed a path of travel to the rest of the units in the building. Within the first week of owning the property I received a call from a tenant who believed that "mice" had gotten into their kitchen cupboard and was getting into their food. After setting traps and killing more and more rats in the basement (I never told them this for fear of their leaving) I soon started to realize what I was up against. I mentioned to you that I lived in that basement unit, right? I would hear the rats scurrying through the walls and across the ceiling at night as I lay in bed. I nearly had a mental breakdown. It wasn't so much the thought of dealing with the rats around me; that I could deal with that. But the fact that other people were living in the building at that at any time might come across a rat was horrifying to me. I was sick to my stomach. I eventually managed to get the problem under control, and hopefully none of my former tenants are reading this. These are just two concrete examples. There have been countless clogged sinks, laundry dryers failing, garage doors not working, dripping condensation from ductwork, leaking windows, stoves not working, and on and on and on. You'd think that I own run-down properties, but I assure you these are all fairly normal things that just come along with owning real estate.

The purpose of sharing all of this is to help illustrate the mental cost of self-managing real estate. It's not to scare you, but rather to reinforce the fact that you need to have a high level of tolerance for all the problems inherent to owning real estate. Now one might argue that a lot of this is the same thing experienced by any homeowner, and that is somewhat true. But when managing rentals, it is of course multiplied by however many units you own, as has been discussed repeatedly. Furthermore, the need for a timely resolution to those issues is paramount- your tenants are paying you for that service. The ability to stomach all of this is not something that can be taught, it is, however, something that can be developed over time. With each new problem you encounter, you learn from it, find an effective way to deal with it and the next time it happens it becomes astonishingly less stressful. Without a doubt there is a mental cost associated with managing rental properties. It takes someone who is persistent and refuses to give in. One thing you cannot be is a procrastinator. As alluded to above, real problems require immediate attention, and that can take a toll on you mentally. I'll be honest, there have been times where I've thought about selling my properties and taking a backseat with a "normal" life. But then I get a good night's sleep, and with a fresh mind realize that whatever struggle I was going through is only temporary and that the long-term benefits far outweigh the hardships of the moment. I also know that at some point I will grow to a size that justifies the cost of hiring a property management company, or even employees of my own. It may take some time to get to that point, but in the back of my mind I know the current operating procedure is not indefinite, and that gives me solace during the difficult times.

With all of this in consideration, you may be sitting there with a question floating around in your mind. You're reading all about the fact that as a self-managing real estate investor you have to always be on call and that problems can't wait until it's convenient for you to resolve them. So, naturally, it may cause you to wonder: "What do I do when I'm out of town...?"

Rome, Italy. 1:30 AM Local Time: I had just arrived in Italy only a few hours earlier after 12 hours of flying with a connecting flight through Munich, Germany. Needless to say, the extended time sitting in an airline seat, and the long lines of security, boarding, deboarding, customs, re-boarding, deboarding again, and customs again had me sleeping like a baby in my comfy Air Bnb bed in Rome. It was then, as if the bells of St. Peter's Basilica were right over my head, my phone began to ring and sprung me from my slumber. In a dazed, half-asleep lunge for my phone I looked down to see who could possibly be calling me. I rubbed my eyes, thinking surely I had read the caller ID wrong. I had been out of the country less than a day, yet here I was, on the other side of the Atlantic Ocean, and was already receiving a call from a tenant. "Just my luck" I thought as I slid the screen to answer...

And so, we get back to the question- what do you do when you're out of town? This is a realty that you too will have to face at some time, and if you're at all like me, will face many times. I try to travel as often as possible, and that of course leaves me with the dilemma of how I can self-manage my properties when I'm not physically there to do so. This only further adds to the mental cost we've been discussing. Rest assured, it is indeed possible, but you need to set up a reliable system for doing so and it likely won't be developed until after you've got a bit of experience under your belt.

Early on in my real estate investing career, when I would head out of town, I would simply *hope* that nothing would happen when I was gone and tell myself I'd just figure it out if something did come up. That's' certainly one way of doing things, but if we're trying to minimize the mental stress we take on, a better way of doing things is to develop a contingency plan of sorts so you don't have to "just figure it out". A vast majority of the times you are away, nothing is going to happen. But it's that one time that something does happen that you'll want to have a way of dealing with it effectively.

Depending on where I'm going and how long I'll be away, I may or may not even let tenants know that I'm gone. Being away for 2 or 3 days inherently has less probability of something going wrong than does being away for a week or two. But before I even notify my tenants of being away (since I am their only contact for problems) I must first determine who I can go to in order to help me out when I'm away. You might have a friend or relative that you think of straight away as someone who could be your stand-in for when you're away. And if you do, that's great. But be sure that it's a good friend, or a relative who truly has a familial love for you because you are now making them that person who might potentially be woken up in the middle of the night with a phone call about a clogged toilet. My suggestion is that it should also be someone who at least has some inkling of not just common sense, but also "house sense". What I mean by that is that it should be someone who can make a judgement call on whether or not the "issue" requires professional help, or is something that can wait, or possibly be taken care of by themself.

Let's travel back to Rome briefly. My contingency plan included having my brother as the contact for my tenants to get in touch with should something go wrong. This tenant of course decided to call me regardless, so I took the call. As he described it, he was having "serious issues" with the washing machine. This is the same tenant who at one point required my assistance to reset a GFCI outlet in his kitchen by pressing the rest button, but I digress. I promptly told him to get in touch with my brother and I would follow up with him. The following day I was standing in line at the Colosseum on the phone speaking with my brother (technology is incredible). My brother explained that he simply went to my rental property, closed the lid on the washing machine and fed it another 4 quarters to find that the washing machine did in fact work, and worked fine. I say that your backup contact person should have some "house sense" because in that situation someone else might have defaulted to calling a repair man immediately and I would have paid him to essentially tell me that my tenant is an idiot (sorry Andy from Unit 2...).

But what if you don't have that trusted friend or family member who you feel could be an adequate stand-in for you while you're away? There are still other options that could work out well for you. After you have lived in your neighborhood for some time, hopefully you've introduced yourself to your neighbors and gotten to know them, not only because it's the friendly thing to do, but also because there is a self-enriching outcome from it. These are people who potentially could also be a backup contact for your tenants while you're away. I'm fortunate that my neighborhood is comprised mostly of multi-family apartment buildings, and it just so happens that the buildings on either side of both of my properties are both owned my small real estate investors similar to myself, both of whom live in their respective buildings as well. So not only do they live in the immediate vicinity of my buildings, but they also have the know-how of property & tenant management. I hesitate to burden either of them with the additional responsibility of managing my properties when I'm out of town, but if for some reason my brother is not able to address an issue, I know I have another two contacts I can feel comfortable reaching out to for help. And it's not strictly self-enriching. I lend this same courtesy back to them if they're ever in need of that as well. It's a good system.

Let's also consider if you don't have that trusted friend or family member, and you're not lucky enough to have other property managers living nearby. Then what? My final suggestion would be to describe this scenario at your local real estate meet-up group or to an online forum. I've done this with success too, although I have not had the need to implement it yet. I simply posted a request for another investor like me who would be interested in an agreement to stand in for each other while either of us were out of town. I was pleasantly surprised with how many responses I got, so clearly there is a real need for this. Again, you'd be getting someone who has property management experience, not to mention you're expanding your network to boot.

Once I have my backup person identified, I then decide if it's worthwhile to notify my tenants. If I'm traveling abroad or for an extended period of time, and I know it's likely I might be unavailable for certain periods of the day (a drastically different time zone, for instance) I will then send out an email to all tenants mentioning that I will be out of town and let them know who they should reach out to in my absence, along with the phone number and email address of the contact person. Similar to when you first purchased a property and attempted to "train" your tenants with a proper chain of communication, you should instruct your tenants to only reach out to this person in the event of an emergency or things of moderate concern that require prompt attention. All other things that can wait, should wait for your return. But clearly everyone has their own definition of emergency. Hopefully your backup person is competent enough that they are able to resolve any issue without any assistance from you. If I'm travelling locally or only away for a short period of time, I don't even bother with letting my tenants know, given that I know I can respond to the situation with relative ease and call on my backup person myself.

There are a couple other things that will only serve to help you in these scenarios as well. The first being having a short list of trusted contractors should professional involvement be required. That's not to say your backup person won't be able to find a contractor willing to come to the property to inspect the problem, but you want someone you are familiar with and know is not going to take advantage of you on price. Your backup person is there to help resolve problems, but it is not necessarily their top priority to ensure a cost-effective method to resolving that problem. Better to just provide them with your approved list of a plumber, electrician, and general handyman should something go wrong that is beyond their ability of handling on their own.

Lastly, if/when travelling abroad, I suggest you cough up the couple hundred dollars to purchase a short-term international data plan for your phone. Clearly, I had this in place when talking with my brother while in Rome, and have also used it two other occasions while in the vast emptiness of Iceland and the remote jungles of St. Lucia. On both of those occasions it provided me the ability to screen tenants and setup showings for when I returned, something my backup person could not have done effectively for me.

As you will at some point experience, in addition to the more obvious costs of Operating Expenses and Capital Expenses, there is the less obvious "expense" in the form of the mental cost of self-managing real estate. But this should be an encouraging narrative of how it is manageable, and how in time the seemingly insurmountable problems become "no big deal". When I find myself particularly frustrated with a maintenance mishap or a problem tenant, in my head I calmly say "Thank you for paying my mortgage. Thank you for helping to make me wealthy". With that attitude it's hard to remain frustrated in any circumstance for very long. Time, a willingness to learn from each experience, along with a solid contingency plan for when you're away, will transform the things that keep you up at night now into things that you can manage in your sleep.

CHAPTER SEVENTEEN – GROWTH: THE NEXT STEPS IN BUILDING AN EMPIRE

Two years had elapsed since the purchase of my first building, and like most things, it seemed to pass in the blink of an eye. One day I was a greenhorn homebuyer with zero landlording experience, and the next I was a on my way to becoming a real estate mogul. Ok, well not quite, but I had acquired up two years-worth of invaluable on-the-job training, learning how to manage a building and tenants, all the while with my ever-present goal of scaling my newfound real estate business into something much larger. The time I spent living in the basement unit of that first building, while certainly not the only way to do it, I feel was the best way to do it, for me. It allowed me to be immersed in my investment, and as a result I had no choice but to learn, develop and fine tune my landlording skills. But I was starting to get the itch for more. I felt that after two years I was comfortable in my position and wanted to challenge myself further. During that time, I faithfully continued to save every spare penny I had, with the hope of being able to afford another building as soon as possible. And if I thought the process to purchase my first building was challenging, I had no idea what was in store for me on the next.

Scaling Up and Turning $60 into $42,000 (A Short Story of a

Long Process)

Two years living in a basement apartment, as anyone who has done the same will tell you, was not very pleasant. The low ceilings and even lower amount of natural light seemed to give me a tangible sense of depression (not to mention the story of the rats I described earlier, and I was ready to get the hell out). But there was no way I was going to occupy one of the other units in my building given how much rent they were bringing in. My goal continued to be the expansion of my real estate "empire". Although I had been a casual observer of property listings for a while, I decided now was the time to get serious and begin to search in earnest for a second building. In doing so I was hoping I could upgrade my living situation to something that actually had a decent view of the outside world.

My previous realtor had since moved out of Chicago so I was also facing the challenge of finding a new realtor who had a keen sense of the multifamily market and could provide guidance along the way. Not being able to find someone who I thought was a comparable replacement, I ended up settling on a recommendation just so I could get the process started. Through the first two showings I knew she was not quite the right fit. But I seemed to have a bigger problem on my hand: despite having paid attention to trends in my area, I was blown away by the steep asking price for the listings that were coming up on the MLS. This was in 2018, a full 10 years after the depths of the Great Recession, and real estate values were soaring. That seemed to be especially true for the multifamily market. I just could not stomach what I was seeing. Relying on my studies from early on, it seemed like the rents could not possibly support the asking price for most of the properties that appeared on the MLS. Add to that the competition from other buyers and it was a situation ripe for potentially grossly overpaying. I had to find another way.

On a whim I decided that I would start walking my immediate neighborhood and jotting down the addresses of every single 3 and 4 unit building around. I printed a map of my neighborhood, put on my headphones, and started walking. I went up and down every single street in an area approximately three miles square and as I went along, I highlighted that street on the map and moved to the next. This was a process that took many weekends to accomplish. An hour walk here, an hour walk there and I'd add a handful of properties to the list. In some cases, I would get lucky and see a sign on the front of the building that mentioned the property manager and a phone number. I wrote this all down as well. For those properties that didn't provide this information I had another plan.

Once I was satisfied with my list of well over 150 addresses, which doesn't seem like a lot but is significant considering the size of the area and the fact that they were very much targeted and not just a list of random addresses, that's when the work really began. I created an Excel spread sheet and listed every property address. I then went online and pulled up the county tax assessor's website to perform a property address search. Once I did this, I was able to determine a few pieces of key information:

1. Number of units - If the property had fewer than three or more than four units, I would usually eliminate it from the list. Sometimes a property might appear to be 3-4 units from the street but would turn out to be more or less. As I did this, my list started to shed the properties that no longer fit my criteria.

2. Basement Status – What might seem like a non-essential piece of information could actually provide the caveat to the previous rule. The county assessor's website would list whether or not a property had a basement. In Chicago it's very common to have a non-conforming unit in the basement of a building. While this space is considered a rentable unit in the eyes of the owner, it is not in the eyes of the city. So, if I noticed a 2 unit building with a basement, I would keep it on my list knowing that there's the

potential of a third unit existing, though not officially recognized by the city.
3. PIN – the third and final piece of information I obtained was the Property Index Number, or PIN. The PIN identifies the property type, location and is used for taxation purposes. Those uses for the PIN did not interest me though; I had a different use in mind.

My list that started off as about 150 addresses now contained about 125, and along with those addresses I now also had the PIN for each. The next step in this process was to determine the owner's name. You could potentially stop here and send letters to each building addressed to "current owner", but I suggest you do the extra legwork I'm about to describe.

With the PIN in hand, I then went to the website of the county recorder of deeds. Every single real estate transaction that takes place is recorded by the county and is associated with that PIN. Each record contains the name of the deed grantee (owner) and the year in which the deed was transferred to that owner, which is another valuable piece of information. If I noticed a property was purchased within the past 3 years, I removed it from my list. My thought was that this person was less likely to be willing to sell after such a short time frame. My list shrunk again to 101 total addresses. For each entry on my spreadsheet, I noted the name of the owner and the number of years he or she owned that property. This was a tedious process that required a lot of back and forth between multiple websites. I would chip away at my list each night until I had all the information I needed.

Armed with this information I then sat down to write a letter to each and every one of those owners. The body of the letter itself was generic in that each letter contained the same description of who I was and why I was interested in the property. I would describe that I am a young, hardworking, entrepreneurial, and aspiring real estate investor and not a large investor or broker. People are better able to relate to you in that sense, especially if it's an owner who has blazed a similar trail that you are starting down. I've provided a sample letter in Appendix. The personalized part of each letter came in that I not only knew the first and last name of the owner, but I also knew how long that person had owned the property, and I mentioned it too. I would explain that I admire their ability to manage a property for "X" number of years. Furthermore, I would mention a specific quality of the building I really liked, such as limestone accents or a Spanish-tile roof. Imagine reading that letter and feeling as though the writer knows you on a personal level (I imagine it was unsettling for some). On top of this, I handwrote the name & address on the envelope. This too becomes more compelling for an owner, who may otherwise see a printed mailing as another piece of junk mail.

The goal was to find a willing seller who perhaps was considering selling their property but was not yet listed on the MLS. It also eliminated my competition. Between the stamps and the envelopes, this process cost me about $60 total. To be quite honest I thought my efforts would be futile, so you can imagine my surprise when I received three responses. The first response I got was from a lady who was a tenant of the building to which I had sent a letter (definitely not the target audience). I think she had a few screws loose because she said she hated her landlord and had been opening and reading his mail. I think she just wanted to talk with someone- anyone. Lucky me. The second response was from an older woman who owned a building a few doors down from me. We chatted for a while, but nothing came of it; I don't think she was fully committed to selling at that time. The last response came from an older gentleman who, as I would learn from listening to a voicemail response, owned a 4-unit apartment building he had been considering selling. This seemed promising! When I found his name on my list and looked at the details, I was stunned to see that not only was the building number 101 of 101 on my list, but it was also directly across the street from my current building. Could this be too good to be true?

The owner and I scheduled a day to meet to tour the property.

At the time we were only able to see the common areas of the building, such as the basement and front & rear entry stairwells, etc. He took the time to show and/or describe the improvements he had performed over the years including a new roof, brick tuckpointing, air conditioning units, copper piping, and so much more. I knew without a doubt he had taken meticulous care of the building and could see it in the limited areas we viewed. We also seemed to connect on a personal level over the difficulties involved with being a landlord and how other people just couldn't possibly understand the unique frustrations. I had one goal in mind for the meeting and that was to not show my cards first when it came to discussing price. I mentioned to him that it seemed like he had been thinking about selling for a while, and he admitted he had and that his wife was pushing him to sell it now as he was getting older. I asked him if he had a number in mind. This was the pivotal moment. To my relief he willingly provided that information and said he was looking to get about $500,000. I couldn't believe what I had just heard. Similar sized buildings in the area were asking $600-$650k, and almost certainly were not in as good of condition. I knew instantly this had the potential to be a grand slam but didn't allow myself to express my excitement. I simply acknowledged his "ask" and said I would crunch the numbers and get back to him. I offered to take him to lunch, and we continued to build further rapport and talk about things unrelated to real estate or the potential transaction.

After intentionally waiting a couple days, I reached back out to the seller and mentally prepared him for something that was far lower than his asking price. I started the conversation with "You're not going to like my offer...". In doing so, this set his expectations extremely low. The idea was to create mental turmoil for an offer that was so low, so ridiculous, that it couldn't possibly be considered.

I countered with $475,000. I knew the purchase would be a bargain at the $500,000 that he was asking, but the psychology of any transaction is such that if I had yelled out "DEAL!" right away he of course would think he undervalued the property and likely would have found a way to kill the deal. Furthermore, after setting the expectations low in his mind, a difference of only $25,000 was likely a huge relief for the seller, and his fears of an insultingly low counteroffer were unfounded. I explained that since we were not using realtors to broker the transaction, I was discounting the price 5% to account for that fact. He acknowledged my point and countered at $490,000 to which we came to a verbal agreement on. I was in shock that the efforts of my handwritten letter campaign were about to pay off. I found an off-market property, had no competition, and got a hell of a deal to boot. It was coming together very nicely. Could the financing and closing of the deal be just as easy?

> **LESSONS APPLIED**
>
> Prior to entering into any negotiation, I highly recommend you read *Never Split the Difference – Negotiating as if Your Life Depended on It*, by Chris Voss.
>
> Voss, a former FBI hostage negotiator, provides a wealth of knowledge with actionable steps for coming out on top in any negotiation. I had previously read his book but decided to page through it again to refresh myself on some of the key negotiation tactics before I met with the seller. Below are some of the tactics I found to be helpful and was able to apply to my situation:
>
> -Create empathy by speaking to someone with deference. Understand the seller's motivation.
> -Label their emotions with a phrase like "It seems like..."
> -Let the other party go first.

With a signed letter of intent from the owner, the real work was about to begin. All along I had been working under the assumption that I was going to use a low-down payment program like I had on my first property purchase. After sharing details of the property with my lender it came back as a complete shock to me that I was *not* going to be able to use the loan program I had previously used, as that was only available to first-time home buyers, and an FHA loan was also unavailable. My only option at this point was a conventional loan with a 20% down payment. I was furious with myself for not having researched this further before getting into an agreement. At a purchase price of $490,000 I was going to have to come up with $98,000 for the down payment. I had about $45,000 saved up. "There's no way," I thought to myself, "the deal is dead". I spoke with my lender, and she walked me back from the edge of the cliff. She laid out some options for how to come up with the balance. The first was a gift from my parents. Even if my parents had been willing to give me that much money, there was no way I was going to accept it. Another option was to partner with someone, but at the time I was steadfast in "going it alone". I had to figure out how to accomplish this without the involvement of another investor. My last option was to utilize the equity I had built up in my first property. This option seemed promising. I could either do a cash-out refinance, resetting my loan maturity date and also increasing the monthly principal & interest, or take out a home equity line of credit (HELOC). In my mind I didn't want the purchase of this new property to negatively affect the cash flow of the first property, so I opted for the HELOC, with the plan to use the cash flow of the second property to pay down the HELOC on the first.

A HELOC works similar to a cash-out refinance in that the process determines the amount of equity you hold in a given property. The difference is that a HELOC simply works like a credit card; you have a certain amount of credit from which you can utilize that you must pay back, with interest. It is an open line of credit that can continually be drawn upon, whereas a cash-out refinance is a one-time lump sum amount. The bank that was offering the HELOC scheduled a date for an appraiser to tour the property and provide his valuation. Given the soaring real estate market at that time, the improvements I had performed, and the two years of inflation since having purchased the building, I was confident the appraisal would come back with a high number, solidifying my strong equity position.

The appraisal came back at $560,000. Pretty good, right? I was devastated. I had purchased the property two years prior for *$550,000*. I thought, at a minimum, the appraisal would come back at $580,000 from inflation alone. The new appraised value, minus my initial down payment and the loan pay-down of two years, left me with roughly $59,000 in equity in my first property. Although I didn't know it at the time, the $59,000 equity line plus the $45,000 in cash I had saved up left me with just $467 in excess of the required cash-to-close on the new purchase. Talk about squeaking by. Thinking back on it, this was an extremely risking move because it completed depleted any reserves I had for normal repairs and maintenance.

With the financing fiasco behind me I could now schedule a professional inspection of the building I was getting ready to purchase. Although to my eyes the building appeared to be in great shape, it is always advisable to have a professional inspection performed as well. On the day of the inspection, I followed the inspector around to see what he'd uncover, prior to receiving his report. The inspector should present an unbiased view of the property and provide an opinion on the current state of the building. He typically won't recommend repairs or how to correct deficiencies, but simply make you aware of any issues. While touring the building and out of earshot of the owner, the inspector turned to me, and in a hushed voice said, "This place is immaculate. You could eat off the floors". He validated what I already knew to be true; this building had been meticulously cared for over the years. I was feeling more and more confident about the purchase.

Finally, after multiple delays and various hiccups along the way in getting to a closing date, we were ready to sign documents and finalized the purchase. Prior to the closing date I took a draw on my home equity line of credit so that I had the required total funds to close. My attorney provided me with the title company to whom I needed to transfer the money to, along with the appropriate account and routing number. His email included big, bold letters that read:

PLEASE VERIFY THE ACCOUNT INFORMATION WITH THE TITLE COMPANY PRIOR TO TRANSFERRING FUNDS.

His recommendation was that I call and speak with a live human being at the title company to verify the wire instructions. These types of transfers are a preferred target of cyber criminals. So, I called the title company, got a prerecorded message with the account information, and was unable to get through to someone on a subsequent call. I figured it was good enough and thought "what are the odds?"

Throughout the closing process, as I signed one document after the next, the title company representative would periodically let us know that the funds had still not cleared, and that they were waiting for them to arrive into the account. "This is normal, right?" I thought to myself. By the time all documents were signed and notarized the funds had *still* not cleared. I was beginning to get nervous, second guessing my decision to trust that calm, inviting voice at the other end of the prerecorded phone message. I started to sweat. The second hand ticked in thunderous succession around the clock on the wall across from me. Thirty minutes went by like an eternity, but finally we were given word that the funds had cleared. I had closed on the property and was now the proud owner of my second building.

So, what about the $60 into $42,000 you ask? Well, fast forward about a year and I decided to do a cash-out refinance of the second building. (You will remember that the $60 was the cost of stamps and envelopes to send out letters that landed me this building). This time around the appraisal was certainly what I had hoped for. I purchased the building for $490,000 and after the appraiser was finished, he gave an appraised value of $630,000.

Purchase Price:	$490,000
Appraised Value:	$630,000
Equity:	$140,000
Down payment:	$98,000 (cash plus HELOC funds)
Equity increase:	$42,000

The cash-out refi provided a loan-to-value of 75% of the new appraised value, which netted me about $77,000 in cash after the initial loan was paid off. On top of that, the equity I pulled out was tax free. With the cash I pulled out I could have paid off the balance of the HELOC and still had money left over, however with the relatively low interest rate of the HELOC and the ability of the second property to cash flow even with me living there, I decided to set it aside to be ready for an eventual third purchase. In 4 years, I had purchased two properties and recuperated a substantial amount of the down payment money I had put in.

To File or Not to File… That Is the Question

Often times when new investors get into real estate they are fixated on the idea of "legitimizing" their business by setting up an organizing structure in the form of a limited liability company, or LLC. While owning real estate in an LLC as opposed to your personal name does have its benefits, the question that should be asked is whether or not the benefits outweigh the costs to make it worthwhile. Perhaps it does, but you should consult with your attorney and tax professional before trying to answer that question on your own. So why would someone want an LLC in the first place?

Simply put, and LLC is an entity structure that protects your personal assets in the event that your business, in this case the real estate, gets sued. The LLC acts as a barrier between you as an individual with other assets, and the property as a standalone asset of its own. If, for instance, someone was to get injured while on your property and decided to sue you, they might potentially sue you for the value of the property as well as any other assets you have, such as savings, personal residence, your car or other assets. Logically this may lead you to wonder, why wouldn't all real estate investors own their properties in LLC's? This answer is complex. First, you have to consider that your homeowner's policy or landlord policy on the building already provides you with liability coverage, often as high as $1,000,000 in protection. For most people this is more than enough to protect against any lawsuit that may come their way. Secondly, there are costs associated with forming an LLC. These costs will sometimes outweigh the potential for risk. There is a filing fee with the state in which you organize the LLC, typically a cost to have an attorney draw up the documents and articles of organization, and the ongoing cost of the annual fee to keep the LLC active with your state. Additionally, if the liability coverage provided in your homeowner's/landlord policy isn't sufficient another viable option may be to purchase an umbrella policy to increase your protection. An umbrella policy very well could be cheaper than the combined costs of created an LLC.

> When purchasing each of my first two properties, I did so in my personal name. However, each property is now owned in the name of my real estate LLC. I was able to accomplish this by performing a Quit Claim Deed. A Quit Claim transfers ownership from one entity to another, in this case from my personal name to my LLC. In addition to the costs already described for setting up the LLC, there is also the cost to have an attorney perform the Quit Claim. Furthermore, there is risk that doing so will trigger the "Due on Sale Clause" in your mortgage. Most residential mortgages contain this clause, and it allows the lender to call due the balance of your loan upon the transfer of ownership of the property. This should not be taken lightly when considering setting up an LLC for ownership transfer.

There are other challenges with setting up an LLC aside from the initial costs. After reading the preceding paragraph you may be inclined to go set up an LLC prior to even purchasing a building. However, doing so would likely prove to be a wasted effort. When obtaining a conforming residential loan to purchase a property, the loan must be in the name of the individual (you), *not* an LLC or other corporate structure.

Alternatively, the LLC could obtain a commercial loan, however now you'll end up paying a higher interest rate and almost certainly be required to put 20-30% down.

For most new investors just starting out, creating an LLC for your first property just doesn't make sense. There are other ways to protect your assets as described. The reason I've included a discussion of this topic at this point in the book, rather than earlier, is because with the addition of a second property to my portfolio, the risks now outweighed the costs for me to set up an LLC. I needed to provide protection to both properties, *from each other*. As your real estate business continues to grow, each property added to your portfolio creates an additional avenue for lawsuit-happy individuals to target. Now, instead of just the value of one property, a lawsuit could potentially go after both buildings, as well as other assets. Setting up an LLC for each property will limit your liability (as the name entails) to just the value of the property where the lawsuit originates. So instead of being able to sue you for everything you're worth, the most a person could go after is just the one LLC in which the property is owned. While this all may seem a bit unlikely, I view the cost of setting up and maintaining LLCs as an additional, cheap insurance policy to protect myself and my assets from a worst-case scenario. You need to evaluate your own situation to see if and when it might make sense for you to do something similar. There are plenty of real estate owners who never create an LLC and go through the life cycle of owning a property without incident.

That being said, LLC ownership of real estate is a common practice in the real estate world. Typically, an owner will set up an LLC for each and every property they own, with a slight name variation for each new property, i.e. 123 Main Street LLC, 456 Park Avenue LLC and so on. I was introduced to a fairly new concept of an LLC structure called a "Series-LLC". In a Series-LLC, the managing member will create a "parent" LLC. The parent LLC will then give birth to various "series" or sub-LLCs. Let's look at an illustration to help depict the structure.

Although there are not *significant* advantages to a Series-LLC over a traditional LLC, there are a couple that might make it a more attractive option. First, regardless of the series, all expenses and revenue are paid or collected through the parent-LLC. So, instead of your tenants writing checks to various LLCs, they write checks to the parent LLC. That being said, it is still advisable to have your tenants note the series name on the check so as to allow you easier management of rent checks coming in. Similarly, taxes are filed for the parent LLC only, rather than a separate return for each property. I like Series-LLCs for the simple fact that it allows me to operate as "one company", rather than many. Another benefit of operating Series-LLCs is the cost. As compared to setting up a brand-new LLC for each property, Series-LLCs are typically cheaper for the initial set up and also typically cheaper for the annual fee. This can add up over time and with the addition of more and more properties.

With each LLC/Series-LLC you setup you will then need to obtain an employer identification number (EIN) assigned by the IRS (even if you have no employees, contrary to what the name implies). Your EIN is a unique number that separates each entity for tax purposes. With the EIN number you can then open a business checking account for each LLC/Series-LLC to keep funds separate. Be aware that some banks will not allow business checking accounts for series LLCs, however there are plenty that will.

Economies of Proximity

As you grow your real estate investing business and get to the point at which you are ready to purchase an additional property, whether that be your second or tenth, it is my firm belief that doing so in the area immediately surrounding your other investment(s) will allow you to be more efficient, more knowledgeable about your area and reduce the overall burden of self-managing. We are familiar with the concept of economies of scale in minimizing costs. The example we used earlier was 3 units in one building as opposed to 3 units in 3 separate structures. The economy of scale by owning multiple units in one building can produce financial savings in various ways. But what about the time savings when managing multiple buildings with multiple units in one area? I call this an economy of proximity.

As a self-managing landlord, the closer your properties are together the easier it will be for you to manage them. Properties in close proximity are inherently more efficient to manage than properties that have a great distance between them. It doesn't mean that you will magically have problem-free properties if they are close by. The number of problems does not reduce, rather, the amount of *effort* to manage those properties reduces as they get closer. I want to reiterate this is under the assumption that you are still self-managing your properties while also living in one of them. If at some point you hire a property management company or hire managers of your own, the proximity of properties becomes less important, and in fact the properties could be on opposite sides of the country and it wouldn't matter.

Prior to having found my second property, in desperation I started to search in areas of the city that I had absolutely no experience investing in, no knowledge of the neighborhood, and most importantly in areas that were nowhere near the one property I owned at the time. As self-managing real estate investors it is in our best interest to group the properties as close together as possible. For me, it didn't get much closer than right across the street. The value of being able to look out my front window and keep an eye on my other property cannot be overstated. I do recognize that this is a rarity, however. That being said, you should strive to purchase properties as close to your other investments as possible. When considering properties now, I typically do so within a one-mile radius of my current properties. This is possible for me because of the density of housing in Chicago. Your radius may vary depending on the density of your area. I like to think that if I have to spend more than 10 minutes in my car to get from one property to the next, I probably don't want to buy it. And it's not just for the inconvenience of having to drive around the city. Rather, it's the hassles of having to collect rent checks, doing visual inspections of a property, moving around a lawnmower/snowblower/tools/paint or any variety of other items. I cannot tell you how many times I have gone to fix something in one building and had to walk across the street for a tool I forgot at the other. And while that might not seem like a big deal, think about doing that with buildings that are miles apart. Also consider the showings you'll need to do every time there is a lease that is ending. You could find yourself driving back and forth between properties on a daily basis. Not only is there a considerable savings of your time, but by investing in your immediate area you will be more in tune with the neighborhood as well. This will help you in staying competitive with market rents, being able to know precisely the amount that a certain size apartment can rent for in your specific neighborhood. Similarly, it helps in analyzing the value of properties for purchase.

All this is not to say that eventually you shouldn't consider expanding outside of your immediate area, and in fact you may decide instead that it is a better use of your money to hire a management company to manage your properties so you can continue to find good deals, regardless of the location. Keeping your properties close by is merely a suggestion in the early years of self-managing your real estate so you can maximize your efficiency and ability to provide reasonable response times for your tenants.

Taxes and Cost Segregation

As real estate investors we are always looking for ways to reduce expenses and increase revenue. We discussed various methods for reducing expenses earlier, but there is another method that was not discussed. With the addition of a second property to my portfolio, my tax professional recommended I consider having a cost segregation study performed for my properties. A cost segregation study is an analysis of a property and all components within it. The analysis "segregates" all components for means of depreciating each on its own. Those components can be a furnace, appliances, kitchen cabinets, even flooring, and more. Now why would you want to separate each of these components from one another, and what is the benefit?

Similar to how to IRS designates a useful life of 27.5 years for a structure (also known as a "recovery period"), the IRS also designates useful lifespans for specific components within a structure. Without a cost segregation, all of those components are depreciated along the same straight-line method of 27.5 years. With a cost segregation, the eligible components are depreciated over a much shorter timeline, either 5, 7 or 15 years, depending on the specific component. This accelerated depreciation method, also known as front-loading, allows the owner to capture the depreciation deduction for the components much faster, resulting in a lower tax liability and a higher likelihood of a tax credit. There are four categories into which a component can be segregated into:

1. Personal property (non-structural items)
2. Structures
3. Land improvements
4. Land

Of those four categories, only Land is not depreciable. Personal property, which can consist of furniture, fixtures or other items not necessary for normal operation of the building, can be depreciated over an accelerated timeline of 5 or 7 years. The next category, Structures, are not just the building itself, but also the components such as a roof, water heater, or furnace that are required for normal operation of the building. These items are depreciated over the same 27.5-year timeline as the building itself, but the benefit is that if one of those components becomes non-functional or obsolete during that time, it can be written off immediately (whereas without a cost segregation the write off for that component cannot be captured on its own). This makes logical sense because most of these items have a much shorter useful life than 27.5 years. The Land Improvements category is just what it sounds like and can be depreciated over 15 years.

There is a lot to digest here, and it can easily become confusing. To help illustrate the power of a cost segregation study let's take a look at an example to contrast a property with cost segregation applied versus one without.

> Our novice real estate investor purchased an apartment building for $650,000 in the prior year. Not only has she never heard of a cost segregation study, but she also does her taxes herself, so there is not a tax professional that might make the recommendation of performing an analysis. The value of the non-depreciable land is $130,000 with the remaining $520,000 value of the structure being depreciable. Using the straight-line method of 27.5 years, our investor is able to capture a depreciation deduction of $18,909 to help offset any net income produced by the building that year, and therefor lower her tax liability. Who would complain with that?

> Well, let us say that our same investor, in a parallel universe, decided a tax professional would be much better suited to take on her taxes. After consulting with her tax professional she decides to pay him to perform a cost segregation study and depreciate components of the building on an accelerated timeline. Through his study, the

tax professional determines the following values can be attributed to the building:

Land: $130,000 (non-depreciable, as before)
Personal Property: $50,000 depreciable over 5 years = $10,000 annual deduction
Structures: $465,000 depreciable over 27.5 years = $16,909 annual deduction
Land Improvements: $5,000 depreciable over 15 years = $333 annual deduction

With the cost segregation study applied, the total annual depreciation deduction for that year adds up to $27,242 which is an additional $8,333 compared to the straight-line method. You can see how advantageous it can be to have a cost segregation performed on a property.

* * *

In order to understand the full scope of this subject, we need to take a deep dive into IRS code, as it is not as simple as it has been described in the examples. Afterall, why would someone want to invest in an asset that loses money? As classified by IRS Section 469, rental real estate is considered a passive activity. This is an important distinction because Passive Activity Losses (PAL) can only offset *passive income*, not earned W2 income. That is, unless the taxpayer qualifies for one of two exemptions:

1. Real estate professional (750 hours worked in real estate annually)
2. The taxpayer's Modified Adjusted Gross Income (MAGI) is less than $100,000

For our purposes, we will assume that the reader is not a real estate professional (nor am I). This leaves us with the MAGI exemption. Passive Activity rules limit the taxpayer to deduct up to $25,000 of passive losses from real estate against earned W2 wages, *if* the MAGI is less than $100,000. For every dollar earned over $100k, the deduction amount is decreased by $.50. So once the MAGI of the taxpayer reaches $150,000 the deduction decreases to $0.

To be able to take full advantage of the losses generated by the depreciation deductions resulting from the cost segregation, it is in the taxpayer's best interest to keep his or her earned income less than $100,000. If the taxpayer's earned income is over the threshold, a strategy may be to defer earned income to a pre-tax retirement account in the amount that will decrease the gross income below $100,000.

Further complicating matters is any amount of loss beyond the $25,000 limit. In our example, the investor had a depreciation deduction of $27,242 resulting from the cost segregation study. As we now know, only $25,000 of that can be utilized against earned income in the current tax year. So, what happens to the balance? The additional $2,242 is carried forward, indefinitely, into the following tax year(s) until it has been "used up".

All things being equal, the property in both scenarios will produce the same amount of depreciation over the 27.5-year lifetime. The significance, however, is the time value of money. The deprecation is captured much faster using a cost segregation than the straight-line method, which permits the property owner to put that capital to work much faster, allowing him or her to reinvest in the property or further scale her real estate portfolio.

Cost segregation studies do not come without their own costs, of course. They can be expensive. Depending on the value of the property, the price of the study may outweigh the benefits produced in depreciation captured. Additionally, once the depreciation for any particular component has been fully utilized (for instance, the $50,000 of personal property after 5 years in the second example) no further depreciation can be taken on those components. As a result, the owner will have less and less depreciation to offset tax liabilities as the building continues through its lifecycle. Cost segregation studies further complicate matters in the event of the sale of a property. Depreciation recapture for the components that were placed on an accelerated timeline will be assessed by the IRS accordingly, meaning the net gain on the sale will be lower than if that same property had been depreciated using the straight straight-line method. Before considering a cost segregation you must first recognize how you stand to benefit, as well as asses how it could affect your future plans and goals. It goes without saying that it's a discussion that should be had with your tax professional.

CHAPTER EIGHTEEN – LANDLORDING THROUGH A PANDEMIC

As the clock struck midnight on December 31st, 2019, not a single person on earth could have predicted how the following year would play out. As happens every year, people were getting ready to commit to their New Year's resolutions and start the year off on the right foot. I was among those. One of my goals for the upcoming year was to make a third purchase and further scale up into larger real estate. But there was a problem looming that would put the world on its head and destroy the hopes and dreams of many.

We are now all too familiar with the Covid-19 pandemic that swept over the world like a tidal wave. But it's easy to forget how things manifested in the early days of the outbreak. As the number of infected and death totals continued to increase exponentially, China and countries across Europe imposed lockdowns to mitigate the spread of the virus. Entire cities looked like post-apocalyptic ghost towns: highways free of cars, national monuments barren of tourists. There were images on TV of people in hazmat suits walking

empty cities fogging the streets with disinfectant. It was a truly surreal feeling to watch the world spiral out of control, as if we were caught up in a dystopian sci-fi movie. But it was anything but science fiction, and it was only a matter of time before the outbreak ravaged through the US. The case numbers started off small, but soon grew to a point at which states in the US followed suit with the lockdowns that were taking place in the rest of the world. Along with the lockdowns came Great-Depression-esque layoffs. Certain businesses were considered essential, while others that were considered non-essential were forced to close. In a matter of mere months, the unemployment rate went from a near record low 3.8% to an earth-shattering height of 14.7% in April 2020. More than 20 million Americans were without work.

The federal government, which normally moves at the rate of molasses on a cold winter day, acted quickly (by normal standards) to pass a two-trillion-dollar stimulus package, known as the Coronavirus Aid, Relief and Economic Security Act, or CARES Act, aimed at lessening the blow to the economy. In that package was money for the Paycheck Protection Plan, or PPP, to persuade small business employers to keep workers on their payroll. But there was only so much PPP money to go around, not to mention it was wrought with fraud. Another provision of the stimulus package was the federal supplemental unemployment benefit of an additional $600 per week on top of the amount normally provided by state unemployment. Furthermore, direct payments of up to $1,200 per person were sent out to all citizens making up to $99,000 for single filers and up to $198,000 for joint filers, with stepped-down payment amounts for those with higher incomes. On top of that, parents received $500 per dependent age 16 and under. The Treasury ran the printing press to issues millions of checks, equating to hundreds of billions of dollars. All of this did little to ease the markets, as the major stock market indices went on daily roller coaster rides and saw 35% drops from their peaks at the start of the year. Recognizing the potential for disaster, local governments also moved quickly by imposing eviction moratoriums to ensure those who were out of work and unable to pay rent would not be put on the street. It was an uneasy time for landlords as we were left wondering whether or not we would be caught holding the bag.

As real estate investors it can be difficult at times to forecast costs. We can set aside money for capital expenditures and unanticipated repairs. Preparing for a pandemic is an entirely different crisis to manage. As the pandemic worsened and more people were out of work, there were calls for rent freezes and petitions to cancel rent altogether. The impending possibility of renters not paying put an immediate highlight on the absolute need to have sufficient reserve funds. Yet it also begs the question; why should a real estate investor have to tap into reserve funds to continue paying the mortgage and property taxes if he or she is not receiving rent that is due? The argument was made that it is the responsibility of the landlord to have money for such instances, yet

none of the responsibility should be placed on the renter to have similar emergency funds. It all seemed absurd as the landlords were painted in the all too familiar "greedy" hue.

Our job as landlords is not only to manage the financial aspect of our properties but also the *relationship with our tenants*. I had sufficient funds to continue paying my expenses for quite some time even if all tenants decided to stop paying, but that certainly didn't mean that I wanted to. I didn't go out of my way to tell tenants to pay if they were able, rather I took a different approach; I mostly stayed silent, meaning rent was still due. For those tenants I knew were at risk of losing their jobs or having hours cut because of the industry they work in, I reached out to them personally to let them know I would be willing to work something out in the event they were going to have difficulty paying their rent. As the months passed by, we would stay in touch to see how their financial situation was working out, and the tenants seemed to appreciate it. I wanted no surprises. During the depths of the crisis, I am thankful to not have missed one rent payment from any of my tenants. I think when tenants are able to see you as a person, rather than just someone responsible for collecting a substantial portion of their income, they are more likely to ensure they are capable of meeting their responsibility to pay rent. This comes from fostering a relationship with tenants not only when times good, but also during times of crisis.

I had one tenant whose lease was expiring during the depths of the lockdown. The monthly rent at the unit was well below market and was due for a sizeable increase. He knew it too but wanted to stay. So, I was in the awkward position of determining whether or not I would increase rent for someone I knew had his hours at work cut. What I offered instead was to keep the rent locked in at the current rate until a later phase of reopening was reached, which at the time was a complete unknown. I knew it wouldn't affect me financially in a significant way, but it seemed to make all the difference to him.

In another similar morality situation, I had a tenant who was granted rent assistance from a local non-profit organization. For circumstances I am unaware of, this non-profit covered her rent for several months. One month I was sent two checks for her rent. The first was for the current month's rent, and the second was for the previous month, which had already been paid by the tenant from her personal checking. I had a few options:

1. Destroy the check
2. Cash the check for myself. After all, rent had already been paid, and the non-profit won't lose over it, right?
3. Cash the check and then immediately send that same amount to the tenant.

I'm sure you can guess where this is going, but I decided on option three. The money was not mine to keep, and if the non-profit intended for it to cover rent for a particular month, then that's how it should be allocated, regardless of the fact that the tenant had already paid for that month on her own.

I share these stories not to signal my "moral righteousness", but rather as examples of real-life scenarios where we can show compassion for others as landlords. Perhaps you don't find yourself in the exact same situation, but small acts of kindness can go a long way, pandemic or not. These are the kind of things that will earn you a good reputation as you continue to grow, but will also make for a tenant who returns the favor in continuing to be an exceptional tenant, which as landlords is the best thing we can ask for.

> **A Strange Correlation**
>
> In 1937, as America just began to emerge from the depths the Great Depression, famed author Napoleon Hill wrote his book Think and Grow Rich. The book was intended to be a personal development template for Americans who fought for their survival through the Great Depression, and how they could come out better prepared for a changed world. More than 80 years later, the book has an unexpected, yet appropriate relation to the 2020 Covid-19 pandemic. Undoubtedly the world will be a changed place once the realty of the pandemic becomes a memory.
> The following excerpt is as true today as it was in 1937:
>
> "Never, in the history of America has there been so great an opportunity for practical dreamers as now exists. The six-year economic collapse has reduced all men, substantially, to the same level. A new race is about to be run. The stakes represent huge fortunes which will be accumulated within the next ten years. The rules of the race have changed, because we now live in a changed world that definitely favors the masses, those who had but little or no opportunity to win under the conditions existing during the depression, when fear paralyzed growth and development…
> …there is one quality which one must possess to win, and that is definiteness of purpose, the knowledge of what one wants, and a burning desire to possess it. The business depression marked the death of one age, and the birth of another. This changed world requires practical dreamers who can and will put their dreams into action. The practical dreamers have always been, and always will be the pattern-makers of civilization."
>
> If that isn't motivation that rings true today, I don't know what is!

Mortgage Relief

The Covid-19 pandemic brought to light numerous inadequacies in our country; from locally producing personal protective equipment and the need to stockpile it, to the ability to produce a reliable, readily available test to combat the spread.

But it also brought to light inadequacies to small landlords alike. I mentioned before the absolute need to have sufficient reserve funds, however there are plenty of scenarios where those reserve funds could be wiped out in one fell swoop, global pandemic being just one among them. Congress recognized the seriousness of the pandemic for property owners and made moves to prevent a repeat of the 2008 mortgage crisis. In their response to the pandemic and as a requirement of the CARES Act, banks began offering property owners with government backed mortgages two methods for delaying their mortgage payments in the event they too, similar to renters, were unable to meet their financial obligations. Property owners facing the possibility of a missed payment had two avenues for assistance: deferment or forbearance. Let's take a look at each to understand the differences between the two.

> **Mortgage Deferment** – A mortgage deferment allows a borrower to temporarily defer payments to a later date, typically at the end of the loan period. During the time in which payments have been deferred, interest is typically still accruing, though not always, depending on the lender. The repayment at the end of the loan may be in the form of one lump sum payment or spread out over time. Let's look at an example.
>
> Loan Amount: $500,000
> Interest Rate: 4%
> Monthly P&I: $2,387
> Deferment Period: 6 months (6 payments)
> Loan Origination: January 2020
> Original Loan End: January 2050
> Start of Deferment: April 2020

During these 6 months, no payment is due, however interest is still accruing, totaling $9,918. At the end of the deferment period (October 1st, 2020) payments continue as they normally would, but the payment amount is slightly higher to account for the amount of interest during the deferment. There is also a new loan completion date of July 2050, so instead of 360 payments over 30 years, there are instead 360 payments over 30 years and 6 months. It is important to note that those payments do not disappear, they are simply *deferred* to a later date as the name implies.

Mortgage Forbearance – Similar to a deferment, mortgage forbearance temporarily delays payments during the forbearance period. The difference is that at the end of the forbearance period the amount paused becomes due in one lump sum, in addition to interest that accrued during the paused period. Let's take a look at another example with similar numbers.

Loan Amount: $500,000
Interest Rate: 4%
Monthly P&I: $2,387
Deferment Period: 6 months (6 payments)
Loan Origination: January 2020
Loan End: January 2050
Start of Deferment: April 2020

During these 6 months, no payment is due, however on October 1st, when the forbearance period is complete, all 6 months of paused payments (principal and interest) in addition to October's regular payment, become due in one lump sum. In this example, that means a payment of $16,709 is due from the borrower (6 months x $2,387 plus October payment). As you can see, unless the borrower is able to come up with the money to make those payments in one lump sum, a forbearance may just be delaying the inevitable.

While it is the hope to never be in a situation requiring either mortgage deferment or forbearance, it is vital to understand the difference between the two so you can correctly understand your obligations as a borrower and what it means for your repayment.

The Cost of Money – Macro Economics 101

If there is one word that would describe the Covid-19 pandemic, and one that all would agree was grossly overused throughout, it is the word "unprecedented". The ensuing layoffs, closing of businesses and general mayhem that was prevalent throughout caused such turbulence that "unprecedented" certainly seems appropriate. However, the way the Federal Reserve (the Fed) reacted to the pandemic was anything but unprecedented. Indeed, the Fed had precedent from the way it responded to the Great Recession only 12 years prior.

The stated goal of the Fed is "...to promote a strong U.S. economy. Specifically, the Congress has assigned the Fed to conduct the nation's monetary policy to support the goals of maximum employment, stable prices, and moderate long-term interest rates. When prices are stable, long-term interest rates remain at moderate levels, so the goals of price stability and moderate long-term interest rates go together. As a result, the goals of maximum employment and stable prices are often referred to as the Fed's "dual mandate"..."

One of the tools of the Fed to promote said strong economy is the manipulation of the federal interest rate. The federal interest rate, also known as the federal funds rate, is the rate (typically defined as a range) banks charge each other for overnight loans. Without getting into too much of the minutia, banks are required to meet a reserve requirement with the Federal Reserve bank, based on a certain percentage of their deposits. If, on a nightly basis, any particular bank will be unable to meet that reserve requirement, they must borrow from other banks within the rate range specified by the Fed. This reserve requirement is dictated to ensure a bank will be able to meet the obligations of its depositors.

The fed interest rate has changed drastically over time. The graph below, produced by the St. Louis Regional Federal Reserve

Bank, shows a general upward trend peaking near 20% in the early 1980's, followed by a general downward trend into the 2000's, plummeting to near-zero.

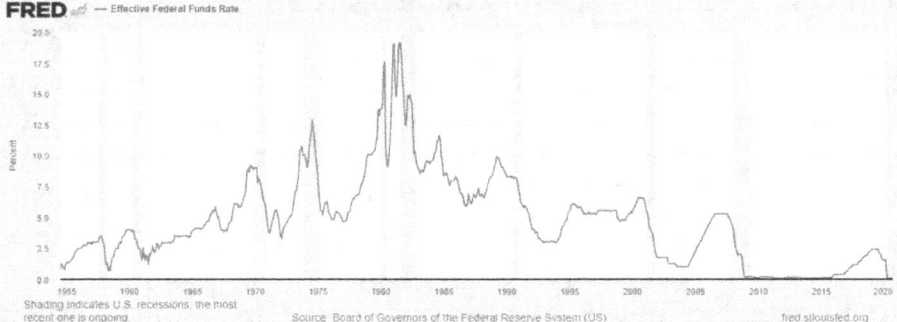

The gray vertical shading indicates a U.S. recession. As can be seen, each recession is met with a steep decline in the federal interest rate. But why is this?

During periods of economic uncertainty, those times during recessions, lenders become more hesitant to lend money to businesses and individuals, as the risk of default increases. To help spur additional lending, and thus additional liquidity into the financial system, the Fed cuts the federal interest rate. A lower interest rate incentivizes business to borrow money from banks, in turn stimulating economic activity. Similarly, during these times of economic uncertainty and higher risk, the yield on a 10-Year Treasury Note also falls. A Treasury Note (T-Bill) is a loan made to the federal government. As the economy faulters, investors are willing to accept a lower yield for less risk, knowing that a loan to the federal government is as close to a guaranteed return as one can receive. Although not inherently linked, there is a general correlation of the yield on a 10-Year note to follow the federal interest rate, as seen in this graph also produced by the St. Louis Regional Federal Reserve Bank.

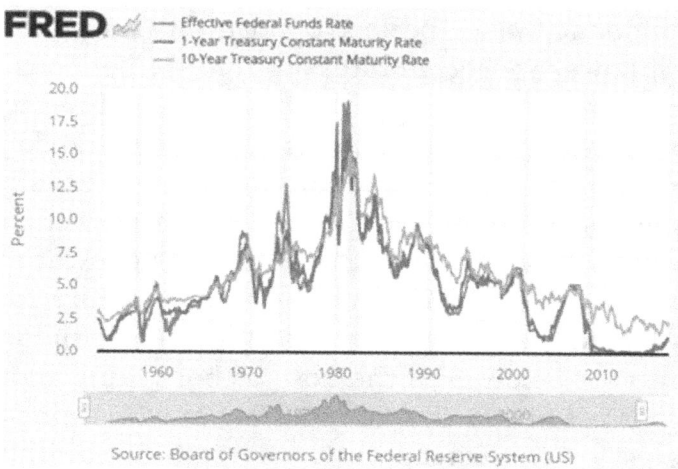

Source: Board of Governors of the Federal Reserve System (US)

Leading up to the Great Recession of 2008, while still comparatively low, the federal interest rate was gradually increasing. As a reaction to the recession, the monetary policy of the Fed was to cut the federal interest rate to near-zero levels, something that had never been done before. In addition to the rate cut, the Fed implemented a strategy called "quantitative easing" by which the institution aggressively bought back treasury notes in order to flood the financial system with additional liquidity. This was the precedent set in 2008 that was mimicked following the recession that ensued during the Covid pandemic, but to far greater extent in 2020.

In the years following the 2008 recession, the federal interest rate again began to slowly tick back up, although it was still maintained at historically low levels. When the Covid pandemic began its stranglehold on the US economy, there was not nearly as much room for the Fed to cut rates, but rates did come back down to near-zero levels. *Important to understand is that residential and commercial mortgage rates closely follow the yield on the 10-Year T-Bill*, and as we have seen there is a correlation between treasury yields and the federal interest rate. As the Fed interest rate dropped, and in correlation the 10-Year treasury yield, so too did mortgage rates.

For buyers, although it seems like a strange dichotomy, the

Covid pandemic was a perfect opportunity to either buy or refinance. Lower mortgage rates spurred tremendous amount of demand for real estate, and the competition drove up prices. It was extraordinarily unusual that in a time marked by people losing jobs left and right, real estate was simultaneously coming off the shelves left and right. The real estate market continued to be exceptionally strong all throughout. The lower mortgage intertest rates essentially provided an opportunity for buyers to borrow money at nearly no cost. With residential mortgage rates hovering below 3%, the cost of borrowing money was practically the same as that of inflation, only marginally more. The interest on a mortgage is nearly paid for by the annual inflated purchasing power of a dollar. That being said, recessions do tend to cause short-term deflationary conditions for an economy, however, long-term the rate of inflation tends to creep back up. For buyers ready and able to pull the trigger, the Covid pandemic created very favorable conditions to invest in real estate.

CHAPTER NINETEEN - WHAT'S NEXT?

The first five years of my real estate investing journey have certainly supplied no shortage of learning experiences. Through that time, I have developed an insatiable hunger to grow and challenge myself. Year after year, as I lay out my goals, I ask myself a question that remains pervasive throughout the year; what's next?

With two properties to my name, my "what's next" was to purchase a third property, which I just recently accomplished. My ambition was to graduate from the residential multifamily space into the small-commercial space of 5–10-unit apartment buildings. This of course comes with its own unique set of challenges. For starters, there are far fewer of these small-commercial apartment buildings in my market, so supply is limited. However, being able to overcome these challenges has the potential for significant reward. In my mind, this small-commercial space is a niche market in which competition is greatly reduced. As one would expect, the price range for these larger buildings is higher than that of the 2–4-unit residential multifamily buildings. Along with that, a building with 5 or more units is considered a commercial property in the eyes of a lender, which carries the burden of a down payment that is often 25% of purchase price, or higher. Those two factors (higher purchase price and higher down payment percentage) will, for the most part, eliminate a lot of the mom-and-pop landlords that you are otherwise competing against on the smaller 2–4-unit residential properties. On the other end of the spectrum, I have found that these size buildings are often unable to create a return that is high enough for the larger institutional investors, and that they typically seek buildings with a greater number of units to give them more bang for their buck. I, however, and willing to accept a lower return in order to build my portfolio, plus I know I can increase my return by self-managing. As a result, there seems to a be a window of opportunity to purchase a 5–10-unit apartment building with considerably less competition that one would face otherwise. This of course is beneficial to any buyer.

So, what did I do to overcome those challenges? As business great Robert Kiyosaki says, "Inside of every problem lies an opportunity". My problems are twofold, and no different than any real estate investor: finding a deal and financing a deal.

Unfortunately, I have no secrets to reveal about finding a deal. First and foremost, I searched the MLS. The trouble is, everyone else looking for a similar deal is doing the same. That certainly doesn't you can't find a deal on the MLS, but it just introduces more competition. Although they can be found, commercial properties of 5 units or more, in most instances, do not trade on the MLS. Most of these types of properties are bought and sold through commercial brokerages that advertise specifically from their website, but also directly to their list of known buyers, not on the MLS. This is common in most markets. In Chicago there are about a half dozen commercial brokers that sell commercial properties. When dealing with small multifamily properties of 2-4 units, you're usually working with a real estate agent who will interact with the seller's agent. In commercial properties, this is usually not the case. There is one broker who acts on behalf of both the buyer and the seller as a dual-agent. The challenge then, of course, is becoming familiar with these brokers in order to get on their list of buyers. Building these relationships is a slow process. Not only do you need to find out which brokers are selling the types of properties you are seeking in your area, but perhaps more importantly they need to be familiar with you. They need to know the criteria of what you're looking for as well as what kind of experience you have as an investor, which we'll discuss in greater detail later. My process for this involved finding properties for sale on the brokers' websites that came close to fitting my criteria. I would use that as an opportunity to reach out to the selling broker to introduce myself and describe what it is that I was looking for. They in turn would send me the offering memorandum (OM) for the particular property, describing the details of the deal, and I would foster that relationship to stay engaged with them and let them know I was a willing buyer with the hopes of being sent future opportunities. This can be more difficult than it seems. What I found was that in the world of commercial real estate, unless you have done past commercial deals or have a previous relationship with a broker, getting attention from a broker can be challenging. They seem to want to work with known buyer clients and not dedicate time to someone they have no history with. My recommendation is to request the OM for properties that come close to fitting your criteria so that you can analyze the deal, and to then provide feedback to the broker as to why it does or does not work for you. Through this process they will learn more about what you're looking for as well as be able to vet your ability to analyze a deal. Building that confidence can take time, and there's a fine line between pursuing meaningful dialogue and simply wasting the broker's time.

My other method for finding a deal was to repeat the process I performed to find my second deal, and that is to send letters. I again methodically canvased the neighborhood to create a list of all the 5–10-unit apartment buildings in my immediate surrounding area. Of the over 300 letters I sent, I received 8 responses, which equates to a response rate of less than 3%. Of those 8 responses, only two were actually interested in selling. Each of those two preempted with an asking price that was so outrageously high that it didn't make sense to pursue any further. However, a handful of the other responses said they would keep me in mind should they be interested in selling in the future, which is a small win in and of itself. One of those owners, as it would turn out, happened to be the seller of my next purchase (though he had decided to sell through a broker and not directly to me).

Short of finding a deal from sending letters, my next move was to cold-call owners. I zeroed in on owners who have owned their property for more than 15 years in hopes that they will be more willing to sell than those who have owned for fewer. My method for tracking down their phone numbers was simple, but not very productive. In Chicago, owners of buildings with more than 5 units are required to post their phone number in a visible location somewhere on the building. To me, it's an open invite to call to see if they are interested in selling. Most of the time I found the other end of a voicemail, to which I rarely received a response. On the rare occasion that I did reach someone, I was mostly met with disinterest, other times with outright anger for even calling them, and other times still an owner who is just interested in knowing what his or her property is worth, with no intention of selling. If you decide to follow a similar method, be sure to fine-tune your valuation skills to be able to provide a quick (yet fairly accurate) napkin-sketch estimate based on cap rate, rents and any information you can uncover during the length of your conversation. There is always the possibility of catching an owner off-guard by presenting a value that is much higher than they would have anticipated, which might just convince them to further entertain the thought of selling. As is said earlier, everything is for sale at the right price.

My other problem, the challenge of financing a deal, proved to be a far more difficult task to overcome, as one might expect. Following the purchase of my second building, I had two years to set aside cash for my next purchase. Add to that the equity I pulled out in a cash-out refinance, and I still didn't have enough for a down payment on the size building I was looking to purchase in my market. What I have identified is three different strategies to help get over the financing hurdle. These aren't the only options, but just a few strategies to consider in order to fund the purchase of a small commercial apartment building.

Owner Financing – The basic premise of owner financing is that the seller acts as a "bank" loaning you money, either in part or in whole. In exchange for foregoing the full purchase price of the property upfront, the seller may be willing to accept a better than average interest rate on their money. Let's look at a couple simple examples to help illustrate.

Complete Owner Financing
Purchase Price: $1,000,000
Buyer Cash Available: $100,000

Owner Financed Amount: $900,000 (Scenario assumes property is owned free-and-clear by owner)
Interest Rate Offered to Seller: 6%
Amortization Timeline: 30 years
Monthly Principal and Interest Paid to Seller: $5,396

Partial Owner Financing
Purchase Price: $1,000,000
Buyer Cash Available: $100,000

25% Down Payment: $250,000
Down Payment Shortage: $150,000

Bank Financed Amount (75% LTV): $750,000
Owner Financed Amount: $150,000

Interest Rate Offered to Seller: 6%
Amortization Timeline: 15 years
Monthly Principal and Interest Paid to Seller: $1,266
Seller Proceeds: $1,000,000 purchase price - $532,000 loan balance - $150,00 loan to buyer = $318,000 gross

In either scenario, a seller might not need all of the cash right away. Rather than selling outright and parking their money in a savings account that might get 1% as a best-case result, a seller might be enticed by the promise of a 6% return while also no longer having to deal with the hassles of owning real estate. Furthermore, the seller still gets a substantial amount of cash up front and continues to receive the consistent monthly income they have become accustomed to. As a buyer, you are paying a higher interest rate than you would otherwise find from a bank but are able to make a purchase with significantly less capital than is normally required.

With large commercial transactions, not only is owner financing typically asked for, but it is also usually expected. Oftentimes a seller-financed deal is structured with a balloon period of 3-7 years, at which time the balance of the loan is due, which will necessitate a refinance on the part of the new owner. The duration of the balloon period can provide the buyer time to improve the property, increase its net operating income and therefore its value, and secure traditional bank financing by the time the balloon period expires. A balloon period does not come without risks, however. It must be enough time for the buyer to improve the property, *and* there must be enough upside potential to make it feasible. If both of those conditions don't exist, you may be unable to drive enough value into the property in order to create a sizeable equity position and in turn be able to secure bank financing at 70-75% loan-to-value. In such an instance the seller may be able to foreclose on the property if you are unable to secure bank financing to pay off the full loan balance, or you may be coming out of pocket to fund the portion in excess of the established bank LTV.

The challenge is finding an owner who is willing to agree to owner financing, though. When an owner is selling a property, typically it is because they no longer want to be involved with it. By financing some or all of the deal the owner is no longer able to make a clean break from the property. They are still tied to it financially and to a lesser extent mentally. Sometimes an owner is wanting to use the proceeds of the sale of their current property to help purchase another property. Having a portion of their capital tied up in a deal to loan you money could prevent the seller from purchasing their next purchase. Your objective is to pitch the owner on the benefits of utilizing seller-financing, some of which have been discussed already.

- Interest rate paid on the loan far exceeds bank savings rates, and is much more secure than the stock market
- Continuation of a stable monthly income without the hassles of ownership & management
- Delay a large tax bill on the sale of the property. Long term capital gains are delayed until the balloon period expires or can avoided entirely if the loan comes to full term. Taxes are spread out and lower the seller's taxable income.
- The loan is secured by the property and title can be reclaimed if the buyer defaults on payments.

Finding a seller who is willing to entertain owner financing is like the proverbial needle in a haystack. A lot of things have to go right in order for it to work out for all parties. That is not to say those sellers don't exist, but they are certainly more difficult to come by. On rare occasions I have actually seen properties that advertise an owner's interest in providing seller financing. If nothing else, an owner-financed deal could just be one more arrow in your quiver to provide an alternative offer to a seller once you've identified a property. It could provide you an angle to negotiate terms in order to provide the seller with their full asking price. When compared side by side with a traditional offer at a lower price, the seller may be more agreeable to the concept.

Partnership – The next strategy for financing a small commercial apartment building is to secure an equity partner; someone who can bring a substantial amount of capital to the table but enjoys the benefits of not needing to be involved in the day-to-day management. We touched on partnerships briefly early in the book, but I want to diver deeper into how this can be applied specifically towards a much larger transaction that doesn't have the benefit of residential, owner-occupied financing as an option, as small multi-family purchases do. Partnerships are very common in real estate transactions, but I have always had an aversion to them. Part of this is out of fear of losing someone else's money, but also out of a desire to be in full control of all decisions regarding the asset.

The struggle to find traditional commercial financing from a bank forced me to rethink my distaste for getting involved in a partnership. I've come to realize that the fear of losing someone else's money should be viewed as a motivational driver to ensure failure is not an option. This is true of my own money in my own deals, but it is magnified to a much greater extent when someone else has entrusted you with their money. Being financially responsible for the return on someone else's money should provide a heightened sense of diligence, hard work and commitment to something you already have in interest in seeing succeed. And giving up full control of the asset in exchange for getting into the deal in the first place seems like a small price to pay. As the saying goes, "for better is a half loaf than no bread."

So how does one find someone who:
   a. Has a lot of money
   b. Is willing to invest it in real estate, and
   c. Will entrust you with the success of the asset?

Finding a partner who meets all those criteria could prove to be even more difficult than finding a seller who will agree to owner financing. The obvious and easy first answer is to look to friends and family. A partnership could be a combination of multiple people coming together with varying amounts of money. Partnering with friends and family can be dangerous territory though. Like the game of Monopoly, a small disagreement could lead to bitter resentment, but now the stakes aren't over Monopoly dollars. I don't want to scare you away from partnering with friends and family. Certainly many

CHAPTER NINETEEN - WHAT'S NEXT?

people make it work, but you need to really analyze who it is you might be getting involved with and how things could play out when things go sideways. Part of the struggle is convincing friends & family to go into a deal with you. No one likes to be sold on something that they are not actively shopping for. In essence, you need them much more than they need you.

Another, perhaps better, option for finding a partner is utilizing someone who is already committed to the idea of investing their money in real estate. Presumably, if the person is willing to invest with a partner in a real estate transaction, they are already aware of the inherent risks and obstacles to overcome. The best place to look for someone like this is going to be at your local Real Estate Investors Association (REIA) meetings. There are plenty of people who understand all the benefits that real estate investing provides but are unwilling or unable to get into a transaction on their own, or do not have the desire to manage it on their own. In this instance the relationship is less one sided; you both need each other.

Attending REIA meetings will expose you to numerous potential partners who are already seeking real estate deals. Your objective is to network with as many people as possible. You need to have a clear, defined vision of what it is you're looking for. Not every person is going to be wanting to enter into a partnership that fits your exact needs, and in fact most won't be, but each person you communicate with has the potential to open up conversations with other people they know who may be looking for something that aligns with your goal. This isn't a one and done thing either. Consistently showing up and networking at REIA meetings will be required to make inroads. Not only will you continue to meet new people, but it will also establish your dedication and legitimacy with those who you've already met and continue to engage with.

Other times, as could end up being the case for me, you find a partner from sheer dumb luck. I received a response to one of my mailing letter campaigns from an investor who was selling one of the properties in his portfolio. The property had been listed to the public for well over a year, and at a price that was too expensive for me to acquire on my own. I thought it could be a good opportunity to pitch the benefits of owner financing to the seller, knowing nothing about him at the time. He responded to my letter expressing interest in providing owner financing to structure a deal, but in the course of the few days of our communication he received a traditional offer that was good enough that he went under contract (if only I had reached out to him a few weeks earlier). Having already established communication with the seller I decided I didn't want to let it go to waste, so I asked if he'd be willing to get coffee to learn more about him and how he got his start in real estate investing.

We ended up meeting on a few occasions, during which time we discussed his impressive real estate portfolio and how he managed to grow it over time. We toured some of his investments and even a brewery project he was involved in, and along the way he seemed to take a general liking to me and a shared interest in my success. What I never anticipated, nor was the desired outcome of meeting him, was that he expressed interest in partnering on a deal in the future. His proposal was that he would bring a majority of the cash required for a purchase. My contribution would come from not only the cash I would be able to contribute but in larger part by way of me managing the day-to-day operations of the property. He could provide guidance and advice but would remain mostly uninvolved in the management of the property itself. From my standpoint it seemed like a great way to not only expand my own portfolio but to also acquire a mentor in the process.

The partnership has not come to pass yet. This is in part due to the lack of inventory for small commercial apartment buildings that have presented themselves, and also in part to the fact that he has stricter criteria for the financial return on the asset. Whereas I may be willing to receive a lower return on investment going into it alone, my potential partner is looking for a higher return on his money and so the search for a deal becomes that much more challenging. Of course, a higher return is a good thing, it will just take more time and effort to find the right property.

Portfolio Lender – Bank financing for a larger purchase is still attainable, but you need to find a willing lender. A portfolio lender is one who instead of selling their loans to the secondary market (i.e. Fannie Mae/Freddie Mac or mortgage-backed security funds) keeps the loans on their balance sheet. Many small regional banks or credit unions will retain loans on their books rather than selling them off. The reason you would want to seek out a portfolio lender is that as a result of keeping the loans in-house, a portfolio lender may be able to establish lending criteria that differs from conforming loan standards. What does that mean for you? It means that you could potentially find a lender who is willing to lend on an asset at a higher loan-to-value, meaning you may not need to bring as much cash for a down payment. Or, perhaps a lender can be more lenient on the required debt-service coverage ratio, or the property's ability to service the debt based on income. In exchange for more flexible lending standards, you can typically expect to pay a higher interest rate.

Small banks and credit unions can be much more flexible in their ability to make a good deal work. In comparison to large, national banks, a local portfolio lender is more likely to lend based on relationship alone. A fruitful relationship may be difficult to cultivate, and will likely require a proven track record or other means of making the deal more attractive to the lender. Perhaps as a new investor acquiring a loan with a portfolio lender for a smaller 2–4-unit apartment building could be your first step in an extended plan to continuing working together in the future, building that relationship, track record and trust along the way. You may not get as favorable of terms as you might with a larger bank, but if your end game is to create a relationship you can rely on in the future, it may be worth it in the long run. But what if you already have a couple properties under your belt, and you have not worked with this portfolio lender in the past? How do you then make the proposition more attractive?

In this scenario, an option could be to investigate the possibility of cross-collateralizing your existing loan(s) with the new portfolio lender. In a cross-collateralization deal, you can introduce one of your current investment properties as additional collateral to the loan for the new property. Doing so will decrease your overall debt-service coverage ratio (DSCR). With a mortgage on the secondary investment property held by another lender, the new portfolio lender would have to be willing to take a "secondary position" to the primary lender. In the event of a default on the new investment property, a secondary position holder could place a lien on the cross-collateralized property, but would only be entitled to collect their debt due *after* the first position lender has been paid off in full. This of course presents some additional risk to the secondary portfolio lender unless you can demonstrate you have paid down the existing mortgage to a low enough level or have established substantial equity in the property.

If you do have other investment properties, those properties could also provide you with an opportunity to refinance the existing loans with the new portfolio lender, bringing the lender additional business through the servicing of those loans. In doing so you could either take cash out during the refinance process to apply towards the new purchase or retain the equity in the property to again decrease the DSCR on the overall deal. These are sometimes known as blanket mortgages. A blanket mortgage may be attractive to a lender who is trying to get more loans on their balance sheet, but it could also be viewed as riskier to overextend on a single borrower.

Finding the right lender, like every other option we have discussed, is going to take time and a lot of work. I ended up reaching out to dozens of small community banks in an effort to find a banker who was willing to work with me. I pitched all the above strategies and was consistently met with "no's". It took nearly two years of fostering a relationship with a community banker who would ultimately provide financing for my third deal, and it was a combination of many of the strategies mentioned. After having built rapport with the banker through the analysis and discussion of a variety of properties, the terms he was able to offer (subject to the specific deal) was a 20% down payment and a DSCR of 1.15. Compare this to typical terms of 25-30% down and a DSCR of 1.20 – 1.25, and you can understand my elation with what he was offering. It did not come without its concessions of course. In exchange for the favorable terms, I had to agree to place a secondary lien on one of my current properties. Doing so would help hedge the risk of the lender. It was a calculated risk I was willing to take in order to finance the next deal. Having closed on that third property I have now found a willing lender who I continue to strengthen that relationship with and plan to continue utilizing for future deals. Part of the lesson here is to not give up. You will also have countless interactions with lenders who are just not willing or able to provide the terms you are looking for. But you have to be persistent, painfully so at times, if you are to find that banker who is willing to place their trust in you and your abilities.

Selling Yourself

Regardless of which route you may pursue (and there are many) to acquire the financing needed to purchase your next building, be it a small commercial apartment building or a residential multi-family, one of the most important steps you can take is to establish yourself as a worthwhile and trustworthy borrower and/or partner. You can only convey so much about yourself during the length of a conversation or within the body of an email. You need to do more to demonstrate that you are a serious investor who brings a certain amount of knowledge, ability, and dedication to the table. Similar to a resume presented to a prospective employer, as a potential borrower or partner you need to create a portfolio describing who you are and what you do in real estate.

The portfolio should illustrate a few aspects about yourself and your investing to briefly summarize why it is that someone should give you the time of day. Furthermore, it should present you as an established and credible investor and highlight the property(s) you already own. You should describe your vision for not only the next purchase but for the future as well. The effort is wasted if the portfolio doesn't look truly professional, so if that means you need to spend a little bit of money to buy a portfolio template or hire a freelance marketing professional, you should do it. Lastly, you want to describe your financial standing as well. A personal financial statement detailing all assets and liabilities provides a sense of transparency that helps bring another level of comfort to anyone who would consider lending you money or entering into a partnership.

After each and every conversation you have with a lender or potential partner you should follow up with an email including your investing portfolio. Additionally, the portfolio can and should also be sent to commercial brokers you reach out to in search of a deal, though you may consider leaving out the personal financial statement. This further highlights your qualities as a potential buyer who has the ability to close on a deal. Compared to someone else in a similar position as yourself, you will undoubtedly get more return calls and open the door to more possibilities by presenting your portfolio to everyone you can.

Final Thoughts

What is going to be your next step? Is it researching the market and analyzing deals to get more comfortable with the numbers? Is it getting pre-approved to understand what you can afford? Or is it making that first (or next) offer on a property you've identified?

If there is one attribute that I believe is vital to success in real estate, it is the ability to persevere. Undoubtedly you will be faced with an uphill battle at times. But at any moment, your next success could be right around the corner. Chasing your goals and doing so with persistent tenacity, not just becoming focused sporadically but rather being laser focused at all times, is what is going to move you closer and closer to achieving those goals. The hope is that the stories and strategies presented in this book can serve as a blueprint to establishing success in your own real estate investing career.

Dream big! Perhaps your name will one day be in the upper echelons with the likes of Rockefeller, Carnegie and Ford, but as the real estate mogul of the 21st century- he or she who is the master of The Landlord's Game.

"Make no little plans; they have no magic to stir men's blood…"
-Daniel Burnham (Chicago city planner), 1907

APPENDIX

A1: Recommended Reading List:

- The One Thing – Gary Keller and Jay Papasan
- Secrets of the Millionaire Mind – T. Harv Ecker
- The Millionaire Next Door – Thomas J. Stanley
- The ABC's of Real Estate Investing – Ken McElroy
- A Year of Growing Rich – Napoleon Hill
- Landlording on Autopilot – Mike Butler
- How To Win Friend and Influence People – Dale Carnegie
- The Richest Man in Babylon – George S. Classon
- The Millionaire Real Estate Investor – Gary Keller
- Crushing It In Apartments and Commercial Real Estate – Brian Murray
- Never Split the Difference – Chris Voss
- Think and Grow Rich – Napoleon Hill

A2: Personal Letter to Seller

February 20th, 2016

Mr. Livingston,

I would like to take a moment to introduce myself and why it is I am interested in your property. My name is W.R. Cheltenham. You don't know me from the next potential offeror, but I imagine I am at the younger end of the spectrum of buyers you may be considering. At 27 years old and a new (potential) owner, a lot of people think I am crazy for trying to pursue a building like yours. However, what I may lack in experience, I make up for in enthusiasm and determination to succeed.

One of the biggest things that stands out to me about your building is the classic charm, character, and vintage details you kept while still updating the building. It's a beautiful property to walk through and I imagine the original owners felt the same pride viewing it much like it looks today, only many years ago. The bathrooms are beautifully updated but retain a classic feel. The original built-in hutches display craftsmanship rarely seen today. I would be proud not only as the individual who owns the building, but even as a renter living there! I will also say that your choice to update the electric and install new copper plumbing, though hidden behind the walls, does not go unnoticed. It is a huge selling point for your building and will provide for many more years of continued operation.

I've seen a lot of properties over the past few months and have yet to have the feeling of "this is the one for me", until I came across yours. I aspire to one day own multiple buildings and hope this particular property can be my first step in realizing that dream.

Thank you for your time and consideration in reviewing my

offer. I hope we can ultimately come to an agreement for this wonderful opportunity. Best regards,

W.R. Cheltenham

A3: Residential Real Property Disclosure Form

Illinois REALTORS®
RESIDENTIAL REAL PROPERTY DISCLOSURE REPORT
(765 ILCS 77/35)

NOTICE: THE PURPOSE OF THIS REPORT IS TO PROVIDE PROSPECTIVE BUYERS WITH INFORMATION ABOUT MATERIAL DEFECTS IN THE RESIDENTIAL REAL PROPERTY. THIS REPORT DOES NOT LIMIT THE PARTIES' RIGHT TO CONTRACT FOR THE SALE OF RESIDENTIAL REAL PROPERTY IN "AS IS" CONDITION. UNDER COMMON LAW, SELLERS WHO DISCLOSE MATERIAL DEFECTS MAY BE UNDER A CONTINUING OBLIGATION TO ADVISE THE PROSPECTIVE BUYERS ABOUT THE CONDITION OF THE RESIDENTIAL REAL PROPERTY EVEN AFTER THE REPORT IS DELIVERED TO THE PROSPECTIVE BUYER. COMPLETION OF THIS REPORT BY THE SELLER CREATES LEGAL OBLIGATIONS ON THE SELLER; THEREFORE SELLER MAY WISH TO CONSULT AN ATTORNEY PRIOR TO COMPLETION OF THIS REPORT.

Property Address: _____

City, State & Zip Code: _____

Seller's Name: _____

This Report is a disclosure of certain conditions of the residential real property listed above in compliance with the Residential Real Property Disclosure Act. This information is provided as of _____, 20___, and does not reflect any changes made or occurring after that date or information that becomes known to the seller after that date. The disclosures herein shall not be deemed warranties of any kind by the seller or any person representing any party in this transaction.

In this form, "am aware" means to have actual notice or actual knowledge without any specific investigation or inquiry. In this form, a "material defect" means a condition that would have a substantial adverse effect on the value of the residential real property or that would significantly impair the health or safety of future occupants of the residential real property unless the seller reasonably believes that the condition has been corrected.

The seller discloses the following information with the knowledge that even though the statements herein are not deemed to be warranties, prospective buyers may choose to rely on this information in deciding whether or not and on what terms to purchase the residential real property.

The seller represents that to the best of his or her actual knowledge, the following statements have been accurately noted as "yes" (correct), "no" (incorrect), or "not applicable" to the property being sold. If the seller indicates that the response to any statement, except number 1, is yes or not applicable, the seller shall provide an explanation, in the additional information area of this form.

YES	NO	N/A	
1.			Seller has occupied the property within the last 12 months. (No explanation is needed.)
2.			I am aware of flooding or recurring leakage problems in the crawl space or basement.
3.			I am aware that the property is located in a flood plain or that I currently have flood hazard insurance on the property.
4.			I am aware of material defects in the basement or foundation (including cracks and bulges).
5.			I am aware of leaks or material defects in the roof, ceilings, or chimney.
6.			I am aware of material defects in the walls, windows, doors, or floors.
7.			I am aware of material defects in the electrical system.
8.			I am aware of material defects in the plumbing system (includes such things as water heater, sump pump, water treatment system, sprinkler system, and swimming pool).
9.			I am aware of material defects in the well or well equipment.
10.			I am aware of unsafe conditions in the drinking water.
11.			I am aware of material defects in the heating, air conditioning, or ventilating systems.
12.			I am aware of material defects in the fireplace or wood burning stove.
13.			I am aware of material defects in the septic, sanitary sewer, or other disposal system.
14.			I am aware of unsafe concentrations of radon on the premises.
15.			I am aware of unsafe concentrations of or unsafe conditions relating to asbestos on the premises.
16.			I am aware of unsafe concentrations of or unsafe conditions relating to lead paint, lead water pipes, lead plumbing pipes or lead in the soil on the premises.
17.			I am aware of mine subsidence, underground pits, settlement, sliding, upheaval, or other earth stability defects on the premises.
18.			I am aware of current infestations of termites or other wood boring insects.
19.			I am aware of a structural defect caused by previous infestations of termites or other wood boring insects.
20.			I am aware of underground fuel storage tanks on the property.
21.			I am aware of boundary or lot line disputes.
22.			I have received notice of violation of local, state or federal laws or regulations relating to this property, which violation has not been corrected.
23.			I am aware that this property has been used for the manufacture of methamphetamine as defined in Section 10 of the Methamphetamine Control and Community Protection Act.

Note: These disclosures are not intended to cover the common elements of a condominium, but only the actual residential real property including limited common elements allocated to the exclusive use thereof that form an integral part of the condominium unit.

Note: These disclosures are intended to reflect the current condition of the premises and do not include previous problems, if any, that the seller reasonably believes have been corrected.

FORM 108 (05/2019) COPYRIGHT ILLINOIS REALTORS®   Page 1 of 4

A4: Contract Modification Letter

Attorney at Law

Chicago, IL 60613
Telephone:
E-Fax:
Email:

April 20, 2016

VIA EMAIL

Chicago, Illinois 60613

Re: ████████████████ Chicago, Illinois
File No. 16-11 7

Dear ████:

Pursuant to the attorney approval and inspection contingencies of the April 10, 2016 contract (the "Contract") (as extended by agreement of the parties), we are requesting the following modifications to the Contract:

Contract Issues:

yes 1. Sellers represent that the subject property is not subject to any past judgment or injunction or pending court litigation or other administrative action filed by any governmental entity relating to building code or other code violations or that would prevent the use of the property as a three-unit residential residence.

yes 2. Please confirm that the Sellers will be provide a plat of survey dated not more than two (2) months from the date of closing.

April 20, 2016
Page 2

[handwritten: To The Best of Their Knowledge]

3. Sellers represent that any renovations and modifications to the structure undertaken by the Sellers were in full compliance with all applicable building code regulations and that all necessary permits were obtained in conjunction with those renovations and/or modifications. *[handwritten: yes as allowed]*

4. Sellers represent that all plumbing, heating, electrical and other mechanical systems will be fully operational at the time of the closing. *[handwritten: yes]*

5. The Contract is contingent upon the Sellers providing prior to or at closing a certificate of zoning compliance showing the property is zoned as a three-unit residence. *[handwritten: yes]*

6. Sellers have no knowledge of any notice from any governmental body relating to any alleged violation of any applicable zoning, building, fire, health, electrical, plumbing codes. *[handwritten: No knowledge]*

7. The balance of the earnest money will not be due until one (1) business day after the parties have resolved all contractual issues. *[handwritten: ok]*

8. Please confirm that this property is not subject to foreclosure or short sale approval. *[handwritten: it is not]*

9. The Contract is amended to state that the Sellers' sole remedy in the event of a default by the Purchaser is a claim to the retention of the earnest money. Purchaser shall have five (5) business days to cure any default. *[handwritten: OK]*

10. Sellers to assign any existing lease agreements to the Purchaser at closing along with providing appropriate notice to tenants (three business days notice to the tenant). *[handwritten: ok]*

11. Sellers to credit Purchaser at closing with the rent for the month of the closing prorated to the closing date) (if applicable). *[handwritten: at closing; corrected]*

12. Sellers to credit Purchaser at closing with the entire security deposit for any tenant, along with interest from the date of commencement of the tenancy. Sellers agree to indemnify Purchaser for any violations of the Chicago Residential Landlord-Tenant Ordinance occurring prior to the date of closing. — Purchasers to Indemnify *[handwritten: No security deposit; Seller for viol after clos]*

13. Please provide a complete copy of any current leases (including any amendments and/or riders). Our final approval of the Contract is subject to receipt and review of any lease. — Within 48 hrs of Receipt *[handwritten: as amended]*

14. The Sellers agree not to enter into any lease amendments and/or extensions without the prior written consent of the Purchaser. *[handwritten: ok]*

15. Please confirm that none of the units have any current options to extend lease agreements. *[handwritten: they do not]*

16. Paragraph 8 of the Contract is amended to state that the Contract is contingent upon the property appraising at or above the purchase price set forth in the Contract. In the event the property appraises below the purchase price, the Purchasers shall have the sole right to cancel the Contract and receive a refund of all earnest money deposited. *[handwritten: OK]*

April 20, 2016
Page 3

17. In the event the closing date under the Contract is postponed due to re-disclosure under the CFPB regulations, the Purchasers shall not be in default and the closing date shall automatically be delayed for ten (10) business days (unless the lender can close sooner).

OK (margin note)

18. Please confirm if the Sellers have filed any claims under their homeowners insurance policy in the last five (5) years and if so, please provide the details.

Nothing Filed (margin note)

19. Please confirm if the Sellers have had any instances of water infiltration during their ownership and if so, please provide the details.

No Water (margin note) *Agreed* (margin note)

20. Real estate taxes shall be prorated based upon ~~110%~~ 105% of the most recent assessed valuation (39,514) times the most recent state equalization factor (2.7253) times the most recent local tax rate (6.833%).

Ok as amended 4-25-16 (margin note)

Inspection Issues:

Agreed (margin note)

We have attached the inspection report. Purchaser requests a credit of $2,500.00 to address the issues raised in the inspection.

If you agree to the above, please sign below and return a copy of this letter to my office.

These modifications are not to be construed as a counter-offer and may be unilaterally withdrawn or modified by my client. The attorney approval and inspection periods will be extended until the parties have resolved all contractual and inspection issues. I reserve the right to disapprove the Contract.

Please call if you have any questions or comments.

Very Truly Yours,

Attorney At Law

Enclosure

cc:

Agreed to on April 22, 2016 *as amended*

Sellers or Sellers' Attorney/Agent

Agreed as amended
4-25-16

A5: Insurance Quote

Property Location: ▮▮▮▮▮▮▮▮▮▮▮
CHICAGO, IL 60618-2202

Year Built:	1911	Subzone:	07	Quote Effective Date:	05/25/2016
Territory Zone:	31	Construction:	Masonry veneer	Num Families:	4

Rate IV: 100%

Quote Description: 100% Replacement Cost

Quote Results

	Limit	Premium
Coverages		
Dwelling (Coverage A)	560,000	1,803.00
Increased Dwelling - Option ID	112,000	
Dwelling Extension	56,000	
Personal Property (Coverage B)	196,000	
Personal Liability (Coverage L) each occurrence	1,000,000	35.00
Medical Payments (Coverage M) each occurrence	10,000	15.00
Credit Card / Bank Card and Forgery	1,000	
Damage to Property of Others (Each Occurrence)	500	
Loss of Use (Actual Loss Sustained)		
Loss Settlement Provision		
Loss Settlement Option - Dwelling	A1 - Replacement Cost - Similar Construction	
Loss Settlement Option - Personal Property	B1 - Limited Replacement Cost	
Deductibles		
Policy deductible	1% 5,600	
Charges / Credits		
Claim free discount		(162.00)
Policy Options and Endorsements		
Jewelry and Furs	1,500 / 2,500 Option JF included	
Silver / Goldware Theft - Option SG	2,500 included	
Business Property - Option BP	1,500 included	
Building Ordinance or Law - Option OL (% of Coverage A)	10% 56,000	
Firearms - Option FA	2,500 included	
Home Computer - Option HC	5,000 included	
Back-Up Dwelling/Pers Property	Dwl Lmt/10,000	482.00
Fire Department Service Charge Increased Limits	500 included	
Total Annual Premium		2,173.00
Monthly Premium (Service charge not included)		181.08

This example of available coverages and limits is not a contract, binder, or recommendation of coverage. This quote assumes you insure for 100% of the estimated replacement cost of your home. Higher limits are available at a higher premium. Coverage is available in a lesser amount, subject to restrictions and limitations. If information used for rating changes or different rates are effective at the time of policy issuance, this rate quote may be revised. All coverages are subject to the terms and conditions contained in the policy and endorsements. You must choose your limits and coverages.

A6: Pre-Screening Questionnaire

ABOUT YOU

1. Name: _____
2. Current Address: _____
3. Email Address: _____
4. Phone Number: (_____) - _____ - _____
5. If approved, how many people will be living in the unit? _____
6. What kind of animals do you have? _____

PREVIOUS HOUSING

7. Why are you moving? _____
8. How long at current residence? _____
9. Date of desired move: _____
10. Desired length of lease: _____

EMPLOYMENT INFORMATION

11. Occupation: _____ 12. Time at current job: _____

13. What may interrupt your income or ability to pay rent?
    _____

OTHER INFORMATION

14. How many evictions have been filed on you? _____

15. **How is your credit?** _____

A7: Application Requirements

Thank you for your interest in the apartment available for rent. The following are the basic requirements for being approved as a resident of the property, to which we take no exceptions to:
- Minimum credit score of 650
- Total monthly income of all lease signees must not be less than 3x the monthly rent
- No prior evictions
- Applicant must provide contact information for current housing provider
- An applicant with prior conviction(s) in the previous three years will be afforded an Individualized Assessment per the Cook County Just Housing Amendment
- No sex offenders or persons under a current child sex offender residency restriction
- An active renter's insurance policy is required for the duration of the lease. Proof of an active policy is required at the time of lease signing

If you decide you would like to begin the application process, please notify the property manager. At that time, you will be provided a link to a 3rd party company to perform a background and credit check. The non-refundable cost of this service is $40 per applicant.
- If approved, the applicant will have 24 hours from notice by property owner to accept and sign the lease, or risk being passed for the next qualified applicant.
- A non-refundable $375 move-in fee is required at the time lease signing.

If you have any questions, please do not hesitate to ask.

A8: Adverse Action Letter

DATE
Name
Re: Rental Application

Thank you for your recent rental application. Based on provided information, we find that we are unable to accept your application for rental at this time.

This decision was based in whole or in part on the information provided to us in a Consumer Report or Investigative Consumer Report prepared on our behalf by a consumer-reporting agency. Their mailing address and phone number are listed below:

Credit Reporting Agency Name: TransUnion
Toll Free Phone Number: 1-(800)-916-8800
Address: TransUnion Consumer Solutions
PC Box 2000
Chester, PA 19016-2000

The credit Reporting Agency plays no part in the decision to take any action on your rental application and is unable to provide you with specific reason(s) for our action.

You have the right to a free copy of the report within 60 days of receipt of this notice and to dispute the completeness or accuracy of any information in the consumer report issued by the credit reporting agency.

A9: Mail Campaign Letter

Dear Mr. and Mrs. Peterson,

My name is W.R. Cheltenham. Like you, I am a property owner myself, managing two 4-unit buildings near your property at 1060 W. Addison. My fiancé and I are looking specifically for a building ranging from 5 to 12 units to purchase, which is what initially drew my eye to your property. I especially like the limestone accents at the parapet. For a building of its age, it appears to be in great condition, which makes it clear to me that you have continued to take meticulous care of it in your 33+ years owning the property. I admire and respect your ability to do so.

Although I realize your building is not currently for sale, perhaps you have considered the thought of selling recently. There are many advantages to you as a seller to seek an off-market sale, including the following:

- Eliminate the use of realtors. Save 6% otherwise paid to buyer and seller agents.
- No need for constant showings. Minimal disturbance to tenants.
- Building to be purchased in "as-is" condition. No credits or repairs will be requested.
- I will offer you a fair market price, while values are at or near their peak in this cycle
- You would be selling to someone who will care for the property as you have done yourself, and who will continue to do so for many years to come.

At very least I hope we chat by phone to discuss further, but if now is not the right time I would appreciate hearing from you in the future when you are ready to sell.

Thanks for taking the time to read this letter. If you'd like to reach out, I am available via phone or email. I am not a realtor or large-scale investor, but rather a young, determined individual trying to do well for myself, the neighborhood and ultimately for you as well. Thanks again and have a great day.

Sincerely,

W.R. Cheltenham

ABOUT THE AUTHOR

W.R. Cheltenham is real estate investor, renaissance man, and loving husband & father. His life is dedicated to saying things like "Yes!" and "You better believe it!". An unassuming philanthropist, Cheltenham  strives to improve the lives of those around him through education, motivation, and living life large.

www.ingramcontent.com/pod-product-compliance
Lightning Source LLC
Chambersburg PA
CBHW052344220526
45465CB00003BA/940